Sex and Salvation

Sex and Salvation

Imagining the Future in Madagascar

JENNIFER COLE

The University of Chicago Press
Chicago and London

Jennifer Cole is associate professor of anthropology in the Department of
Comparative Human Development at the University of Chicago, a coeditor
of *Love in Africa,* and the author of *Forget Colonialism? Sacrifice and the Art of
Memory in Madagascar.*

The University of Chicago Press, Chicago 60637
The University of Chicago Press, Ltd., London
© 2010 by The University of Chicago
All rights reserved. Published 2010
Printed in the United States of America

19 18 17 16 15 14 13 12 11 10   1 2 3 4 5

ISBN-13: 978-0-226-11330-2 (cloth)
ISBN-13: 978-0-226-11331-9 (paper)
ISBN-10: 0-226-11330-2 (cloth)
ISBN-10: 0-226-11331-0 (paper)

Library of Congress Cataloging-in-Publication Data
Cole, Jennifer.
    Sex and salvation : imagining the future in Madagascar / Jennifer Cole.
        p.   cm.
    Includes bibliographical references and index.
    Summary: As much of the intense political and social change in
Madagascar revolves around urban youth, who view themselves as avatars
of modernity, this book argues that traditional social science offers inadequate
theorizations of generational change and its contribution to broader cultural
historical processes.
    ISBN-13: 978-0-226-11330-2 (cloth : alk. paper)
    ISBN-13: 978-0-226-11331-9 (pbk. : alk. paper)
    ISBN-10: 0-226-11330-2 (cloth : alk. paper)
    ISBN-10: 0-226-11331-0 (pbk. : alk. paper) 1. Urban youth—Madagascar—
Social conditions—21st century. 2. Sex customs—Madagascar. 3.   Women—
Madagascar—Social conditions—21st century. 4. Madagascar—Social
conditions—21st century. I. Title.
    HQ799.8.M33C66 2010
    306.70835'09691091732—dc22   2010004139

⊚ The paper used in this publication meets the minimum requirements of the
American National Standard for Information Sciences—Permanence of Paper
for Printed Library Materials, ANSI Z39.48-1992.

*To Amelia and Jacob, and to the many women who
cared for me in Madagascar, with so much love*

How does newness come into the world? How is it born? Of what fusions, translations, conjoinings is it made?

—Salman Rushdie, *The Satanic Verses*

CONTENTS

This book concerns the role of generational transitions—the many small steps young people take as they move from childhood to adulthood. It also examines personal change, the ways individuals adopt novel orientations toward their social worlds. And it is about how both generational change and personal change shape, and are shaped by, broader historical and cultural transformations. I explore these topics through a focus on women's intimate and religious lives in Tamatave (Malagasy: Toamasina), a large multiethnic port town on Madagascar's east coast. Hence my title: *Sex and Salvation*.

In the 1990s, Madagascar abandoned an isolationist form of state socialism and adopted an aggressive policy of economic liberalization. Previously the life trajectory of aspiring middle-class residents of Tamatave had been fairly predictable: many people attended school and found jobs, then married and had families. They would likely have belonged to Catholic and Protestant churches that, since the nineteenth century, have been a familiar part of the cultural landscape. Now, with massively intensified globalization and new economic pressures, this older way of moving from childhood to adulthood is becoming more difficult. Disillusioned with other options, a generation of young women have embraced what they perceive to be the promise of a sexual economy, taking up practices that some liken to prostitution. Others have sought the alternative path of salvation in the Pentecostal churches that have recently sprung up throughout the country. Participating in these churches requires abandoning ancestral practices that have long been synonymous with Malagasy culture and identity. By following women as they enter the sexual economy or join Pentecostal churches, I trace two common paths through which "newness enters the world" on the mundane terrain of everyday life.

My analysis of how young people seize hold of the cultural, social, and economic resources that enable adulthood, adapting these resources to their present circumstances, and of how slightly older people enter Pentecostal churches when alternative paths prove unsatisfying, takes seriously a level of analysis that is usually elided in broader structural histories. A basic premise of this book is that the many small steps people take as they find new ways to support themselves and build families, and the ways they inevitably seize on and transform existing social and cultural practices, bring together two different but interdependent time scales of historical transformation: the life course and national and global development. This conjuncture of the life course with broader economic and political change not only is produced by but also produces new cultural and historical formations. This is never a mechanical, unreflexive matter of one cohort replacing another as some theories of generational change have implied. Rather, it is a highly imaginative undertaking in which people's desire to be good and to be valued, their culturally shaped dilemmas, and their visions for the future meet the broader forces of history and culture in unpredictable, uneven ways.

This book is based on research that spans from 2000, when people living in Madagascar's cities first began to witness the full effect of the liberalization policies enacted some years earlier, to 2009, when Andry Rajoelina seized power and declared himself the new president of Madagascar. I first went to Tamatave because I wanted to understand young urbanites' relation to the ancestral rituals that were such an important part of the rural life I had studied earlier. Like the rest of Madagascar, and much of Africa, relatively high fertility rates and comparatively low life expectancy mean that the population in Tamatave is disproportionately young. The sheer numbers of young people make what they are doing and thinking highly visible, an important part of how all Tamatavians think about the options available to them. And I soon found myself drawn into Tamatavians' concerns about how to build a viable future amid considerable economic and cultural flux.

Since I had worked in a rural area of Tamatave province in the early 1990s, I already had several points of contact when I arrived in Tamatave city. One of these was at the university, and I soon started to meet groups of young people there, who in turn led me out into the wider community. I also knew many others who came from the village where I had worked previously. Some of those people had lived in Tamatave for years, but others had only recently arrived, owing to hardships at home. Albeit in different ways, it was these two groups—university students and their friends and families in town (most of whom did not go to university), and my connections from rural areas—that directed my attention toward the practices associated with young women and the importance of the sexual economy. At the same time, having studied the role of ancestral practices in shaping social relationships in rural areas, I arrived in Tamatave already curious about the possible effects of Pentecostalism, which is well known in the literature on Africa for its hostility to ancestors. Consequently, I developed and maintained active relationships with members of various Pentecostal churches, attending services and prayer groups and spending time in youth groups.

It was only when I began to recognize such patterns after conducting the bulk of this fieldwork that I initiated archival research in France. That research enabled me to provide a deeper history for contemporary practices. At the same time, the newspapers and other archival materials I consulted raised new questions, which I took back to the field. Having completed the bulk of my research by 2007, I then returned to the village where I had previously conducted fieldwork to get a sense of how rural patterns compared with what I saw taking place in Tamatave. My visit confirmed that many of the patterns I observed in Tamatave were different from what was taking place in the countryside. However, it also revealed that some aspects of urban life were beginning to stretch into rural areas.

Scholars generally agree that, as a social category, generation is a notoriously difficult concept to delimit. It is certainly true that everyone goes through similar processes of biological maturation, whether or not they come to be considered socially adult. But not all people who are born sharing the same times or places share the same problems or the same solutions; not all people "come of age" in the same way, and not all have common formative experiences. In this sense, generational formations are inevitably partial. Moreover, to become visible, the new kinds of cultural formations that emerge as young people enter adulthood must somehow become embodied or institutionalized: the particles that have hung dimly in solution, so to speak, need to crystallize and take form in cultural symbols, laws, or even commodities. My long-term fieldwork in Madagascar enabled me to watch as what was first an inchoate phenomenon, a nascent form of novelty shared and performed by a group of young people on the cusp of adulthood, began to affect the more macro sociopolitical events that are the stuff of typical historical analyses. It remains for a future ethnographer to document how these patterns evolve over time.

My first and greatest debt is to the people of Tamatave, who took me into their lives and generously shared their time, and without whose openness I never could have written this book. I owe a particular debt to Solofo Randrianja and Lucia Razafindrakoto, who helped me find a house to rent and who offered me a place to stay and practical support on many consecutive trips to Tamatave. I also warmly thank my research assistants, Carole Ranaivosoa, Onja Randrianasoloniana, and Cadria Said Ben Amed. Onja and Cadria tirelessly tramped all over Tamatave with me and helped me ask the right questions. Sitting with them transcribing tapes and translating them was a tremendously exciting experience that opened up the world in new ways. I also thank Zoma Laurencia Anastasie, Zoma Franceline, and Lahady Celestin, who took care of my family while we lived in Tamatave. Without them we would never have made it through our stay. I would never be as happy as I am in Madagascar were it not for Simone and Anselme Ralaizonia, who gave me a home in Antananarivo and helped in a million ways.

Research grants from the American Fulbright Program, the Wenner-Gren Foundation for Anthropological Research, and a small grant from the American Philosophical Society funded my fieldwork. Summer grants from the Social Science Division at the University of Chicago helped me return to Tamatave on several occasions and further enabled me to travel to France for archival research. Fellowships from the Radcliffe Institute for Advanced Study (2003–2004) at Harvard University, from the American Council of Learned Societies (2007–2008), and from the American Philosophical Society (2007–2008) enabled me to write up this research. I will always be grateful to these institutions for giving me the time to think and write. Judy Vichniac at Radcliffe provided much needed support in what turned out to be a difficult year.

My work on this book and the engagements it represents span several countries where so many people have offered intellectual companionship, friendship, and practical help. I am grateful to my former colleagues at Harvard University, especially Steve Caton, Michael Herzfeld, and Mary Steedly, for supporting this project and making sure it got under way. At the University of Chicago, I have been lucky to find a home in a most eccentric and wonderful Department of Comparative Human Development. I particularly thank John Lucy, Rick Shweder, and Richard Taub, who have worked tirelessly to build an interdisciplinary department and who let me be me. Jean and John Comaroff have supported this project from start to finish and have always, always made time to help; Jean gave inspirational comments on a panel at which I presented an early version of this work; John generously read drafts of grant proposals and offered comments on some of my very first thoughts on the sexual economy in Tamatave. They have provided incomparable intellectual companionship in African studies, as has Ralph Austen. I am also grateful to Andy Apter and Robin Derby. Though they have perhaps wisely migrated to warmer climes, I continue to value our shared exchanges about African and Afro-Caribbean topics. Comments from audiences in the African Studies Workshop at the University of Chicago have contributed to this project in many ways that I still appreciate.

In France, I am indebted to Dominique Bois for his irrepressible enthusiasm, for sharing a love of Tamatave, and for generously allowing me to use his postcard, "Métisse Betsimisaraka," which appears in chapter 5. Thanks also to Françoise Raison, Fara Rajaonah, and Lucile Dubourdieu for answering many questions along the way and for always helping me to find my way to the right archives. My discussions with Laurent Berger helped sharpen my analysis considerably. Questions from audiences at the Laboratoire du SEDET provided useful feedback on some of the ideas in chapter 5. In England, I thank the participants at the London School of Economics anthropology seminar who asked me tough-minded questions on an early draft of what eventually became chapter 6. I particularly thank Rita Astuti, whose questions during that seminar spurred my thinking in ways that made this a better book.

I have had the great good luck to place this book in skilled hands. My anonymous readers for the University of Chicago Press helped me to sharpen the manuscript in just the right ways, and I remain indebted to them for reading the book so carefully. David Brent has been a loyal and efficient editor, and I thank him for his labor on *Sex and Salvation* and for his support of African studies. Laura Avey good-naturedly answered a thousand tiny questions about photos; Erik Carlson expertly shepherded the book through production. Thanks also to Erin Moore and Elayne Oliphant for helping me prepare the manuscript for publication and for keeping me company through the interminable checking of details. And thank goodness for Alice Bennett and her care, precision, and patience with the copyediting.

Being an anthropologist would be a terribly lonely task were it not for the many friends and intellectual companions I've shared work with over the years. I am indebted to Maurice Bloch for reading several essays, for fetching me from Charles de Gaulle airport when I came home weak from malaria, and for consistently supporting my research in Madagascar. Maurice Bloch and Christine Langlois generously gave me a place to stay in Paris on many occasions. Karen Middleton is a true friend who took the time to read a draft of an article for me when her mother was deathly ill. She continuously helps me think Madagascar better. Saba Mahmood gave me excellent, provocative feedback on a talk that later became chapter 7. Nancy Munn really can see heaven in a grain of sand, and I benefited tremendously from her comments on several chapters. Rosalind Shaw and Christine Walley both read early drafts of the introduction and offered useful suggestions. Tanya Luhrmann generously took time away from her own work to read the whole manuscript and pushed me to the finish line just when I needed it.

I have been lucky to have had the most amazing coeditors, writers' group, and friends in Chicago and beyond, without whom this book would not have come into being. I have learned an enormous amount about youth, Africa, and collaboration from my coeditor Deborah Durham. I treasure her unique way of experiencing the world and making it come into writing. Lynn Thomas was a wonderful coeditor and loyal coconspirator on *Love in Africa*. Rochona Majumdar and Lisa Wedeen both offered terrific comments on chapter 1; they are darling friends who have gone to the gym with me at early hours even in the dead of winter and shared many of the seemingly insignificant events that make up a life. Without them Chicago would not be home. I also thank my beloved writing partners, Jessica Cattelino, Judith Farquhar, Danilyn Rutherford, and Shawn Smith. They saw this book emerge from grant proposals, through inchoate drafts, to final product and inspired me to continue working on it when my own enthusiasm flagged.

My parents, Sheila and Michael Cole, have supported this project throughout. My dad read bits and pieces of many chapters, and my mom graciously let him. I only hope I am as generous to my children as they are to me. Ever since Julian Dibbell walked into my kitchen on a cold October evening and saw me frying chicken, I've felt like the luckiest woman in the world. He has helped make the world beyond the book worth living. My children, Jacob and Amelia Mazzarella, have never really had much of a choice when it comes to their mother's anthropological proclivities, but they have endured Madagascar, even enjoyed it, despite malaria and strange French schools. In part this has been because of the enormous kindness shown to us by so many people. I dedicate this book to the many women in Madagascar who have cared for me, and to Jacob and Amelia, who taught me how to care.

ONE

Imagining the Future: Theorizing Generational and Historical Change

On an early morning in December 2003, I joined a ragtag parade that marched through the city of Tamatave for International AIDS Awareness Day. It was a time when Madagascar's abandonment of state socialism was still fresh in adult memory and the excitement and fear associated with economic liberalization were still new. The participants represented the prostitutes' association, a group that distributed condoms to women working the streets, employees of Top Reseau, a USAID-funded NGO (nongovernmental organization) working to raise awareness about sexually transmitted diseases, and a group of Adventists in favor of abstinence, representing the growing presence of evangelical churches in Tamatave. I had been invited to the parade by the president of the prostitutes' association, so I marched with them. The group wound its way through the city and ended up in the dilapidated building of the Ministry of Sports and Youth. On the first floor, various posters exhorted young people to better protect themselves against AIDS by waiting until marriage to have sex and remaining faithful to their partners. We made our way past the poster display to a room with rough wooden benches facing a blackboard. After we sat down, a man, who turned out to be a member of the Adventist church and who represented a Christian perspective more generally, began a lecture titled "Dare to Be Different with AIDS: Choose Abstinence and Fidelity."

Drawing on a speaking style that church leaders in Madagascar use to deliver moral homilies to their flocks—pacing the floor and regularly interspersing his lecture with asides in which he cleverly ventriloquized the perspective he was mocking—the Adventist speaker began to deliver the following speech:

The reason we should change our behavior is that we need to find a solution to the problem of AIDS. The Bible is our solution. Even if I am tired, I cannot rest but must teach you. Because AIDS is going to ruin Malagasy culture! People start talking about how to prevent AIDS in the streets [implying that it has led people to talk about sex publicly]. We are the "instantaneous generation." We need everything quickly! We need to finish things quickly! And when we go out with someone we need to sleep with them right away. And we use condoms so we can sleep with them right away. This is a sex-worshiping world [*monde sexolatre*]! We sell matches with sex, people are always half naked in the advertisements, we show people wearing their bathing suits on TV, and we have X-rated films now, when we never even used to watch people kiss on TV! We've become postmodern. We see something and we want it. We have the mentality of consumers. We buy girls, and we consume them. We use condoms for our pleasures. "Who should I sleep with now? [Scans the room eagerly, exaggerating the look of a sex-starved young man, eyes popping as he searches the crowd.] Bring on the next one." In the Song of Solomon it says how wonderful girls are! Even God says that it is good to sleep with women. But God said, "If you sleep with a woman you are of one flesh, not two." Because your mind becomes one with the person you have sex with. So that means you should marry the person you sleep with. But the devil speaks, "Do it now [sleep with others] or you will be late" [behind the times or backward].

The speaker's lecture about the evils of unbridled consumption and the delights of sex within church-sanctioned marriage was hardly the only time the topics of sex and religion came up during my fieldwork. At dusk, in an area near the regional truck stop a few blocks from the Ministry of Sports and Youth, young women often milled about, waiting to be picked up by men. Along the strip of road that ran just parallel to the shore, where most of the large hotels and restaurants are, it was impossible to miss the young, scantily clad Malagasy women coupled with much older European men, sipping beer or whiskey in the early evening. All the Internet kiosks in town were filled with young women looking online for foreign men to establish relationships with. Sex, as a way of building social connections and gaining resources, seemed omnipresent.

Yet such activities blatantly contradicted the position the speaker had been preaching, with his allusions to the Bible and his demands for abstinence. His rhetoric bespoke an explosion of new religious enterprises that appeared to use very different, religiously motivated, strategies for earning a livelihood and building a life. Although a Catholic cathedral and several

Protestant edifices had been part of the Tamatavian landscape for decades, several huge Pentecostal churches had sprung up over the 1990s, two of them the size of airplane hangars. On Wednesday evenings and throughout the day on Sunday, I frequently encountered groups of soberly clad men and women making their way to and from these churches. When the pastor of one of the Pentecostal churches died, the road through a middle-class neighborhood was so clogged by his funeral procession that traffic came to a standstill. For many Tamatavians, Pentecostal churches offer an attractive life option.

I doubt the homily delivered at the Ministry of Sports and Youth persuaded many in the audience to abstain from sex until marriage or to remain faithful to their partners, though everyone seemed entertained. Yet if the man's speech failed to convince his listeners that day, his viewpoint nevertheless resonated with many urbanites' sense of what was wrong with life in urban Madagascar in general, and Tamatave in particular. Whether in the newspapers or in day-to-day discussions heard around town, people who came from very different social positions expressed their concern about the issues he touched on. All these different actors also criticized the way the inhabitants of Tamatave had responded to the opening of Madagascar to an aggressive form of consumerist capitalism after almost twenty years of state socialism and comparative isolation.

Repeatedly, laments centered on the "problem" of "youth." One newspaper article, headlined "Malagasy Youth, Don't Throw Away Your Culture," warned: "There are many things coming here from around the world, bringing progress—like computers, new ways of dressing, etc. Youth are most touched by those changes because they really appreciate new things! And starting then we have begun to lose our Malagasy culture. The majority of youth, they are immediately seduced by the new culture coming from outside and they forget the culture of their elders" (*Tribune de Madagascar,* March 15, 1995, 9).

Yet another newspaper article spoke directly about the scandalous behavior taking place in Tamatave. The author described walking into an unnamed nightclub where he was distressed to find "things the day shouldn't see! The worst was this: girls of 13, 14, 15 years old—some just growing breasts. Men were giving them more liquor to drink than one can imagine. The Malagasy youth of Tamatave are ruined. Something must be done" (*Tribune de Madagascar,* March 22, 1995, 6).

Moralists writing to newspapers were not alone in this view. It was widespread among young people themselves. One young man, the son of a postal worker, voiced his frustration about the loss of older forms of masculinity,

which he attributed to the new economic policies. He captured this sense
of loss by referring to the changing value of cattle, traditionally a crucial
means for rural inhabitants, particularly men, to accrue wealth and prestige,
but now displaced by more modern commodities: "Before, Malagasy things
had weight, and if you had cattle, girls would fight over you; but nowadays
if you have cattle they would run away from you because you stink of cow
shit. But if you have a television and brought that home, then girls would be
following behind you. So what makes us Malagasy is diminishing, because
of the currents brought by liberalization."

His friend broadened these complaints to remark on the association between economic liberalization and the loss of cultural authenticity more
generally:

> [Economic] liberalization is a way of scattering things from overseas. For ex-
> ample, books, television, everything that you see in terms of lifestyle, none
> of it is bad in the American way of life [in its original context]. They use it as
> publicity [to show how great they are], but we have nothing that gives value to
> what is Malagasy because our morality was ruined by colonization. And then
> liberalization comes here too with all its ads to say that their foreign things
> are good. And we are hurt and say, "Our ways don't work anymore, let's look
> for our future over there. Let us go toward what is made by Europeans." You
> realize that there are bad consequences from liberalization.

The women who participated in the World AIDS Awareness Day march,
the many more young women who did not participate but whom the
marchers explicitly referred to, the Adventist speaker who lectured them, the
moralists writing to the local newspapers, and the young men who regret
the loss of a Malagasy world—all these parties might easily have blamed
one another for contributing to the circumstances they lamented. Despite
their concerns, however, they actively adopt the very pursuits that create the
situation they decry, even as they share a general perception of what is taking place. Collectively they tell a story of cultural corruption and loss caused
by Madagascar's abandonment of state-sponsored socialism and the switch
to economic liberalization in the 1990s. Though it might seem odd to associate cattle's loss of value with the end of the socialist period, given that
cattle as a cultural icon predates the arrival of state socialism by centuries,
such an association makes sense in the context of recent Malagasy history.
The socialist regime of the 1970s and 1980s claimed to have rescued an
indigenous Malagasy culture from the jaws of the neocolonial regime. Consequently, many likened the economic policies that replaced socialism to a

new kind of colonization, in part because these policies quickly brought an influx of foreign goods, practices, and technologies.

Ultimately these Malagasy commentators believe that young urbanites' attempts to attain adulthood through imported ideologies and consumerism drive this story of rupture, conjuring up an alarming future in which old values no longer matter and money rules. Nor are local commentators alone. Scholars from all over the world have long viewed youth as a source of rupture and as central to the creation of new and different futures. Among the reasons for this are their presumed propensity either to adopt foreign practices and throw off older ones or to reject present practices and recuperate older, newly revivified, traditions.

Both for scholars and for many Tamatavians, particular conceptions are at work that associate youth with rupture and assume that the practices of a subset of young people represent those of an entire generation. This way of interpreting generational change and its effects offers a symbolic shorthand for understanding more complex historical dynamics. But the changes selected for attention and highlighted as characteristic of an entire generation also mask important historical continuity, heterogeneity among young people, and the relation between young people's choices and the futures they create. The actual processes at work are far more subtle than such theories allow.

I suggest that the most effective way to understand a generation and the process of generational change is to focus not only on what young people do in the present, but on how they imagine—and seek to attain—a desired future. By examining how a generation slowly takes shape in relation to an imagined future, we can see that this process does not create a clean break with the past. Rather, cultural practices and ways of imagining what it means to be a proper person powerfully constrain how young people think and act. By expanding the depth of our analysis, we can also understand more deeply why young people seize on certain opportunities in the present, and we can afford to look more broadly at the variety of choices they may make, because we can appreciate the shared vision that informs them.

Generations are not simply social groupings that emerge as people enter adulthood or experience a particular historical event. They also create representations of what the life course is like and what it should be. Young people's own understandings and representations of the life course, of what youth are, and of the futures they envision play a central role. The way we imagine the future shapes the mundane strivings of our daily lives, though what we imagine does not always conform to what we create. As a means of understanding and acting, representations of youth and the life course are intrinsic to young people's actions, providing an experience-near view of how, through shared representations of change, we propel ourselves into the future.[1]

"Youth" in Africa: Beyond Rupture and Crisis

A language of crisis has long characterized modern, and particularly European, analyses of generations and their role in history—one thinks of the "lost generation" of 1914, the "rebellious generation" of 1968, the post-Soviet generation after the fall of the Berlin Wall in 1989, or the emergence of Generation X in the 1980s. Albeit in different ways, these examples foreground the role of cataclysmic events or sharp changes in economic circumstances affecting people's lives, dividing off those who come of age in such moments from those who come of age before or after—creating what we commonly think of as a *generation*. This way of imagining the emergence of a new generation, however, is a product of particular culturally shaped choreographies of past and future, including conceptions of historical progress that emerged in Europe in the late eighteenth and nineteenth centuries (Fussell 2000 [1975]; Wohl 1979).[2]

In recent years a language of rupture and crisis has reappeared in discussions of youth and globalization. Whether analyzing youth as child soldiers, as consumers in a newly globalized economy, as unemployed would-be workers, or as bearers and producers of youth culture, a large body of current work suggests that as young people seek to attain adulthood, they make a fundamental break with the past, as a precondition for a new and different future.[3] Nowhere is this emphasis on rupture more visible than in recent studies of youth in Africa. For example, one edited volume foregrounds "how young Africans today experience the ruptures and breaches in their lives brought about by historical processes of colonization and decolonization, the state of civil war, and the mechanisms of global capitalism" (Honwana and De Boeck 2005a, 2).[4] The authors further argue that "to many young people in contemporary Africa, . . . the order through which the postcolonial world has existed seems to have become entirely devoid of meaning. What is more, it has become incomprehensible, even unknown and totally irrelevant to young people's own understanding of the lives they lead. . . . These youth move in worlds governed by rules, norms, ethics and moralities that seem to have broken quite radically with all kinds of pasts" (2005a, 11). The image produced by such accounts is one in which contemporary youth seem to be cut off from an ongoing exchange between different generations, creating what some have called a crisis of social reproduction (Comaroff and Comaroff 2004).

This way of framing the lives of young people in Africa is useful in many respects. Scholars have been rightly concerned about how ongoing military conflict and economic collapse affect young people across Africa (Abbink and Van Kessel 2005; Christiansen, Utas, and Vigh 2006; Cruise-O'Brien 1996; Honwana and De Boeck 2005b; Mains 2007; Marguerat 2005; Richards 1996; Weiss 2002). They have documented how economic and social instability make it increasingly difficult for young people to attain valued forms of adulthood, drawing attention to the very real problem of "producing African futures" (Weiss 2004). In so doing, they take seriously young people's ways of thinking about their dilemmas, thereby illuminating how large numbers of youth, who make up a significant proportion of the population of the African continent, feel that proper social adulthood is beyond their grasp (Hansen 2005; Masquelier 2005).

It is tempting to rely on this kind of argument to build a theory of generations and generational change. After all, much of this work carefully depicts both the social forces that shape young people's lives and how young people interpret their experiences. In so doing, it implies that youth are crucial actors who link the pasts and futures of their societies. Yet precisely because this research focuses primarily on youth's experience of crisis in the present, it tends to leave unexplored the actual relationships between their actions and temporality more broadly—young people's ongoing and varied relationships to the past, present, and future.[5]

In the absence of an explicit attempt to theorize generational change, youth's experience of change can all too easily be taken as an analytic model of how change happens. And when interpreted as a model for how youth produce social change, a language of crisis and rupture comes eerily close to reproducing certain aspects of what Sewell (2005) refers to as stage theory. Used by a variety of authors from diverse disciplines, this way of thinking implies that change happens through a unilinear progression of stages, each marked by a radical break from the one that came before. Addressing social-historical change, stage theories include the social evolutionism of Spencer and Tylor, the modernization theory of Rostow, the historical materialism of Marx, and more recently, some variants of globalization theory (for recent discussions of the parallels between modernization theory and globalization theory see, for example, Cooper 2001 and Walley 2004). Addressing how individuals change over the life course, stage theories include the developmental approaches of Freud or Piaget. Whether they operate at the level of individual growth or structural and cultural change, stage theories tend to homogenize variation within stages while downplaying continuities that exist between them (Sewell 2005, 101).[6]

In recent years, the assumptions that characterize stage theories have been amply critiqued. Anthropologists, psychologists, biologists, and historians have all shown that there is more heterogeneity, more nonsynchrony, within developmental stages (childhood or youth, feudalism or capitalism) than the standard stage model allows (Castañeda 2002; Cole, Cole, and Lightfoot 2005; Durham 2004; Goody 1982; Gould 1996; Johnson-Hanks 2002).[7] Likewise, the idea that history moves forward according to a fixed progression of simple to complex, savage to civilized, or traditional to modern has long been set aside.

Scholars have sought to develop less linear, more contextually based theories of change over time in general and of change over the life course in particular. James Ferguson (1999), for example, shows how former miners on Zambia's Copperbelt use a complicated "full house" of strategies for organizing social life, ones that belie the linear progression central to stage theories. These strategies include going back to their rural farms rather than remaining the urbanites that modernization theory had predicted. Likewise, Jennifer Johnson-Hanks (2002, 2006) demonstrates how among young Cameroonian women, motherhood does not automatically imply adulthood. Not all women who bear children are mothers; rather, motherhood is a fluid status that women constantly seek to manipulate by keeping some children and giving up others. Her ethnography of Beti reproductive practice challenges the idea that giving birth is an event that automatically propels a person from one stage of life to the next.[8] In cultural and social history and in historical anthropology, stage theory has given way to a more microlevel tracing of patterns across multiple temporalities: here change is gradual and complex.[9]

Yet inadvertently, an uncritical emphasis on rupture tends to reproduce stage theory's overly tidy narrative, downplaying how deeply the "precrisis" past continues to influence young people's experiences in the "postcrisis" future. Nor does it adequately acknowledge how deeply uneven the changes young people experience really are. This way of conceiving the relation between young people and the futures they create all too frequently assumes that "youth" refers to all young people in a certain age bracket who live at a given time in a given place. It also implies that their actions naturally contribute to a clean break from the past. Most modernist accounts emphasized how youth led new nations into a bright new future—the vanguard of the revolution of whatever political stripe (Anderson 1972; Archer 1976; Chow

1967). By contrast, contemporary discussions of youth in Africa emphasize the dismantling of the modern dream and how young people become both victims and agents in this process of breakdown. The two narratives, however, are best viewed as mirror images. Either way, youth tend to be portrayed as a united group naturally predisposed to be agents of radical change.

This approach to the intersection between life course and history simply cannot account for the complex, lumpy patterns of social change in Tamatave—or anywhere else, for that matter. At one level it may appear that all "youth" participate in a given historical moment. But when one starts to examine who actually belongs to the category of "youth" in particular places at particular times, and who actually engages in the practices of "youth," it becomes clear that the term hides a wide range of social positions and interests. Nor are all young people cut off from their kin or others who belong to older or younger age groups. The same heterogeneity applies to historical processes. As Paul Connerton (1989, 9) reminds us in his analysis of the French Revolution, "The rejection of the principle of the dynastic realm, in this case the ritual enactment of that rejection, was still an account of, and a recalling of, the superseded dynastic realm." Even the symbols of the French Revolution were created with reference to the monarchical past. Whether youth are concretely involved in political movements that change their societies or in more mundane practices that transform everyday social life, it seems likely that their relationship to the past and engagement in the present is far more complicated than an emphasis on crisis and rupture allows.

To understand how youth contribute to historical change, we need a different way of conceptualizing the possible relationships of young people to history. We need to analyze their modes of agency and to develop a nuanced vocabulary for thinking about the issues of continuity and change at the heart of the matter. An emphasis on crisis, while often true to youth's experience, cannot do justice to the way young people in Madagascar actually contribute to patterns of social change. It cannot account for how the very idea of urban youth inevitably takes shape in relation to other life paths and trajectories. But it does hint at some of the ways young people create new futures through their actions *and* through what people imagine those actions to be.

Theorizing Historical Transformation: Lessons from the Indian Ocean

It seems fitting that a Malagasy port town offers a place to build a more nuanced account of social reproduction and change with broader geographic relevance. In fact a growing body of work, much of it from this part of the world, uses ethnographic and historical material to illuminate historical processes. Such work challenges the assumptions underpinning overgeneralized concepts such as globalization, modernization, and diaspora as vast, unidirectional historical movements by showing other ways of engaging with far-flung networks (Cooper 2001; Ho 2004; Prestholdt 2004; Tsing 2005; Walley 2004).

These works share the premise that the societies along the edge of the Indian Ocean, which have participated for centuries in networks of trade and have evolved highly cosmopolitan ways of life, offer a good vantage point from which to unsettle unidirectional histories. Christine Walley (2004), for example, has used her study of a marine park off the coast of Tanzania to critique the concept of globalization and its emphasis on the diffusion of modern institutions. She argues instead for the importance of multiple historical and social genealogies in explaining the social dynamics of development. Similarly, Jeremy Prestholdt (2004) examines east African consumption practices to show how seemingly peripheral places such as Zanzibar contribute to shaping global capitalism. He further suggests that by not recognizing the histories of interconnection in east Africans' relationships, we overprivilege the role of Western powers in forging those connections and undervalue the way those societies may have long constituted themselves in direct relation to others across the globe.

In a related spirit, numerous studies in Madagascar have highlighted the distinctive ways that contemporary Malagasy communities forge history and historical consciousness through incorporative practices centered on ancestors. Michael Lambek (2002), for example, has described religious practices in which ancestors play an important role, and through which the inhabitants of Mahajanga forge historical consciousness. Similarly, Laurent Berger (2006), in his study of the interaction between a monarchy in the north of Madagascar and a shrimp fishing company, has shown the highly sophisticated ways that local actors sought to use ancestral practices to negotiate with members of an NGO, local interests, and the national government. Both of these studies indicate long-standing forms of Indian Ocean cosmopolitanism and local modes of agency. This is a part of the world in which people have long integrated bits and pieces of different cultures into their own distinctive mosaics, and where people have always imagined themselves in relation to far-flung others.

Sex and Salvation focuses on young women's efforts to achieve respected adulthood through the sexual economy and the alternative paths they choose when they fail, paths that often lead them into Pentecostal churches.

And it analyzes the ways that young people's quest for success and older women's coming to terms with their failure, and their adoption of new, meaningful religious beliefs, transform older practices and normalize new ways of being, creating a new and different future. Here I focus more on the future than the past. But like the earlier studies cited above, I too use Malagasy practice in part to theorize history making as people selectively appropriate what they initially perceive as foreign practices. And like these studies from the greater Indian Ocean area, I use Tamatavian experience to query unidirectional, top-down histories.

While Tamatavians like the Adventist speaker quoted above attribute worrisome social changes to the influx of foreign ideas, the social practices they decry are not just foreign. Women have long used their sexual and reproductive capacities to create desirable economic and kin relationships in this part of the world. Such strategies are understandable as ways of attaining respected personhood by enabling the accumulation and flow of resources. These are also among the strategies families use to draw their sons-in-law into local networks, gaining access to the resources they might bring (Bois 1997). Likewise, local east coast cultural practice has long construed women as especially emotional beings, an emotionality that Pentecostalism elaborates and valorizes. This is not the familiar scenario in which global forces undermine local ones. Rather, we can see many points of interconnection and resonance between traditions that existed in Madagascar before the 1990s and the new practices brought by globalized consumer culture.

Numerous cultural commentators have pointed out that youthfulness, risk, play, and—I would add—sex are aspects of social life especially celebrated in late capitalism (Harvey 2005; Jameson 1991). So too, many have noted that with the rise of consumerism the young, particularly females, have become an increasingly visible category. Images of young women are constantly used to eroticize and sell consumer goods. As I will show in the following chapters, however, the existence of a distinctive youth culture, women's use of relationships with men to build valued social networks, and the use of foreign goods to mark status long predate current capitalist consumer culture. The ways women forged connections through sex, domestic service, and childbearing in nineteenth-century Madagascar are not the same as the highly commodified exchange of sex for money now found in Tamatave. Nevertheless, there are resemblances that must be taken into account. In complex ways, the past continues to shape how women build their lives.

Rather than using the metaphors of loss or replacement that are common in analyses of global change, my focus on Tamatavian practice foregrounds how social change may also be imagined in terms of synergy. Local, gendered body practices merge with aspects of late capitalist culture brought by recent economic reforms. *The American Heritage's Dictionary* defines "synergy" in terms of biology: "The action of two or more substances, organs or organisms to achieve an effect of which each is individually incapable." Extending this metaphor to social life highlights a complex change, partly indebted to past forms, as opposed to ideas of rupture. Metaphors such as synergy also prompt us to think about how, over time, even partial change can lead to qualitative transformations in social patterns.

Attending to Structure and History

I am arguing that recent economic reforms, and the influx of Western practices and images they enable, do not impose particular ways of being on young urban Malagasy, nor do Malagasy youth deliberately co-opt what they see of the West to create a new world. Rather, I see a series of small, incremental, and highly uneven changes that become transformative over time. In using existing cultural categories that give shape and meaning to the world, actors may inadvertently create new meanings or give different actors new kinds of power. This is the kind of change that studies of culture and history describe. Such studies show that by paying attention to the interactions between cultural structures and the events that make up history, we can create analyses that, unlike stage theory, presume that "social causality is temporally heterogeneous not temporally uniform" (Sewell 2005, 101).

For example, Marshall Sahlins's analysis of the eighteenth-century Hawaiians' encounter with the British explorer Captain Cook and the sailors who accompanied him to the South Seas offers a powerful example of how change can come about when people apply old ideas to new contexts. Soon after the British ships dropped anchor, Hawaiian commoners paddled out to them, the men to trade food for iron goods, the women to have sex with the sailors. The women, Sahlins tells us, were engaged in the traditional practice of "finding a lord: upward liaisons that would establish kinship relations with, and claims upon, the powers that be" (Sahlins 1985, 139). Meanwhile, the chiefs tried to seize control of the trade the commoners had started. They referred to the idea of *tabu*, "things set apart for the god," using it to control the commoners' ability to obtain metal axes. The commercial use of tabu by the chiefs to protect their advantage in trade thus eventually changed the meaning of tabu from "things set apart for the god" to a way to signal property rights. As Sahlins notes, what began as the logical extension of the conceptual category of tabu eventually acquired a new function and meaning (1985, 142). Likewise, because the women who went out to the ships could use their relationships with the sailors to gain precious trade goods in violation of the chiefs' tabus, they contributed to the breakdown of the old distinctions between men and women. As particular actors invoke cultural categories to pursue their culturally shaped projects and interests, they inadvertently change the meaning of those categories.[10]

William Sewell's (2005) rereading of Sahlins, as well as his efforts to theorize temporal complexity more generally, both modifies some of Sahlins's ideas and offers other pertinent examples for thinking about the transformations that might take place when a new generation forms.[11] Sewell points out that Sahlins's theory relies on a singular conception of culture, such that all Hawaiians appear to be incorporated into an overarching cultural structure. Given such an overarching conception, it is difficult to imagine how change can come about in the absence of an external event—like that provided by the arrival of Captain Cook.

This point is particularly relevant to what is taking place in Tamatave, a multiethnic port town where there clearly is not one site, but several competing arenas in which actors of different ages seek to build meaningful and successful lives. "Cultural structures," Sewell writes, "correspond not to distinct societies" (like the Hawaiians) but rather to "spheres or arenas of social practice of varying scope that intertwine, overlap and interpenetrate in space and time" (2005, 206). Second, Sewell suggests it is possible that the symbolic manipulations Hawaiians engaged in were more complex than Sahlins's discussion implies. *Islands of History* emphasizes how actors classify new phenomena within existing categories. But as Sewell points out, it is entirely possible that people might also splice together old categories to create new schemas or classifications. There can, in fact, be many creative conceptual permutations.

At the same time, there is always a complex, uneven relation between resources and cultural schemas that may further enable new patterns and new social relationships to emerge. Resources are always subject to social dynamics different from the ones that assigned them value in the first place (Sewell 2005). Young Malagasy women, for example, value European men, whose availability fluctuates in relation to political and economic factors— the ease of getting a visa to come to Madagascar, the convenience of starting a business there—that have little to do with any local system of cultural categories. Likewise, when older women join Pentecostal churches, they hope that Jesus will grant them new riches. But when they stay in the churches, they find new meanings that have little to do with material resources. At the same time, their new friendships may in fact bring new material opportunities. This multiplicity of disjunctive structures means there is always the possibility of unpredictable outcomes that may cumulatively lead to change.

These discussions about how groups change over time direct analytic attention to contests over meaning and resources in social life. The example of how the Hawaiians interacted with the British sailors, and Sewell's rereading of it, highlights the multiple interpretations that emerge as people encounter new events and liken them to earlier ones, transforming existing categories. They point to how struggles over resources may inflect cultural processes in unexpected ways. And they show that some structures may endure even in the midst of radical change.

Imagining the Future: Generations, the Life Course, and the Experience of Change in Everyday Life

Attending to how emergent generations participate in history making in the present shifts the emphasis from long ago, faraway events recorded in archives to the more experience-near domain of everyday life. It brings into view a multitemporal social field, because when we think about generations and the individual life course, we can no longer assume that cultural structures or social practices are all perceived or lived in the same way. Such a shift makes actors' representations of change—how they understand what is happening and how they imagine the future—a part of the analysis. We can begin to see that how people imagine the future via the life course shapes how change happens.

In his famous essay on generations, Karl Mannheim (1993 [1927]) notes that because the creation of cultural concepts and their transmission over time are never accomplished by the same individuals, we are constantly faced with both the problems and the advantages of what he calls "fresh contact"—the fact that there is a certain distance in how each new generation approaches and assimilates shared cultural material. For example, when young women in Tamatave enter the sexual economy to attain successful adulthood, they take up a way of engaging the world that was always a potential for women in Tamatave. At least some of them, however, develop and transform this strategy in ways quite different from what their grandmothers would have done. Mannheim further suggests that young people coming of age are particularly susceptible to this effect because they lack memory or ballast (1993 [1927], 371). Consequently he argues they are more open to adopting new ways of being and new practices, much as many folk theories of youth imply.[12]

The emergence of a new group of adult actors is surely central to this pattern. Equally important, however, are the stories people tell themselves about what some imagined entity called "a generation" is doing. In Tamatave, both older people and many young adults claim (like Mannheim) that the choices and behavior of young people uniquely produce change. They fear that all young people are abandoning school because it no longer provides jobs and that all young women risk becoming prostitutes in their pursuit of wealthy Europeans. I call this kind of simplifying discourse a synoptic illusion because it condenses a great deal of actual heterogeneity, making a subset of practices stand in for a more complex whole.[13] In reality, not all women seek Europeans. Nor do all young people who go to school fail to find jobs. And the slightly older women who participate in Pentecostal churches promote changes that are in some ways more radical than those initiated by their younger, European-seeking counterparts.

That representations of generations involve synoptic illusions and that it is impossible to define who really belongs to a given generation are not problems we need to solve simply to understand who the "true" members of any generation are (Newman 1996). Rather, we need to consider the social and subject-making work that those representations enable. After all, talk about maturation, the life cycle, gaps between generations, and such is not confined to social scientists theorizing regular patterns of change (Mead 1970; Newman 1996; Ryder 1965; Shanahan 2000; Wohl 1979). Popular representations and talk about bodily, individual change over time—what it means to be an adult or a child, to belong to the baby boom generation or to move between one status and the next—create a powerful, naturalized link between time and the body.[14] Conceptions of generations and of the life course help constitute subjects, because people imagine their capacities in part through the gender- and age-relative representations made available to them. The choices faced by a twenty-year-old woman in Tamatave in 2003, for example, are very different from those open to a woman of sixty. Cultural representations of the life course tell a person what he or she is supposed to be doing at a given point in life. They are integrally tied to people's efforts to achieve valued forms of personhood.

In their everyday lives, actors draw on the metaphors of human growth and change to interpret and transform their historical circumstances and life course. This is the domain of everyday practice in which all people—whether they have children or not—constantly read their own historical experience in relation to the young people around them and vice versa. Once we think of generations in part as representations rather than as natural groupings, we can begin to understand that there is a politics to how representations and perceptions of the life course work. After all, any representation is partial, highlighting some dimensions of social life and occluding others.

More important, we can begin to inquire into the effects of these ideas about the life course and how they become a causal force in social life. In this regard, I argue for the causal force of generations-cum-synoptic illusion—in the loose sense of causal either as something that makes other things happen or as "telling a story about how something came to be" (Sewell 2005, 111). Talk about generations does not exist separately from the social world: such discourse has consequences for how people experience their lives and how they act. It shapes choices and trajectories. Timothy Mitchell (1998, 2002), for example, has shown that while the idea of a national economy is often thought of as "a material substrate with an existence prior to and separate from its representation" (1998, 84), in fact representation of the economy has profound practical implications. Today, of course, experts constantly invoke "the economy" to justify particular political policies; it is regularly used to effect change in the world.

So too, imaginings of the life course and our fantasies of what the future might look like based on young people's actions have effects. In Tamatave, public discourse decries the fact that young women enter the sexual economy as a way to get ahead. Although this discourse oversimplifies what is actually taking place, it also shapes young women's actions because it privileges certain models to which other young women relate. As I show in chapters 5 and 6, these simplified modes of representation based on a synoptic illusion operate as stereotypes that popularize sexual strategies. Whether they emerge from scholarly theories or local theories or combine the two, representations of the life course are part of how history happens, because they make certain paths, certain social trajectories, easier to imagine than others. Perceptions of social change focused on a particular group work in a representational feedback loop with actors' beliefs about what is possible, influencing their own efforts to achieve their goals. Tracking how generational change contributes to social change means attending to the ways that discourses about age groups simultaneously obscure and make possible certain kinds of actions among actors differentially positioned within various temporal trajectories.

Yet there are always multiple paths that do not necessarily map neatly onto representations of generational transitions. In the same way that focusing on a select group of young people as embodying historical change obscures and simplifies actual heterogeneity, so too focusing on generational emergence obscures how people continue to adopt new social and cultural practices throughout their lives. These other kinds of personal changes may also have consequences for wider public culture. In Tamatave, slightly older women who join Pentecostal churches actively adopt novel practices. Like the young women who pursue European husbands, these women too seek their fortune in the sexual economy, but for the most part they are a few years older and have traveled a bit further down that path. They have often married Malagasy men, borne children, and settled down. Like the young women who seek European husbands to build a happier, more secure life, these women also want the resources that signal the ability to support others. Pentecostalism appeals to them at first because it promises comparative wealth. But when such promises fail, Pentecostal churches give members unexpected ways to create new meanings in their lives. Examining women's participation in these churches reveals still other ways of creating the future, ones that are different from, but in some ways respond to, the opportunities and constraints encountered by younger women.

Such a multipath approach enables a perspective on social change that attends both to people's representations of their experience and to the role these representations might play in everyday life. It also captures the contingent play of multiple temporalities, not only those offered by local cultural processes or the rhythms of global capitalism (though these are very much apparent), but also those shaped by the social tempo of how human bodies and capacities change, or how people encounter new ways of being that they may actively embrace. The women who pursue European husbands in the sexual economy and those who enter Pentecostal churches hold up a mirror to each other, so that the life course of one group unfolds in relation to other possible patterns. These alternatives exist in dialectical relation to one another, further contributing to changes in the social landscape and the emergence of new futures.

Why Women?

In the following chapters, I focus primarily on women. Men do figure among my informants, and in one of my return trips to Tamatave I spent the entire time talking to young men. Nevertheless, my focus on women merits preliminary comment.

When Tamatavians talk about change in their daily life, when they worry that young women in nightclubs are selling themselves or that everyone now lives in a "sex-worshiping" world, they often talk about women. This is not to say they never use men as examples; recall the young man who remarked that, before, men wanted cattle whereas now they want televisions. Nevertheless, on balance women figure in this discourse more frequently than men. My earlier work on memory (1998, 2001) privileged the perspectives of men because the rural Betsimisaraka villagers I lived with constructed their memories primarily through male ancestors (even when some of my best informants about those stories or practices were women). Likewise, this book goes into more depth about the changing lives of women because during my fieldwork everyday popular discourse on change by women and men alike foregrounds the particular young women who seek, and sometimes find, European husbands.

There are, of course, many comparable historical and ethnographic examples where women's behavior generates anxiety and women become the object of moral discourse. One thinks of the figure of the unwed African American teenager in the 1980s, prostitutes in Victorian London, or, in the case of Africa, numerous public scandals over rural women who moved to the cities during colonial rule (Hodgson and Mcurdy 2001; Mutongi 2007; Rose 1999; Rubin 1984; Smith-Rosenberg 1990; Thomas 2003; Walkowitz 1992; White 1990). Scholars often interpret such upsurges in public concern as "moral panics" or "sex panics"—"the process of representing and demonizing scapegoats in popular culture and media" (Herdt 2009, 7).[15] They have shown that such moral panics often provide a way for dominant groups to mobilize state resources and reestablish control over group boundaries (Rose 1999).[16]

Though there is much of value in this kind of analysis, it does not map easily onto the situation I discuss for Tamatave. Not all anxiety about women's behavior is generated for the same reasons, nor does it always lead to the greater control of women, as much of the international literature on the topic implies. We need to understand the symbolic and historical resonances that give rise to a particular discourse. In Tamatave there are specific kinship practices and ideas about subject formation that make women particularly fit subjects through which to imagine social change. East coasters reckon kinship bilaterally even though they privilege patrilineal connections. Marriage is supposed to be virilocal—women should follow their husbands when they marry. The result of this system is twofold. First, women have a good deal of freedom in their relationships with men. Second, women are always symbolically and practically associated with movement away from the ancestral land, the locus classicus of continuity and timeless reproduction in Madagascar (Bloch 1971). In addition, east coasters often claim that women and men are differently constituted. As I noted earlier, women are commonly said to be more volatile than men, more prone to excesses, and supposedly less likely to control their emotions (see also Feeley-Harnik 1984;

Keenan 1974). Rural inhabitants regularly invoke this conception to justify why women should not have the same access to ancestral power as men do. These ideas make women particularly resonant subjects through which east coasters imagine social change and give it form in their daily lives. And that imagining is an important part of how change actually happens.

Conclusion

The everyday ways people experience time and create a sense of the future are fundamental to a cultural analysis of how change takes place. If, as a long lineage of scholarship has argued, the "body is the first and most natural tool of man" (Mauss 1973 [1935]), providing humans with endless metaphors through which to imagine social relations, then transitional moments in the life course associated with rapid bodily change are the most "natural tool" for how human beings imagine social and historical change.[17] Cultural representations of how people change over the life course are not only about how we come to experience ourselves in time. They also provide an experience-near view of how, through shared representations of change, we propel ourselves into the future. But insofar as the formation of a new generation provides a natural tool and draws our attention, it may also inadvertently obscure other ways personal change contributes to broader patterns of historical transformation over the life course.

Once we begin to realize that the emergence of a new generation does not inevitably produce discontinuities in existing patterns, that sometimes people adopt new practices much later in life, and that youth constantly interact with, and respond to, people of other generations, we can begin to explore how the life course and change are imagined in relation to one another in particular times and places. Doing so reveals that actors' perceptions of their role in the life course create a feedback loop between their representations and their actions that contributes to the larger process of social change. How actors imagine change and how it happens, as seen from an external point of view, always exist in tension with one another. The views of those who track changes overlap with the views of those caught up in its throes, but in ways no one can predict. But it is a tension that historically informed ethnographic research can illuminate.

In the pages that follow I trace these strands to show the subtle ways local conceptions of gendered personhood, the life course, and recent economic change all converge to make entering the sexual economy an appealing way for some young women to get the resources that enable adulthood. Some go on to attain one widely shared ideal of female Tamatavian adulthood, even as they transform the wider social terrain and the range of acceptable cultural practice. These women's strategies and the new futures they enable can be understood only in relation to their families and the wider social world. Consequently, the first three chapters focus not on young people per se but on ideas about personhood, political and economic change, and the gendered life course more generally. Insofar as the changes wrought initially by urbanization, and more recently by economic liberalization, affect many dimensions of social life, I return to these themes from different angles in all of these chapters. At the same time, women's choices also need to be examined in relation to the other options for forging a viable life in Tamatave. For many women, new kinds of Pentecostalism offer a powerful and appealing alternative path to the future. Following these different paths, and watching as these women creatively seek to forge viable futures, we will begin to see how new, initially inchoate dimensions of social life gradually take form and solidify, and how different options come to coexist.

TWO

Making Modern Life in Tamatave: Shifting Paths to Social Mobility

The first impression most people get of Tamatave is dilapidated colonial splendor. The city was rebuilt in the late 1920s after being destroyed by a cyclone, and wide boulevards lined with palm trees and the occasional flame tree transect its heart. Colonial-style concrete buildings, including the mayor's office, the post office, and the train station, frame the boulevards. Until the tracks became unusable in the mid-1990s, the station marked the end of the railway line from the capital city of Antananarivo. Many of the fancier hotels and old colonial villas, some designed by the French architects Georges Cassaigne and Jean Henri Collet de Cantelou, are also in this area. Today government officials, wealthy merchants, and high-level executives in various businesses live in these buildings. Nightclubs also line the boulevards that run from north to south. At night, women looking for men stand beneath the widely spaced streetlights, giving them one of their many slang names—*mazava alina*, "lit at night."

Toward the southeastern edge of the town lie the port, the commercial houses, and the "big bazaar" (*bazary be*)—this is the marketplace that was formerly intended for Europeans and is still used primarily by expatriates, wealthy Malagasy, and Chinese and Indian merchants. Farther to the west is the small bazaar where most Malagasy shop. Moving away from the port and nestled between the boulevards are the various residential neighborhoods: Tanambao II (close to the port, and reputed to be where the women who worked the boats as prostitutes lived in the past), Tanambao V, Tanamakoa, Ankirihiry, and Ambolomadinika, to name just a few. Much farther north, near the airport, where flights arrive daily from Antananarivo and biweekly from Réunion, is a neighborhood called Tahiti Kely—Little Tahiti—where many expatriates and wealthy Malagasy live. As you move past the downtown boulevards and enter the residential neighborhoods, the broad

N

Cap d'Ambre
Antsiranana

Ambilobe
Daraina

Nosy Be
Ambanja
Andravory

Sambava
Bealanana
Andapa
Antsohihy
Antalaha
Befandriana-Nord
Cap Est
Baie de Bombetoke   Mahajanga   Maroantsetra
Katsepy
Marovoay   Mandritsara
Cap Saint André   Soalala   Mampikony   Cap Masoala
Besalampy   Baie d'Antongil
Lac
Kinkony   Ambato-Boeni
Maevatanana   Ile Sainte Marie
Soanierana-Ivongo
Lac Alaotra
Fénérive-Est
Maintirano   Ambatondrazaka
Ankazobe   Didy
Anjozorobe   Toamasina
Antsalova   Tsiandro   Andasibe   "Tamatave"
Lac Bemamba   Tsiroanomandidy   Antananarivo   Brickaville
Lac Itasy   Moramanga   Ambila-Lemaitso
Bekopaka   Beforona
Ambatolampy   Vatomandry
Belo-sur-Tsiribihina   Miandrivazo   Tsinjoarivo
Betafo   Antsirabe
Morondava   Mahabo   Marolambo
Malaimbandy   Fandriana
Belo-sur-mer   Ambatofinandrahana   Ambositra

Ifanadiana
Fianarantsoa
Ambalavao
Morombe   Ikongo
Lac Ihotry   INDIAN
Ihosy   OCEAN
Ivohibe
Sakaraha   Ilakaka
Farafangana
Ifaty   Betroka
Toliara
Anakao   Vangaindrano
Betioky-Sud

Bekily
Beraketa
Itampolo   Ampanihy   Ranomafana-Atsimo
Isaka-Ivondro
Beloha   Amboasary   Mandena
Tsiombe   Tolagnaro
Cap Sainte Marie   Ambovombe
Faux Cap

Figure 2.1. Map of Madagascar.

Figure 2.2. A street scene in Tamatave, 2009. Courtesy of Laura Tilghman.

empty spaces and graceful colonial style switch abruptly to intense crowd-
ing as the streets narrow and become filled with buses and trucks, tiny taxis,
men pulling rickshaws (*pousse-pousse*), and people on bicycles. Small stands
where traders sell everything from used cigarette lighters and plastic combs
to tea and coffee crowd the edges of the road. Moving even farther from the
big boulevards, you stumble into the sand paths: narrow, winding unpaved
streets often marked off by hedges of *hasina* plants. This is the terrain across
which men and women, young and old, rich and poor, the lifelong inhabitant and the visiting day migrant all travel in their various life courses. It is
an experienced, social landscape, not an objective one.

Wealth starts at the port and moves outward, first in comparatively large
quantities controlled by European, Chinese, Indian, and Merina (one of the
largest ethnic groups in the country) merchants. These businessmen, who
often live in the villas near the large bazaar and along the shore, own many
of the import-export businesses around the port. The money gained from
this large-scale business is used for still other transactions. It gets divided
into smaller portions as it is spent among more modest Chinese and Merina
merchants who live on the larger streets that crosscut the neighborhoods.
Lower-level employees of the major mercantile firms who live in some of

the better-appointed houses with electricity and running water also receive a share. Finally, various transactions bring some of the money into the depths of the sand paths. Here, if you go far enough, you might believe you were in the Malagasy countryside. The inhabitants, if they are employed at all, work as maids, security guards, pousse-pousse pullers, or very petty traders. The status urbanites receive from working in the state bureaucracy as doctors, midwives, teachers, or secretaries crosscuts and intertwines in complex ways with this uneven flow of wealth from the port. While this spatial and monetary snapshot offers a glimpse of some aspects of life in Tamatave, it does not tell us much about the social processes and the longer history of layered interactions that have formed it.

To understand the way people imagine and create change in the present, we must begin with the way social life flowed forward in the past. This chapter offers a history of Tamatave. At first glance, the periodization I use (precolonial, colonial/neocolonial, socialist, and post–economic liberalization) may appear idiosyncratic, since most histories of African nations divide the past into precolonial, colonial, and postcolonial periods. However, this division makes sense with respect to Madagascar's history. Historians of the island generally accept that the structures French colonizers put in place continued to operate during the years of the First Republic (1960–1972), making neocolonial an appropriate label. Each of the periods I examine here offers different sources for building a historical narrative. Some are richer than others in what they tell us about the history of youth and the gendered life course. But when read together, these disparate sources offer a sense of how Tamatavian social reproduction has changed over time and provide insight into the cultural concerns that have shaped it. Exploring the long history of creolization and métissage, particularly among elites, the dramatic formation of "youth" as a new, more visible social category through the colonial institutionalizing of schooling, and finally the more recent period of economic liberalization that has changed the social and economic landscape and sharpened social inequalities remains profoundly important for understanding contemporary processes of social change. Contemporary Tamatave is a palimpsest, and the inhabitants of the city draw on bits and pieces of the precolonial, colonial, and state-socialist past, endlessly reworking them into new patterns.

Precolonial Contexts: From the Zanamalata
to the Créoles Malgaches

Tamatave is on Madagascar's east coast, facing the Indian Ocean and the Mascarene Islands of Mauritius and Réunion. It has been a port of call for ships traveling throughout the Indian Ocean since the seventeenth century. During the eighteenth century, many lineages, each an independent political entity, together occupied the area that stretched from Tamatave in the south up to the Bay of Antongil in the north. At the time, settlers from France and England had already established planter colonies on the Mascarene Islands of Bourbon (later Réunion) and Isle de France (later Mauritius). These previously uninhabited islands had neither a ready supply of food nor a source of labor, so European settlers relied on Madagascar for slaves, cattle, and rice. The trade in these items proved lucrative for middlemen in both locations. It also led to constant fighting among the lineages seeking to control the ports that gave access to this trade. Numerous Europeans also came from the Mascarenes to set up concessions, and European pirates hid out in the inlets along the coast and attacked ships heading to the Indies (Deschamps 1949). The historian Manasse Esoavelomandroso described the area in the eighteenth century: "It was thus a contact zone, in which populations of diverse origins mixed. . . . The littoral band, the hills and the forest region all possessed varied and complementary natural riches that were sought after by European traders. This explains the arrival and installation of numerous traders from Europe and the Mascareigns. To this natural wealth was added that of pirate booty—the riches stolen from the Arab and European ships making their way to the Indies" (1979, 42).

Madagascar's natural resources, along with its suitability for trade and agriculture, drew numerous groups of foreigners to the region. There they often married local women and settled down. The children of these unions were referred to as the *zanamalata*, literally mulatto or métis offspring. They were considered the leaders of eighteenth-century east coast society (Sylla 1985).

In 1712 the competing ancestries in the area forged a political alliance called the Betsimisaraka Federation, literally, "the many that won't be sundered." The alliance sought to control the east coast ports, securing their profits from the slave trade against ancestries from farther south. During the colonial period (1895–1960), French administrators generalized and ethnicized the name, applying it to even to those inhabitants of the central east coast who had no part in the original political organization (Cole 2001).[1] The unity implied in the name was always more notional than real, how-

ever. By the turn of the nineteenth century, the federation had already succumbed to internal conflict, provoked in part by competing slave traders.

The federation's social disorganization made it easy prey when the Merina king Radama I (r. 1810–1828), who was expanding the Merina kingdom of the high plateau, conquered the east coast and took control of the
ports.[2] The conquest of the port enabled the Merina to negotiate directly
with foreigners and gain greater control over the resources that came from
those connections.[3] In the first half of the nineteenth century the traveler
Legueval de Lacombe guessed the population at 800 to 1,000 inhabitants
(Lacombe 1840). By 1883, with the Merina firmly implanted and a brisk
trade flowing through the port, the population had already grown to approximately 7,000 to 12,000 (Lacaze 1881). The Merina conquest of Tamatave in the nineteenth century marked the beginning of an ethnic-cum-class
distinction that endures to this day.

Yet the Merina state's conquest of Tamatave and its control of the port
never entirely stopped other foreigners from coming. By the late nineteenth
century, however, the reasons for their arrival had changed. As a nascent
plantation system began to replace the pillage and slave trading of the past,
the foreign men who now came to the east coast were not pirates or slave
traders but would-be farmers and traders from Mauritius and Réunion. The
Merina state, however, forbade foreigners to own either land or slaves. This
problem could be addressed through local marriage, which was already a
long-standing custom. The bilateral inheritance patterns practiced along the
coast allowed women to inherit land from their kin, though less than their
brothers received. Foreign husbands could gain access to capital through
their wives' inheritances. Over time these unions resulted in a new group
of commercial intermediaries. Unlike the earlier zanamalata, these métis
tended to make their livelihood from trading in cattle and the beginnings
of a concession economy. At the same time this new group—sometimes referred to as *créoles malgaches*—was more attached to connections in Réunion
and France than the zanamalata had been. They sent their children to be
educated in the Mascarenes or in France, raised them as Catholics, and
generally sought to cultivate their foreign connections. Many of the créoles
malgaches spoke fluent Malagasy, French, and English as well as the creole
dialect (Esoavelomandroso 1980).

Although most of these in-married men and their sons earned their livelihood by farming and perhaps making rum, some sought upward social
mobility by entering the Merina bureaucracy. As their state expanded in Tamatave and along the east coast, the Merina created various administrative
posts (Esoavelomandroso 1979). These posts included the *adriambaventy*

Figure 2.3. Women played a central role in both precolonial and colonial-era Tamatave. This photo depicts a woman returning from Mass.

and the *manamboninahitra*—men who represented the Merina king or queen, collecting taxes, overseeing customs, and transmitting government orders. Although such posts did not bring a salary, they did give occupants some prestige and added control over local resources, including access to manpower. Consequently, the creation of a state bureaucracy offered one route through which a few men—créoles malgaches in particular—might acquire power under the new conditions. Esoavelomandroso (1979) describes how, during Merina rule of the east coast, Radama appointed Corroller, a member of an important local métis family, to be the grand judge of Tamatave. Clearly, the brisk trade through Tamatave's port, and the rich agricultural possibilities along the east coast, fostered a thoroughly hybrid, métis social world, particularly among elites.

In the second half of the nineteenth century, the relative openness of Tamatave shifted constantly in response to tensions between the Merina, who sought to retain and expand their control in Madagascar, and the French, who tried more aggressively to formally colonize the island. Nevertheless, a distinctively cosmopolitan way of life remained characteristic of Tamatave. The leaders of local society established their socioeconomic dominance by forging alliances with outsiders. Tamatavians often used clothing, as well as the style and materials of their houses, to signal the social privilege that came from these connections (Bois 1996, 2001). It is not surprising, then, that nineteenth-century Tamatavians regularly showed interest in foreign goods and practices. William Ellis (1858, 135), a missionary for the London Missionary Society, described Tamatavian youth's keen interest in the outside world. They were also fascinated with his camera and wanted to learn to take photographs. Landing in Tamatave in 1862, he described a bustling scene:

> The conduct of the Merina King—who had not only invited foreigners to settle in the island for trade or other purposes, but had abolished all duty on exports and imports—had caused quite a rush to the country from almost all parts of the world, and something like an inundation of merchandise. Many houses had been built in Tamatave, and others were in the course of erection; traders from Europe and from America had increased; Moors and Arabs I had seen there before, but now I noticed a sort of chandler's shop kept by a Chinaman, the first of his race that I had ever seen in the country. As signs of progress, there was a hotel, one or two bakers, who supplied good bread everyday, and there was a billiard table, though, as I was informed, not much frequented by the natives. (1862, 12)

Even with these colorful details, it is difficult to know what the life course looked like in the past, given the paucity of sources. What we do know is that by 1881 the Merina Royal Code fixed the end of schooling obligations, and hence the assumption of adulthood, at sixteen years of age (Esoavelomandroso 1992). To be sure, the economy and political organization of the central east coast differed considerably from that of Imerina, the area of central Madagascar inhabited by the Merina ethnic group. Nevertheless, this ruling may reflect Tamatavian views of adulthood as well. Though we cannot assume that contemporary rural practices mirror the life course of the past, based on my rural fieldwork and the evidence of earlier Merina practices, it seems likely that individuals on the east coast also moved from a phase of relative dependence to a complicated network of interdependencies established in their late teens. The movement between these social statuses differed according to gender, with women achieving adult status mainly through marriage and men acquiring it as they amassed the resources to support and control dependents. By the end of the nineteenth century, then, east coasters were seeking social mobility and locally respectable adult status through connections with foreigners. Intermarrying, adopting foreign material culture, and controlling external resources were already visible as strategies for achieving socioeconomic and cultural dominance.

Colonial and Neocolonial Contexts: Schooling and Making a Petite Bourgeoisie

France's formal colonizing of Madagascar in 1895 introduced new pathways to social mobility and social distinction, including new kinds of education and new job opportunities. At the same time, many old social strategies remained, as Tamatavians continued to adopt foreign practices as a way to achieve and mark social mobility. Under French colonial rule, elite Malagasy sought to emulate their French colonizers, at least in certain respects.

Political and economic structures in Tamatave diversified over the course of the colonial (1895–1960), and neocolonial (1960–1972) periods. Although producing rice for their own consumption was still important, more families in Tamatave province began to farm cash crops introduced by the colonial state, including coffee, lychees, and cloves. By 1931, 15,000 people inhabited Tamatave, 3,500 of them either Europeans or Malagasy who had been legally assimilated to European status (Frenée 1931). Tamatave's economy remained closely tied to the port even as the town grew as an administrative center, providing customs control, a courthouse, and veterinary services. Although the area around Tamatave still relied on colonial cash crops (vanilla, coffee, cloves, cocoa, sugarcane), there was also some mining of graphite and mica. The French also established several industries in and around Tamatave to process local products: a coffee processing plant, rum distilleries, and a fish refrigeration plant.

The expansion of the government bureaucracy as well as the growth of Christian missionary presence created new jobs and new levels and forms

Figure 2.4. Likely introduced during the colonial period, the pousse-pousse
is one of the most common means of transport in Tamatave.

of social status. With the growth of a colonial bureaucracy that relied partly
on Malagasy labor, some elite Malagasy sought government jobs as sub-
alterns, health professionals, and teachers. The continued importance of
various missions, however, made it possible for other east coasters to move
up the social hierarchy by becoming pastors, priests, or nuns, or in other
ways affiliating themselves with Christian missions. While French repub-
lican sensibilities encouraged French colonial administrators to limit the
power of the church, for Malagasy, civil and religious paths to social status
were never mutually exclusive. Whether one sought social mobility through
the state or through the church, it became increasingly necessary to have
literacy and numerical skills. With colonization, schooling began to hold
the key to advancement.

Missions, Schools, and the Colonial Bureaucracy

Perhaps more than any other change during the colonial period, wider
schooling radically reshaped conceptions of young people, producing new
notions of youth as well as new kinds of generational cohorts. Over the
colonial period, regardless of whether a family could afford to educate its
children, those aspiring to move upward came to see schooling as a sure

path to social ascension and prestige, the sign of a modern young man. The following description by Marc André Ledoux, a Protestant missionary to Madagascar who was active in the Boy Scouts movement in the mid-twentieth century, gives some sense of the overwhelming social significance attributed to school as a collective instrument of modernization:

> The existence of even one modest school is a revolution, a radically new element in village life. The school introduces practices, rhythms, schedules and calendars hitherto unknown. It also introduces a new hierarchy, where the prestige of a diploma replaces the hierarchy based on age. . . . School opens a door before young people enclosed in the static world in which they have lived and tempts them into the world beyond the village. . . . they can go to the regional school, where they may get their diploma. "To have the certificate" confers a certain prestige and opens the door to numerous jobs, whether public or private. The first step in social ascension is attained. (Ledoux 1951, 197)

Ledoux's observation reflects an ideology that contrasts the traditional with the modern and assumes that schooling is synonymous with modernity. Tamatavians widely embraced this ideology.[4]

In the late nineteenth century, the missionaries first promoted schooling; Catholic schooling was the privilege of an elite few. By the end of the nineteenth century, though, the Catholic mission operated a school adjacent to the cathedral of Saint Joseph in Tamatave. The Catholic sisters, Les Soeurs de Cluny, ran another school for girls. Finally the London Missionary Society (LMS) created a separate Protestant school for Merina, though the LMS was not particularly active in colonial-era Tamatave. The school was by the old Merina fort and later was taken over by the Anglican mission. Generally, however, the missionary effort was less intense in Tamatave than in Antananarivo (Esoavelomandroso 1978). Consequently there were fewer parochial schools in Tamatave than on the high plateau. Young people in Tamatave had less access to schooling and the opportunities it offered.

French colonization softened, but did not eradicate, this nineteenth-century disparity in schooling. When the French officially colonized Madagascar, Governor-General Joseph Gallieni built a network of lay schools, mostly in the coastal regions. He intended the schools both to counter missionary education and to offset Merina dominance by helping coastal people gain the skills that would let them become functionaries in the colonial administration. Trying to balance the colonial budget, subsequent governors Victor Augagneur (1905–10) and Albert Picquié (1910–1914) closed many of the schools Gallieni had created (Thompson and Adloff 1965). During the first half of the twentieth century, in fact, only one school, Le Myres de Villiers in Antananarivo, remained for the express purpose of training Malagasy government workers. Despite the vagaries of French colonial policy and funding, however, institutionalized state schooling expanded during the colonial period.[5] In 1931 Tamatave boasted a primary school for Europeans, a regional school, and several primary schools for Malagasy children (Frenée 1931). Although rates of schooling were proportionately higher around Antananarivo, an estimated 31 percent of youth in the province of Tamatave attended school (Randrianja 2001).[6] Over the colonial period, schooling and literacy became the primary route through which east coasters sought to raise their social status by participating in what was initially seen as a foreign institution.[7]

The spread of schooling had both a practical and a symbolic dimension, producing new age groupings and resymbolizing youth and what it meant to achieve a successful adulthood. The introduction of schooling took children and youth out of their families, where they were expected to work and contribute to household production. For those east coasters who hoped to achieve success through the routes laid out by the colonial system, youth came to be regarded as a period when young people and their families were supposed to invest in education to guarantee their futures. Sending a child to school marked the first step in transforming young people from producers into consumers. It was in the context of colonial, and later neocolonial, schooling that a nascent consumer youth culture emerged, though on a restricted scale and with the characteristic colonial dynamic of drawing models from metropolitan France. Speaking of elite youth who attended school in the early 1950s, Ledoux remarked, "The high school students try, at the beginning of each school year, to dress themselves according to the style of their peers who have recently arrived from Europe" (1951, 191). He also noted, "They dream of getting a good job, think that anything is possible, argue about basket-ball matches and go to the cinema. They are now like youth in any country" (1951, 187).

Like their European counterparts who worried that industrialization and urbanization caused moral corruption, educators in Madagascar worried that in a society that already figured in the colonial social imaginary of the time as "young" and only partway along the path toward full "adulthood," Malagasy youth would be easily seduced by the superficial glitter of civilization rather than absorbing its moral substance (Esoavelomandroso 1992; Hatzfeld 1953). One missionary, for example, worried that because Malagasy never came into contact with European peasants or industrial workers, but saw only wealthy administrators, they would gain a false sense of European wealth, to the missionary's detriment. "We have to recognize," Hatzfeld wrote, "that the missionary cuts a poor figure. He is not a big vazaha [European]" (1953, 302).

Seeking to prevent such moral corruption, the major missions established institutions like the Boy Scouts (called Jeunes Éclaireurs in French or Tily in Malagasy, meaning scouts who light the path) and youth hostels, in order to educate youth beyond the classroom and create model Christian citizens. In the primarily Protestant and Anglican context of youth groups in Antananarivo, they sought to create the *olombanona*—"the good man."[8] The "good man" was someone who was intelligent, educated, deeply Christian, and sensitive to the broader demands of social life, and who never lived beyond his means. Revealing the deep connections between this model and a Protestant emphasis on thrift and sober consumption, one pastor remarked, "It is better for a young man to have paid the head tax and wear a simple shirt, than to not pay it and have a suit made of serge" (cited in Esoavelomandroso 1992, 406).

It is not clear whether the Catholic priests and nuns who were responsible for much religious education in largely Catholic Tamatave entirely shared these Protestant concerns about moral development. Nevertheless, many ideas regarding the proper formation of spiritually vulnerable young people circulated in the wider, educated urban public sphere. In 1931 Father du Mas Paysac became head of the mission in Tamatave, starting a local branch of the Boy Scouts and opening one likely path for diffusing these ideas across Madagascar (Delval 1992). What is certain is that by the mid-twentieth century, schooling, possibly giving entry into the lower ranks of the colonial administration, was one of the most coveted routes to social mobility. Joining the church offered an alternative path to the same ends, a point that will become relevant again in chapter 7, where I discuss the opportunities offered by contemporary Pentecostal churches.

Marriage and the Intimate Domain

If men could acquire prestige from careers in the church or state bureaucracy, new kinds of marriage that accompanied French colonization opened up avenues for women to gain higher status. As more women gained some education, they signaled their upward mobility by new marriage practices that were symbolically marked as both foreign and modern (see Cole and Thomas 2009; Thomas and Cole 2009).

Aspiring east coasters' desired to adopt French marriage forms in a context where missionaries and colonial administrators alike scorned local Malagasy practices. During the nineteenth century, missionaries regularly attacked what they saw as the promiscuous ways of east coast women, citing their perceived sexual license as evidence of moral turpitude. In 1838 the LMS missionary William Ellis lamented, "Their sensuality is universal and gross, though generally concealed: continence is not supposed to exist in either sex before marriage, consequently it is not expected, and its absence is not regarded as a vice" (Ellis 1838, 138). Missionaries and educators in the church also railed against what they saw as the practical, nonspiritual nature of Malagasy marriage, which so frequently ended in divorce and remarriage. Folkloric descriptions of indigenous marriage written for colonial audiences, like one that appeared in *La Femme Coloniale*, failed to see how the exchange of goods might carry a moral-emotional dimension and a material dimension simultaneously.[9] As a result, they consistently depicted marriage practices as simply a haphazard quest for the material goods of bridewealth, misunderstanding the local importance of marriage exchanges.

Judging local marriage practices inadequate, missionaries sought to reform them and create proper Christian wives, better suited to the "new men" being fashioned in schools and church groups. They opened housekeeping schools, and they also produced a rich didactic literature for women. These pamphlets taught women how to arrange their homes ("put the radio in the bedroom, arrange decorative objects prettily in the salon") and how to care for their families ("always finish your outing and change your clothes before your husband returns home, so that he is happy with you, otherwise he might be tempted to have an affair"). Much of this writing also encouraged Malagasy families to treat marriage as a spiritual bond. For example, in a booklet aimed at preparing youth spiritually for marriage, a section titled "Fanamboaranatena," which might translate loosely as "The Care or Arrangement of the Self," explained the spiritual transformations young people needed to make before marrying and setting up their own households (Rakotonirina 1960, 15). Conforming to such ideals of modern marriage became yet another way for Tamatavians to mark status and attain prestige. But as the account below demonstrates, such ideals articulate in complex ways with mobility strategies and gendered and economic constraints on marriage options.

By recognizing only civil marriages in providing spousal benefits and pension disbursements, French civil law encouraged still other transformations. Young men and women aspiring to modern lifestyles sought to add French customs to local ways of solemnizing marriage. In addition to the traditional ceremony in which the groom's family comes to beg the bride from her family (*vody-ondry* or *fangatahana*), many aspiring urbanites also adopted French custom and were married legally in a civil ceremony, a practice referred to in Malagasy as "to write down" (*misoratra*). At the same time, missionaries promoted church weddings as well.[10] All three ceremonies solemnized the highest-status marriages. Certainly it was a sign of wealth and prestige for a young couple to have a church wedding. Among those who were not tied to state institutions, however, the traditional ceremony, in which the two families come together to formally acknowledge the exchange of children, continued to be the primary way to mark a union.

It is difficult to know exactly how these missionary and colonial efforts to reform marriage affected local practice at the time. A generation of historical scholarship on the colonial encounter has shown that we cannot assume any direct relation between what French colonial officials or church members preached in their didactic literature and how Malagasy interpreted these ideas in practice (Burke 1996; Cooper and Stoler 1997; Hunt 1999). Tamatavians may have adopted form and not content or appropriated aspects of French marriage practice to their own ends. The oral histories I conducted with Malagasy living both in Tamatave and in rural areas of the east coast suggest that these practices were always more visible among middle-class functionaries and employees of private businesses than among the poorer families who engaged in petty commerce or worked as maids or security guards. They were virtually absent in rural areas in the twentieth century.

Urbanites also competed to display the modern goods that marked social status. Recalling Thorstein Veblen's (1992 [1899]) observation that a wife's consumption habits reflect her husband's pecuniary standing, married women engaged in competitive consumption most fiercely. If educators of young men in the 1920s wanted men to pay their head tax before buying a new serge suit, they expressed comparable concern regarding young women's consumption. Meditations on *la mode* from France (in Malagasy, *lamoady*) fill the women's magazines of the period. From at least the 1920s on, columns appeared in journals such as the *Catholic Paris Bulletin*, *La Vigie*, or just before independence, in journals like *Isika Vehivavy* (We Women), encouraging appropriate consumption. Especially around the time of national independence in 1960, such newspapers urged proper consumption as a contribution to the nationalist cause. They defined it as aimed at long-term household production rather than short-term, selfish pleasure. These journals and women's magazines constantly harangued women not to give in to the immediate personal delights of fashion (see Cole 2008a).[11]

Women's increasing desire for commodities, like the desires of school-going youth, clearly prefigures contemporary consumerism. Yet despite

Figure 2.5. The cover of this women's magazine reveals the widespread understanding that women often build relationships with men to obtain money. The caption running across the woman's face reads "Women are blind," implying that women are easily seduced by men's money.

growing competition over consumer goods, these new ways of displaying wealth through mass-produced commodities did not entirely displace older signs of social status. When I asked one fifty-year-old woman what people used to spend their money on when she was young, she responded, "Oh, for us Betsimisaraka, cattle were really still the most important thing. Even people who lived in Tamatave would buy cattle to leave with their relatives in the country, and only then would they buy the Formica furniture set that was all the rage. The people who had money but did not have cattle weren't respected by their relatives in the countryside." While acquiring new consumer goods was clearly important, older ways of constituting value were still significant.

By the end of the colonial period, a high-status, modern life trajectory had emerged in which men attended school—an institution often closely intertwined with Christian youth groups, or supplemented by them—in order to obtain a salaried job, preferably in an office. Women aspiring to modern social status sought to marry these men, then stay home and care for children or work to supplement the family's income. In this petit bourgeois urban world, social competition for the material signs of modern life remained fierce, but urbanites were not cut off from rural relatives. The opinions of rural kin mattered, as shown by the continuing importance of cattle as a symbol of wealth. While some variation was likely, this picture nevertheless represents a widely shared, if less widely achieved, ideal path to social mobility that coalesced over the colonial period. Some Tamatavians could still traverse this path in the early years of independence.

Political Transitions to Independence
and the Neocolonial Regime

Madagascar negotiated independence in 1960, thirteen years after the failed anticolonial rebellion of 1947. The rebellion had been part of a larger independence movement led primarily by the political party MDRM (Mouvement de la Rénovation Malgache). The colonial government crushed the rebellion, and an estimated 80,000 people died, primarily starving while living in the forest (see Tronchon 1986; Fremigacci 1999; Cole 2001). The rebellion and its suppression left inhabitants, especially in rural areas, profoundly traumatized and fearful of political action, which had come to be synonymous with violence (Cole 2001). In place of the MDRM, the colonial government created what critics saw as a puppet party, the PADESM, or "the party of the disinherited of Madagascar," supposedly representing the interests of those coastal peoples previously dominated by the Merina. The thirteen years between the rebellion and formal independence are widely said to be years of political apathy, as the indigenous independence movement ceded power to the colonial government and its puppets in the PADESM (Raison-Jourde 1997).

As this account implies, colonial officials essentially created the political regime that eventually negotiated independence from France. The newly independent government was friendly to French interests, and French expatriates continued to occupy many positions of power. The French government continued to take an interest in, and shape, Madagascar's economy. Today, those who lived through this neocolonial period (1960–1972) nostalgically remember it as a golden age of prosperity, in contrast to the scarcity that characterized the socialist regime to follow. Economic difficulties had nonetheless already started to appear in the last years of the First Republic, including a new tax that quickly raised food prices (Gogul 2006, 311).

These tensions notwithstanding, schooling still offered the primary way to achieve social mobility and a modern lifestyle. Despite Madagascar's new political independence and the claim that Malagasy and French citizens were now equal, the education system continued to be two-tiered, with French degrees considered more valuable than Malagasy ones. Many urbanites could not achieve the social mobility they aspired to through education alone. This inability, paired with the fact that French colonization had created a larger class of people who desired such privileges, eventually created the tensions that led to the downfall of the regime (Covell 1987).

In May 1972 students at Befelatanana, the medical school in Antananarivo, went on strike and were quickly joined by other school-age youth, as well as by workers and peasants. Their immediate demands were for the reform of the education system, which favored the established elite (Covell 1987; Sharp 2002). These protests eventually swelled to link students, peasants, and lumpenproletariat in an uneasy alliance. On May 14, 1972, President Philibert Tsiranana resigned, marking the end of the neocolonial period of the First Republic.

The Revolution of 1972 and the State Socialist Period

The protestors that caused Tsiranana's downfall accused the regime of being neocolonial: it had continued to favor French economic and political interests even after political independence. In response, opponents of Tsiranana's government advocated a three-pronged policy of Malgachization. First, Malgachization meant the adoption and explicit valorization of "Malagasy ways" (*fombagasy*) as opposed to the "foreign ways" (*fombavazaha*) brought by the French. Second, it meant that Malagasy nationals would replace foreigners in positions of power. And finally, it meant that the official Malagasy language, which in this case meant the Merina dialect of Malagasy, would replace French as the language of instruction in schools. This desire to valorize nationalist culture was further visible in slogans like "Malagasy but beautiful" (*gasy ka manja*), which mocked the neocolonial idea that anything made locally was bad (Raison-Jourde 1997).

This effervescence of nationalist culture in the early 1970s never fully succeeded in papering over local and regional divisions. In December 1972, for example, Tamatavian school youth rioted against the policy of Malgachization that institutionalized the Merina dialect within schools. The rioters burned and looted merchants' stalls, and some six thousand Merina fled Tamatave in fear of their lives. According to Tamatavians who lived through the events, a particular incident set off the riots. A Malagasy language teacher, who also happened to be married to a prominent Merina who owned a pharmacy at the small bazaar, uttered an ethnic slur. As the now mythical story has it, the teacher held up her fingers and said, "You see my fingers, how they are not the same height? So too you Betsimisaraka will never be the equal of us Merina." Others, however, represented the riots as part of a ploy by local politicians to destabilize the newly emerging government.[12]

After several years of political turmoil, Didier Ratsiraka, a former naval officer, declared himself president and instituted Madagascar's Second Republic (1975–1991). Inspired by the principles of scientific socialism that he sought to adapt to the Third World context, Ratsiraka's government deliberately rejected foreign institutions and practices, instead celebrating local, nationalist culture. Ratsiraka laid out his goals in a series of radio addresses that were collected and published in the Charter for the Malagasy Revolution (also referred to as the *Boky Mena*, or Red Book). These included economic and political development and social and cultural autonomy. In theory, it was to be a revolution that "impregnated daily life," creating a "new man" who would build a truly liberated Madagascar (Ratsiraka 1975, 9). Adopting a new foreign ideology continued to enable the creation of new institutions and the reshuffling of existing hierarchies in Madagascar.[13]

To achieve his development goals, Ratsiraka quickly nationalized the major industries (banks, insurance, water, energy, and transport), including the port of Tamatave (Covell 1987, 143). He also doubled the national bureaucracy. He opted for massive state-led development projects, focusing national energy on investment in industry rather than agriculture. Although in theory internal resources were supposed to fund these development projects, in practice the projects relied on loans from the International Monetary Fund (IMF). He also realigned Madagascar's diplomatic connections with the Soviet Union and North Korea, both of which provided military, technological, and educational assistance to the island.

Like the missionaries and the colonial administrators before him, Ratsiraka especially attended to young people and women as part of his project of social renewal. In addition to the institutions of school and church that remained in place, he created a Revolutionary National Service that required urban youth to work for a year in the countryside. Having enjoyed the fruits of the nation in the form of state schooling, government grants, and the like, students were now supposed to sacrifice themselves to build that nation (Jaofeno 2006). In one of his radio addresses, Ratsiraka noted, "It is natural that youth as privileged citizens of the nation who have enjoyed the populace's sacrifice to guarantee schooling and grants should in turn give almost freely of eighteen months to two years of their life to the service of the people. In this way, we can provide the areas that are underserved with doctors, nurses, teachers, mechanics. . . . In return, our youth will learn about the reality of rural life" (Ratsiraka 1975, 114).

If the dominant rhetoric throughout the socialist period suggested that youth, conceived of as a distinct cohort and unitary whole, renewed the nation, divisive tendencies challenged this unity. Specific interest groups and political parties repeatedly recruited young people—particularly young men—to serve their interests. For example, in Antananarivo the minister of Youth and Population organized, and paid, a paramilitary organization that drew its members from unemployed young men. Ratsiraka's party, the AREMA, paid this group, referred to as the TTS (Tanora Tonga Saina), or Young Politicized Youth, to do battle with groups organized by other political parties and to protect Ratsiraka's interests.

Ratsiraka also argued for women's participation in local-level collective bodies referred to as *fokon'olona*, through which the government sought to remake local governance (Condominas 1960). For the most part, however, his policies had little effect on existing conceptions of women. Although his speeches rhetorically emphasized women's contributions to national development, there is little difference between their content and what one finds in women's magazines at independence twelve years earlier. There is relatively little in the oral histories I gathered to suggest a radical break in urbanites' aspirations for what their intimate lives and life courses would look like.

The government's promotion of a very familiar kind of nationalism notwithstanding, the desire for foreign commodities to signal social prestige or to create social distinctions remained an important part of everyday popular practice, as evinced in numerous adults' recollections of their fierce desire for bell-bottom pants and platform shoes. Aspects of Euro-American youth culture—including movies and popular singers—could be seen in the theaters in Antananarivo and Tamatave or heard on national radio. Even popular political culture at the time drew on references to Euro-American forms of popular culture like Westerns (Randriamaro 2008). Already in the late 1960s and 1970s, young people were an increasing demographic proportion of the population (INSTAT 1975).

This growing youth culture, however, did not yet translate into the burgeoning consumerism, paired with participation in the sexual economy, that I will analyze in later chapters. Respectable social opinion still looked askance at girls who were too interested in fashion. One fifty-year-old woman explained, "It was women who were married who ran after fashions to show off that their spouse had money. But if a girl ran after fashions in those days she would have a very hard time finding a spouse." There was even an expression for such young women. According to several of my informants, people would say such a girl was neither fish nor fowl, meaning she was destined to be neither a poor man's wife nor a rich man's mistress.[14]

Over the late 1970s and 1980s, Madagascar's economy deteriorated severely. As the IMF and the World Bank repeatedly devalued the Malagasy franc, prestigious jobs in government administration or work at the port no longer provided enough income to support a family. Even if people did have money, there was not much to spend it on. Stores had few consumer goods, and hospitals rarely had the right medicines. Ratsiraka's policies had also produced a mass exodus of foreigners (though the Soviet Union and North Korea did send foreign technicians). In comparison with both the years before and what was to come in the near future, the island was relatively isolated. Throughout the late 1970s and 1980s urbanites had little access to foreign media. There was only one state-run television station. Few people had television sets, relying for information on locally produced radio broadcasts or the occasional shared television in the open air outside a government building. Very few houses had telephones, and most Tamatavians would go to the post office to place interprovincial or international calls, cueing up until a telephone line became available. They also used national radio to communicate over long distances in case of death or emergency.

As in the years of French colonial rule and the First Republic, socialist policies also brought new constraints and new opportunities to the inhabitants of Tamatave. But there was an important difference. From 1895 to

1972, the lifestyles and aspirations of a petite bourgeoisie emerged and con-
solidated (despite persistent inequalities). By contrast, the 1970s and 1980s
saw the unraveling of the economic conditions that enabled Tamatavians
to realize these aspirations. The impoverishment of the country emptied
schools of books, supplies, and teachers; diplomas no longer guaranteed
employment. These factors helped prolong youth as an intermediate period
between childhood and adulthood. Many young people could not find the
employment that would let them form independent households and support dependents, the hallmark of adulthood in Tamatave. These macroeco-
nomic and political shifts slowly transformed the nature of the life course
and the paths to social mobility open to young people.

Postsocialist Madagascar: Contemporary Conditions

In the early 1990s these social and economic circumstances led to political
unrest in many cities throughout Madagascar as protestors demanded that
Ratsiraka agree to new elections. In some cases the demands were explicitly framed in terms of opportunities for youth. As one newspaper article,
boldly headlined "Crisis," read, "All the unhappiness of the world weighs
on Malagasy youth and the situation is so bad that it needs to be dealt with
before a catastrophe occurs. Our youth want to become adults" (*Tribune de
Madagascar*, January 7, 1991). Following these protests and nine months of
generalized strike throughout 1991 and early 1992, elections were held that
ushered in a transitional government. The new government abandoned the
state socialist ideology that had guided government policy and, in the context of negotiations with the World Bank and the IMF, adopted the language
(if not always the practices) of democracy and neoliberal economics.[15] Zafy
Albert, who replaced Didier Ratsiraka in elections held in 1993, led the first
phase of the transition, though he was eventually impeached. Ratsiraka, no
longer a socialist and now participating in economic liberalization, temporarily returned to power.

Over the course of the 1990s the government privatized most of the major industries—banks, gasoline, the post office, and even the airline, which
had been one of the proudest achievements of the socialist government.[16]
New laws created free trade zones, which hosted Mauritian-owned textile
industries near Antananarivo. Although there were fewer free trade zones
near Tamatave, economic changes associated with liberalization were visible in the increase of service industries related to the port (INSTAT 2003).
According to estimates by the National Bureau for Statistics (INSTAT), only
6 percent of Tamatave's economy is dependent on primary agriculture, and

11 percent is devoted to industry. The rest is mainly related to secondary and tertiary service-sector businesses (INSTAT 2001).[17]

An influx of media, new means of communication, and commodities accompanied these postsocialist economic changes. Whereas in 1990 there was only one state-controlled television station, by 2000 the number of stations in the capital city had grown to eight. Several began showing American serials, as well as Brazilian and Mexican soap operas, which became wildly popular among urban audiences. In addition to foreign shows and local song and dance programs, there were also more advertisements for foreign brands. Drawing inspiration from French styles of advertising, the ads themselves were increasingly sophisticated.

By 1997 the internal telephone system had been extended to many areas previously without service. Public pay phones—unthinkable even in 1994 at the end of my first period of research—became available in major cities. By 1999, when I went to Tamatave for preliminary fieldwork for this project, even cell phones had become widely available. They were still expensive, but people of all ages were coming to consider them a necessity. Over the next several years the networks for cell phones became more widespread. By 2007 a cell phone was de rigeur, and many people had them. Some people even had two phones, one for each company so they could call their friends more cheaply depending on which network they used. From about 1998 onward the Internet became more and more widespread. In Tamatave, pay-per-minute Internet booths are available at the university center. There are also two private Internet providers along Rue Joffre, one of the most elegant commercial streets in town. Chat rooms are so popular, particularly among students, that they have given rise to a new verb: *mitchat*. This new access to the Internet not only has exponentially increased some Tamatavians' access to commodity images but also enables people to forge new connections outside Madagascar.

An increased circulation of foreign-made goods has accompanied the increased communication. In the early 1990s there was only one large supermarket selling foreign brands, and it was in Antananarivo. By 1997 there were several supermarkets in Tamatave, mainly owned by South African business interests and often run by Merina managers. Over the course of my 2001 fieldwork in Tamatave, a South African–owned store called Champion opened. In the sweltering heat of December, it piped traditional English and French Christmas carols through air-conditioned aisles. By 2002 Tamatave offered the discerning shopper three supermarkets and a giant Chinese import store where one could buy electronic goods, including washing machines, microwaves, and rice cookers, on installment plans.[18]

New political arrangements further accompanied this period of rapid socioeconomic change. Although in 1997 Ratsiraka returned to power, having abandoned state socialism for a "humanistic, ecological republic" (Raison-Jourde and Raison 2002), by 2001 he found himself again facing opposition, this time from the self-made yogurt tycoon Marc Ravalomanana, owner of Tiako, one of the most successful Malagasy-owned businesses in Madagascar, and the mayor of Antananarivo.[19] Ravalomanana appealed to people by offering a Malagasy version of economic success and a vision of unbridled capitalism that fit well with the economic wisdom of the World Bank. In 2002, after an electoral standoff that almost led to civil war, Ravalomanana was elected president.[20] In keeping with his position as a transnational businessman, he pursued the liberalizing and the privatizing of the economy even more aggressively than his predecessors.

The temptations visible on television shows and advertisements, and in stores like Champion, are not equally available to all.[21] The liberalizing of the economy has distributed wealth unequally, with the most affluent 10 percent of the population controlling 35 percent of the spending power (Country Profile, Madagascar 2003, 19). The disparities in wealth are sharper in Tamatave than in other Malagasy cities.[22] Those who have jobs in the formal sector generally fare better than those who do not. Older men control most of the stable jobs, and young people and women are more likely to be either unemployed or forced into the volatile informal economy.[23] Men and women, young people and old, all have different opportunities in this new economy, as we will see in more detail below.

Conclusion

I began this chapter with an account of Tamatave's formation in the nineteenth century as a port town. In closing, let me recall the missionary William Ellis's description of Tamatave in 1862: "The conduct of the Merina King—who had not only invited foreigners to settle in the island for trade or other purposes, but had abolished all duty on exports and imports—had caused quite a rush to the country from almost all parts of the world, and something like an inundation of merchandise." Close to 150 years separate Ellis's description of Tamatave and my fieldwork.

Despite the many changes I have examined, there is a curious resonance between the two periods. In both, the economic activity of this multiethnic city relies on the port, its imports and the transfer of cash crops from the surrounding areas into a wider market. Today the government and service industries provide substantial numbers of jobs. Nevertheless, the impoverishment of the government since the late 1980s, combined with the liberalizing of the economy beginning in the early 1990s, means that, as in the nineteenth century, people's sense of where wealth comes from, and how one obtains it, centers on business and the port. As in the nineteenth century, the wealthiest people in contemporary Tamatave are either involved in trade or in high-level government positions. The two are by no means necessarily separate, a tendency we can trace all the way back to the Merina kingdom (Covell 1987, 78).

If the government's economic policies during the socialist period made it difficult for families to follow the usual paths to social mobility, the neoliberal economic policies of the current state have changed the social and economic landscape once again. They have brought new ways of achieving upward social mobility. As in the precolonial and colonial period, many of these entail connecting with the foreign sources of power that new government policies have invited into Madagascar. These new opportunities for accessing power are not evenly distributed. More important, as I will show in the next chapter, they are strongly shaped by a combination of cultural ideas about proper human relations and what it means to be a valued person, a concept that is itself intimately related to where one stands in the life course. In the next chapter, as I turn from the past to the present, I can begin to tease out these conceptions of personhood and the proper life course and show how they inform social, political, and economic changes.

THREE

Disembedding and the Humiliation of Poverty

I was married for the first time at nineteen years of age. I suffered greatly during that marriage, and we separated. I came here to Tamatave to work and met the man I'm married to now. We had a civil marriage. My father didn't react when I decided to get married, and there was no one who came to our wedding except my sister-in-law. I was very discouraged because my family didn't care about me at all. *Before, I'd had money and so they liked me, but when I didn't have any money, they stopped loving me.*

—Mme Florence, thirty-five

There was one girl who used to be my friend, and she used to come here to our house all the time. But now she never comes, though I don't know the reason. One day I was getting water from the pump and talked to her, and she put me down—but she didn't use to do that. I was happy because Maman was getting a telephone, and so I told her. *And she said, "Don't you show off to me! You don't know if I'll succeed or you will, for my family is also going to get a telephone and we're going to build a concrete house." There were many things she said to me, and I was very sad.*

—Vola, fourteen-year-old girl

In social life there are two levels. There are those on top and those on bottom. You know that expression "the thin cow isn't licked by his friends?"[1] *Well, that cow isn't thin—he is poor. What it means is that the rich don't want to know or acknowledge the poor.* That is what happens all the time here in Madagascar. Those who have, they are friends only with one another, in order to increase their wealth.

—Jocelyn, twenty-two-year-old man

When I first started living in Tamatave, one of the hardest things to adjust to was the sadness and anger people expressed when they felt slighted. The word people used over and over was *malahelo*, often translated as sad. But malahelo is more than just sad: it also connotes the bitterness and resentment that Tamatavians say they feel when mistreated. Almost always, money is at issue. All interactions—no matter how apparently trivial— could be used to make people feel inadequate because they lacked material resources. Sometimes it was as seemingly insignificant as a boy being publicly mocked by his teacher because he did not have a ruler. Florence's story, where her family ignored her wedding because she was poorer than in the past, is another example.

At other times the dynamics that produced this sentiment were more anonymous—for example, when a man went into a store and tried to order something but was ignored and served last because his clothes, shoes, or demeanor betrayed his poverty. That poor people do not deserve love, attention, or respect was a lesson many people learned daily as they went about their business.

Particular aspects of the communities people live in contribute to these interactions. The spatial arrangement of houses creates intimacy (and sometimes intimate enmity) among neighbors. Unless they live in a villa (and hardly anyone does), nobody has much privacy. Most of the houses, made either from wood with corrugated tin roofs or from palm thatch and bamboo, are set in a courtyard surrounded by smaller houses used as kitchens, maid's quarters, or sleeping quarters for still other family members. In some cases people who have a bit more money live in *cités*—clusters of small concrete houses that either the government or various businesses built during the early independence period as housing for their workers.

Inside the houses, an entire family may sleep in one room, with curtains hung around a couple's bed to give a bit of privacy. In most houses electric light comes from a single dim bulb, so in the evenings families gather in the rooms with enough light to see by. Although in some neighborhoods people fetch water from the public pump, even where houses have individual water supplies the spigot is in the courtyard. Sinks are set up for washing and cooking, so many household tasks take place outside.

The lack of privacy within homes is replicated within the neighborhoods. Though every effort is made to build fences and mend gates, houses are close together, and music pouring out of one household inevitably trickles into the next. So too do personal secrets and information. Life also takes place in public along the sand paths. Women set up stands to sell food, often at the edge of their courtyards. Children kick balls around, ride old bicycles, or just hang out. Groups of young men squat on their haunches playing cards or dice and smoking cigarettes. Young girls cruise the sand paths, arms linked, tittering and looking back when the boys call out teasingly.

Social opinion takes on incredible force in these conditions. As if they were Durkheimians, Tamatavians constantly referred to the power of the community (*fiaramonina*, from *miaramonina*, "to reside together"). Everyone watches everyone else, especially for signs of social success or failure. How well one does—what kind of job a man has, how much money a woman earns, whether children are well dressed and cared for—is a matter for public discussion. Neighbors gossip constantly, a dynamic that the different branches of extended families replicate.

Yet no one acknowledges treating people in the humiliating ways that evoke malahelo in others. When stories like this were told publicly, the goal was to establish the speaker's identity as a modest (*tsotra*) person, as opposed to a proud (*miavonah*) one. But people also told me such stories secretly, suggesting private anguish rather than public image management. And I did also witness these kinds of interactions. The victim on one occasion could be the perpetrator on the next. Urbanites talked constantly about the differences between those who "have" and those who "have not." In tones that suggested they wished it weren't so even as they knew it was, they implied that those who "have" are more worthwhile, while those who are poor are regarded as worthless, and often feel they are. This social status is expressed in such terms as "having no meaning" (*tsy misy dikany*) or "not considered" (*tsy consideré*). So common is the sense of inferiority that results from "not having," that one popular song cheerfully exhorted people to "not have an [inferiority] complex" (*aza complexé*) as a result of these small hurts and rejections. Most Tamatavians I knew constantly worried about being belittled because they lacked money or other tangible resources. The threat of humiliation loomed large.

Tamatavians themselves argue that these competitive dynamics of material display, humiliation, and withholding resources are uniquely urban.[2] Alongside the discourse of humiliation stemming from variations in material wealth ran another, telling how more generous, reciprocal behavior characterizes rural life. Echoing long-standing modern ideas about the difference between the country and the city, Tamatavians often told me that only in the countryside can one find people who love their ancestral land, not just themselves, so that they behave in socially appropriate ways.[3] They explained this difference by saying that schooling and living in a city lead people to want money. One young man remarked, "People in the country love their ancestral land, but once you've gone to school you just love money."

Many urbanites also attributed malahelo-generating social interactions to the recent changes brought by the new economy. One newspaper articulated this link explicitly:

> [Economic] liberalism has diminished the value of money but at the same time it has made the value of money all the more visible. Our old proverbs that it was better to lose money than human relationships have lost all meaning and weight. Money is the God that governs everything and makes all decisions. There is nothing that can't be done by money and without money you can do nothing. It isn't that it is something that we are used to, or something that "makes the man," as in the old saying "money makes the man" but something that has become our life. You are not a human being, and you are not truly alive unless you have money. But he who has a lot of money lives forever in happiness! In liberalism only those people who have money or who seek their own self-interest can do things. No one cares about the poor. (Raintsoa 1995)

In words reminiscent of Karl Marx's position in the "Economic and Philosophic Manuscripts of 1844," the author blames economic liberalization for creating a social world where money is the only measure of life's value.

I don't know whether the author of this opinion piece had read Marx; given Madagascar's socialist period, he well might have. My point is that this explanation, and that of the young man who said that people who lived in the city and went to school just loved money, attributes malahelo and hurtful ascriptions of social insignificance to a combination of urbanization and more recent economic liberalization. Either way, this account completely erases local historical processes, and local forms of agency, from the analysis.

In my view, my Tamatavian interlocuters are both wrong—and right. The frustrations Tamatavians express in the quotations I began with arise out of a cultural logic that has much wider, deeper roots in rural practice. They are not only a reflex of capitalist processes that originate elsewhere. Nor are these kinds of interactions simply matters of interpersonal selfishness or cruelty. Rather, they are a crucial part of historical processes on the east coast more generally. Ideas of what it means to be a good person who can participate fully in social life—as well as people's efforts to achieve these goals, the obstacles they encounter, and the intense emotions that accompany their efforts—have long been central to how people make and remake communities there.

What has changed is not the existence of these social practices but the way the competitive aspects of rural life get transformed in the city as urbanites are drawn into an increasingly monetized—and now consumerist—economy. In rural villages, the giving and withholding that produce malahelo are one small part of a complex of social, economic, and cultural practices. They are more integrally tied to ancestors than to money. When people settle in Tamatave—and this book focuses on those urbanites who aspire to what they see as a modern urban life—their relation to a whole complex of ancestral practices and the role of money in their life changes. The importance of money has combined with a greatly increased gap between haves and have-nots, amplifying the visibility and transforming the meaning of social inequality in daily life. New ideas from outside Madagascar that are much more pervasive in the city exacerbate these changes. In the city, certain aspects of rural life are retained, but their meanings and consequences change as various elements of the older system fall away and new ones are added. Many distortions and transformations in social relations occur that ultimately separate the children of ancestors from their rural roots, allowing new beliefs and social interactions to emerge.

I call this general process *disembedding*, a term I borrow from Charles Taylor (2007), although I use it somewhat differently. For Taylor, disembedding is a unidirectional historical process that took place in Europe after the Middle Ages, slowly facilitating the growth of a type of person who could imagine himself or herself outside a local social matrix. In Taylor's use, disembedding enables a particular kind of Christian subject and fits neatly with a modern sociocultural formation that emphasizes the growth of individuals.[4] I use "disembedding" to refer to the slow, uneven, and multidirectional ways people can become divorced from old attachments and form new ones. Disembedding has long been an important part of historical change in rural areas of the east coast (Cole 2001). Here, however, I focus on the dynamics of disembedding when people move to the city. This process enables a particular sociality characteristic of life in the sand paths and Internet cafés of Tamatave where urbanites come to participate in a new political economy and where ideas about modernity, tradition, and the power of money powerfully shape contemporary life.

Rural Social Life: Ancestors, Parents, Children, and Caring

Ancestral custom will never be lost. The people who carry the ancestors will change, but their ways will not be lost. Don't you see? The people in the government change, but there is still a government.

—Ramarie, rural elder woman

In many areas of Madagascar, ancestor-descendant relationships provide the central idiom for enacting relations of authority, autonomy, power, and dependence (Althabe 1969; Emoff 2002; Astuti 1995; Bloch 1971; Cole 2001; Feeley-Harnik 1984, 1991; Graeber 2007; Lambek 2002; Middleton 1999; Sharp 1993). Ideally, ancestors are supposed to bless their descendants and make them prosper. In return, descendants are supposed to recognize their ancestors by living in the houses their ancestors built, maintaining their tombs, farming their land, and remembering them with gifts and sacrifice. Fulfilling these obligations keeps the land and the people who live on it *masina*, a word that means both generative and efficacious. Having powerful ancestors is the mark of a powerful person, and having powerful descendants is the mark of a powerful ancestor.

The need to obtain and maintain ancestral blessing—the fact that such blessing is intrinsically tied to a particular place—is central to how ancestral practice both enables and constrains particular kinds of subjects. An instructive example involves taboo. Taboos come about in two ways. People may have a bad experience (for example, a woman chokes while eating a striped eel or a man suffers because his sons moved to the north in search of wealth) and then utter words forbidding descendants to engage in that activity. Alternatively, a taboo may arise because a family goes to a diviner who gives them medicine to ensure good harvests, and that medicine becomes associated with a particular patch of land. In either case, the circumstances that give rise to taboos reflect the historically contingent predicaments of those who created them. As a result, taboos constrain their descendants to repeat their historical experiences, especially by attaching them to particular places.[5] Marx's dictum that the "dead weight" of the past hangs like a nightmare on the minds of the living takes on a peculiarly literal meaning in this context, and it does so in a particularly geocentric way. Such practices also figure the ideal relation between past and future; they are part of how east coasters imbue their lives with a culturally stamped experience of history and time (Munn 1992).

Central east coasters reckon kinship and inheritance bilaterally, so that children are part of, and inherit from, both their mothers' and their fathers' ancestries. Nevertheless, a patrilineal bias is built into the system. The proverb "women do not have an ancestral land, yet they have an ancestral land" captures this tendency to privilege men when it comes to ancestors.[6] On the one hand, bilateral kinship means that women count as important members of both their mothers' and their fathers' ancestries. On the other hand, east coasters devalue kinship traced through women compared with that traced through men. For example, within a given ancestry, *tangalamena*, the older men who mediate between the living and the dead, are supposed to be the "children of men" (*zanin'lahy*), while the "assistant to the tangalamena" (*lefitra*) is usually a "child of women" (*zanin'vavy*).[7] Exogenous marriage, in which women both marry outside their ancestry and ideally go to live on their husbands' ancestral land (even when that means only moving a few houses over in the same village), further contributes to this tendency to associate men with a fixed ancestral location.

In practice, however, east coasters participate in both kin groups. In some cases people break the rule altogether and participate much more in their mother's family than their father's. The bilateral structuring of kinship makes the influence of individual choice significant, and people exercise their options in a variety of creative ways in response to personal, local, and national situations. Although women can never be tangalamena, they still join in the accumulating and flaunting of resources that are part of how families assert their value and importance. Further, a man cannot become a tangalamena without children, for which he needs a wife. If men are more powerful and more likely to be involved in local politics, interdependence between men and women is built into the social and cultural system.

Along the east coast, a full-fledged adult uses the generative capacities bestowed by the ancestors to "make oneself, one's spouse, and one's children living." This lovely Malagasy phrase reaches beyond the simple mechanics of supporting oneself to indicate how a person becomes a generative subject at a particular moment in time. In everyday practice, men's or women's status and position in the life course emerges partly from their position within a network of exchange.[8] Depending on others to fulfill exchange obligations or being unable to participate makes one a child.[9] The ability to "carry" or "complete" (*mitondra, mahavita*) the needs of others defines adulthood.[10] Ideally, adults are positioned at the center of, and hence can command, a socially valued network of material and affective resources. A person's growing ability to exchange marks the progress of social maturation in the endless give and take of "making others live" (Mauss 1990 [1950]; Bourdieu 1977). Recognizing others' human worth means seeing the generative potential or potency (*hasina*) thought to be intrinsic to them. In turn, giving

Figure 3.1. Betsimisaraka inhabitants of the east coast perform ceremonies in which they disinter and rebury the dead to beg for blessing from their ancestors.

to others recognizes their worth and power. Giving also marks the belief that one day the recipients' hasina may enable them to amass resources that they are then expected to give back to you. To respect another human being implies this mutual recognition and exchange.

The proverbs and ritual practices surrounding the relations between parents and children, on the one hand, and ancestors and descendants, on the other, most fully display this ideal of reciprocity and tie it to practices of social life that give rise to one's sense of self. This ideal is expressed in the proverb that "children are like your horns," comparing children to the strength of a bull. When I asked an old man what this phrase meant, he explained, "Whatever you do, you lean on your children. Your children are your protectors, so you say that you have horns, like the horns of a cow. When they are still small you carry them on your back, and later [when you are old] they become your horns." (As I mentioned briefly in chapter 1 and will show in more detail shortly, cattle are perhaps the central indicator of wealth in rural society, and central to ceremonial exchanges with the ancestors.) Rituals similarly embody the reciprocal constitution of hasina through exchange across generations. On Christmas and Independence Day, children visit their parents' houses bringing gifts or food, and the parents respond with food and blessings of their own. In rituals of cattle sacrifice, guests bear small cash contributions and in return receive ancestral blessing. Finally, when the dead are buried for a second time, descendants take the dried remains of their ancestors out of their tombs, change their shrouds, and lovingly cradle the ancestors in their laps, giving them rum, cigarettes, coins, and candy—all in exchange for ancestral blessing.

As in ritual, so in everyday life: the continuing reciprocal exchange of material support and care creates both persons and the sentiments that bind them to one another. To give someone rice you have grown on your own land, to buy clothes for a lover, a parent, or a child, and to pay for a child's school supplies or medical care are well-known forms of *fitiavana*. Often translated as love, the term covers a similar semantic field (including preference and sexual desire) but also includes the attachments formed when others recognize one's generative capacities (Cole 2009). In a context where people acquire resources through the collaborative, labor-intensive work of farming or fishing, and where even small amounts of money are earned through protracted labor, to put one's resources toward the well-being of another is to nurture, protect, and give of oneself. Such giving is the primary way both to create hasina and to build emotional attachments. People expect that by giving their hard labor and resources they will receive fitiavana in return.

In keeping with the idea that the exchange of material support both expresses and constitutes fitiavana, adult villagers constantly talk about their fitiavana for their children in terms of either the labor or the services their children perform for them. When Ramarie, the woman I cited at the beginning of this section, sent her daughter and granddaughter upcountry to help a family friend harvest coffee, she was despondent, even though she had urged the girls to go. Waxing sentimental in their absence, she told me, "Children remove your lice and fleas. To be without children is total poverty; they are your wealth and comfort, and those you raise will always remember you—most especially daughters always remember their mother." On another day she expressed the mutual empathy and interconnection embodied in exchange by saying, "Children are like your mirror. You love to see them glitter." Like a mirror in the sun throwing back light, children are ideally supposed to prosper and give material support back to their parents. Fishing and sharing the catch, working in one another's fields, or picking lice out of a child's hair—all weave sentimental attachments. Money and the lack of it is a constant worry, and people regularly die because they do not have money for medical care. Nonetheless, money is not the medium through which people build their relationships.

Of course there are tensions embedded in these practices. These tensions

Figure 3.2. Children start to help with household labor from an early age.

are closely related to broader patterns of continuity and change within communities and help explain the new meanings associated with hasina and fitiavana that characterize social relationships in Tamatave. They radiate along two axes, one diachronic (between ancestors and descendants), the other synchronic among those who see themselves as contemporaries and thus, ideally, as equals. I consider each in turn.

Tensions between Past and Present

Recall that to obtain ancestral blessing, descendants are supposed to live as their ancestors lived. To inhabit a father's house or till a mother's fields and to respect their taboos maintains both the memory of the ancestors and their sacred efficacy. The problem from the point of view of the living is that to realize their potential, people need to forge relations either with "other people" (*olokafa*) or with sources of hasina outside of those provided by ancestors. They constantly need to reach beyond the past, embodied in ancestors, to propel themselves into the future. One obvious way this dynamic manifests itself is that to have children, considered important evidence of ancestral blessing, men or women need to marry people outside their own lineage.

The need to reach outside your family or ancestry to acquire resources of your own is particularly visible during youth. During youth, individuals are theoretically least attached to the ancestors, least constrained to live within their ancestral land. Consequently, this is when people's projects of self-expansion lay the ground for the transformation of existing social arrangements. Young people "seek" (*mitady*) the resources and social connections that enable them to establish an independent household. Sometimes people say that young people quest for their *anjara*, or personal fate, often used to refer to one's ideal marriage partner. For young men, this requires building up a social and economic base so they can eventually get married and support a household. For young women, it implies finding the man with whom they will create that household and bear children. The need to seek generative power in addition to that provided by ancestors also animates many other kinds of actions—for example, when a man cultivates a new piece of land that unexpectedly generates wealth. This process has transformative potential because it usually requires that the person either abandon burdensome existing taboos, move beyond the confines of ancestral land to farm new fields, or seek wealth in other novel ways.

There are several possible outcomes to the growth and searching that all men and women enter into, although because of their concern with maintaining continuity with ancestors (and the patrilineal bias), rural Betsimisaraka place particular importance on men. In one idealized scenario, a man goes out and searches, then settles in his ancestral land, marries, and has children. He gathers his descendants around him, continuing to till his paternal ancestors' fields, live in his ancestral great house, and maintain his ancestors' tomb, perhaps even embellishing it. In so doing, he not only builds up his own following, he also continuously contributes to his ancestors' power. In this scenario, an idealized reciprocity has been achieved between the ancestors who bless and the descendants who recognize that blessing.

However, it is also possible that a person may never succeed in generating the power base required to be remembered as an ancestor. Sometimes the searching fails, so that instead of amassing the resources that enable independence, a person becomes more impoverished and dependent on others. Some people remain dependent all their lives, similar to slavery in the past, though no one would dare use that term today. Slaves are defined as people who lack the power to invoke their own ancestors, and who get attached to another family. Their labor goes to the growth of that family's ancestors rather than their own. In this state their generative capacities are appropriated by others. Since east coasters imagine full adulthood as the ability to "make others living" and to interact directly with one's ancestors, being a slave is a state of being perpetually junior. Although slavery was abolished in 1896, the metaphor of slavery as a despised junior status in which one can never quite attain full adult personhood continues to haunt contemporary social relations in many parts of Madagascar (see Evers 2002; Graeber 2007; Somda 2009).

Alternatively, achieving local ideals of prosperity can also lead to new patterns and new practices. Men who are successful often find themselves caught between the need to remember their ancestors by living in their houses and tilling their fields and the need to build up a power base of their own by accumulating new resources. Sometimes this situation requires a family to shed taboos that make some actions difficult (such as not farming on Tuesdays). At other times a man may move his family out to new fields, then over time decide he wants to establish a great house and a tomb there. In either case, he needs to use rituals of cattle sacrifice to selectively negotiate between past, present, and future so that his failure to comply with the ancestral injunction to repeat the past, rather than change it, will not incur his ancestors' wrath (Cole 2001).

During cattle sacrifice, the members of a family come together before the assembled community to inform the ancestors of their current undertaking, to ask for their understanding in departing from the ways of the past, and more generally to beg ancestral blessing. In an elaborate speech that precedes the actual sacrifice, they recount their situation to their ancestors. They may explain that, owing to present circumstances, they need to live in a different house than their ancestors chose or abolish a long-standing taboo. They may also explain that they had gone to live in the city, where they had been unable to follow ancestral taboos, and that now they want to resume their relations with the ancestors. Generally, descendants tell the ancestors all the ways their lives differ from the past, asking their forbearance and blessing. They may also take objects that have been marked as foreign in the past—particular materials used to build houses, for example—and rework the associated symbolic meanings to make them "ancestral." As a kind of memory practice, cattle sacrifice enables villagers to realign the idealized past and the imperfect present, letting them construct a continuous identity narrative despite change (Cole 2001). But sacrifice rituals sometimes fail. If you try to seize control of your ancestors and move them to you, or try to eliminate an onerous taboo, everyone knows you have failed if you wind up dead, struck down by ancestral wrath.

Tensions in the Present

But there are also important social tensions between peers or members of the same generation, tensions that become particularly relevant to understanding the malahelo-evoking interactions that began this chapter. This tension begins at home, among siblings who are "children of one stomach." Ideally, as I said, ancestors bless their descendants equally with fertility and prosperity. In practice, however, some are more blessed than others. Although parents are supposed to love and bless all their children equally, some children are more loved, more recognized than others. Injunctions to equality aside, people constantly index which relationships are more valuable to them by allocating resources in particular ways. All those living in a village believe they know which parent-child bonds are strongest, or who loves whom and how much. As evidence, they cite which child or grandchild is held and coddled more than another, who receives the most gifts or material support, or whose fields someone chooses to labor in. Clearly, the ideal of balanced reciprocity—which indicates fitiavana and valued forms of personhood—is difficult to achieve. Recall the proverb Jocelyn cited: the thin cow is not licked by his friends. The saying means that those who have less to give are also likely to receive less: their poverty both signals and reproduces a lack of significant connection to others.[11]

In rural areas these tensions, too, are negotiated through cattle sacrifice. Such rituals mediate relations not only between the living and the dead, but also among the living. They provide a way for members of the community to both differentiate themselves from one another and weave new connections. Not only is almost every sacrifice that takes place a result of the jealous gossip of neighbors, who in remarking about another's success provoke that person's ever-hungry ancestors to come and claim their due, but each sacrifice also works to transform social relations in a community. After all, sacrifices are huge parties, which many people can enjoy. They are not only a means of income redistribution but also a way of symbolically recognizing the importance of the rest of the community—of acknowledging their value (see Cole 2001, especially chapter 6). None of this can happen in the city.[12]

But it is also likely that by holding a sacrifice a family may fuel the basic competitive dynamic that produced the need for the sacrifice in the first place. This outcome is particularly visible in the case of people's adoption of foreign (*vazaha*) practices that have long signaled a family's power and prestige. During the 1990s, the two key foreign-marked practices that men used to signify their wealth and power were roofing houses with tin and building both houses and tombs from concrete rather than wood. When other families see that one family has adopted a new vazaha practice, rather than risk humiliation they are likely to copy it. The practice becomes a model (*lasa maodely*). Once another family succeeds, however, they in turn are subject to the troublesome gossip of their neighbors and the anger of their ancestors, leading to the sacrifice that eventually restores social equilibrium. And so, like wildfire, the practice spreads. Such was the explanation recounted to me numerous times during my rural fieldwork when I asked why people had started building houses with tin roofs, growing cash crops like coffee, using concrete instead of wood to build tombs, wrapping the dead in mass-produced fabric instead of woven raffia shrouds, and so forth. "Why did that custom change?" I asked again and again. "We saw vazaha doing it, or we saw our neighbors doing it, and so we copied." Or, "We saw vazaha doing it, and so we wanted to do it too." From this perspective, the often-quoted proverb "May you be desired by others but may you not desire others" is more than just a reflection on interpersonal relations.[13] It is also a statement about how people make history through the social competition that both fuels and relies on a particular conception of personhood.

Moving to Tamatave: Disembedding

These days it is only those who live in the countryside who still respect ancestral customs. But for those in the city, you hardly see any customs because in the city we all want to follow the practices of foreigners, because we think that means progress.

—Jean Aimé, truck driver, twenty-five

Although these ideas remain profoundly relevant to understanding the social interactions that drive Tamatavians to adopt new practices, ancestors are much less important to their daily lives and self-representations. Tamatavians are also generally more skeptical of the reality of ancestral power.[14] Perhaps the single most important reason ancestors do not play the same role in Tamatave relates to how Tamatavians sustain themselves. In rural areas, where people earn their livelihood primarily as subsistence farmers, people's claims to land are always figured in terms of ancestors and inheritance: to say one's ancestors farmed a particular piece of land is to claim it as one's own. To own fertile land is to ensure one's well-being and the ability to support descendants. In Tamatave, by contrast, the economy revolves around the money from such sources as the port, the transport or sale of produce from the countryside, and the state bureaucracy. Although owning land can still provide resources, it does not have the same central importance as the medium and product of commerce—money.

In Tamatave city, ancestors have less power. Even east coasters who take ancestral power quite seriously when in their ancestral villages agree that once people settle in the city, they no longer are required to obey the same rules. All they really have to do is send money home for the performance of ancestral rituals, including cattle sacrifice and tomb maintenance. For the inhabitants of rural areas, such rituals are only one small part of a complicated exchange of goods and services that constitutes the ancestor-descendant relationship. A rural person who goes to a sacrifice, for example, knows the people who are sponsoring the ritual, as well as the names of the ancestors being called, who are usually members of the immediate family. He or she usually believes the ancestors have power to bless and kill and is excited by the incredible danger and bravery that sacrifice entails, since it calls the dead to walk among the living. These are the moments when people are most likely to have supernatural experiences that prove the existence and power of the ancestors—that make them come alive, so to speak.

Some urbanites do attend rituals for their ancestors that they find deeply moving and compelling and that bring the idea of ancestral power alive in a way that might not otherwise occur. For example, once when I was talking about ancestors with Haja, a high school student who lived with his mother and siblings in Tamatave, and whose family I introduce in more detail in the next chapter, he told me about his father's second burial (*famadihana*). Although the ceremony had taken place three years before, he was clearly still moved and haunted by what had happened. Haja described how, after his father died, he took his father's white cap to wear as a special keepsake. During the ceremony he lost the cap, and he became incredibly distraught. But later he miraculously found it, which he credited to ancestral power. Haja found this experience compelling, since it brought to life ancestral power that might otherwise have seemed distant and irrelevant to his urban life.

In many cases, however, the rituals urbanites attend are not performed for someone they are close to. The daily acts of bending one's practices to ancestral demands fall by the wayside, as do many of the more subtle meanings implicit in these rituals. The contributions of money that most Tamatavians feel obliged to make may be the only remaining indication of the ancestor-descendant relationship. Although most people I knew were quite comfortable with sending money instead of attending rituals (it is considered the polite course of action), this substitution has consequences. It makes their relationship with their ancestors more like a depersonalized transaction, where one can quickly fulfill an obligation simply by paying for it. Simultaneously, their relationships with local kin are reduced. Not only are the daily acts of remembering ancestors eliminated, which would happen anyway, but the power of the ritual to bring ancestors alive and make them relevant is also lost. As a result, it becomes easier for urbanites to have a less embodied, and more objectified, relationship with ancestral practice, an important part of the more general disembedding.

Julienne, a twenty-nine-year-old woman who had moved from Mananara to live in Tamatave, crystallized this interpretation for me:

> We just recently went to do a bone turning [mamadika] for my younger brother. The reason was that [the ancestor's] clothes were wet. At that time we didn't do a party; we just moved him from the old tomb and put him in the concrete tomb. That was it. If there is someone in our family who does ancestral customs, I go to watch them, but that doesn't mean I do everything they do. I only do what I think is right to do. For example, picking through the bones, some people do that, but I haven't done that yet.

Julienne may have seen her attendance at the bone turning as sufficient contact with her ancestors, but rural people I knew consider such an attitude untenable. For rural elders *doing* implies knowing, and the two are the only legitimate way to create real contact with the ancestors, which is why they often insist that younger people participate. Josef, an old man who had spent all his life in a village, once mused to me before I went off to my first bone turning, "You have to get down on your knees and sift through the bones to really know what it is like." Similarly, after we had attended that same bone turning, Ramarie inadvertently echoed Josef's perspective by telling me that you couldn't just "stand and watch like a fancy lady [Madame Be]"—you had to lend a hand and take part. To do was to know. Julienne may have seen her attendance as sufficient to establish connections with ancestors and make rural kin happy, but they likely found it profoundly distancing. Although there are always exceptions, urbanites generally are not as embedded in the world of their ancestors as are their rural kin. Yet it is not just moving to a new place with a new political economy that makes reconnecting with the ancestors difficult. Ideas and practices that are more present in Tamatave further weaken and transform ancestor-descendant relationships. I focus on two of these sources: Christianity and conceptions of modernity and tradition.

Christianity: From Catholicism to Pentecostalism

Catholicism first came to Tamatave in the early nineteenth century with the establishment of the Catholic mission. Historically, Catholicism was the dominant religion there, an artifact of the town's close ties to Réunion and, indirectly, to France during the eighteenth and nineteenth centuries.[15] In addition, many Tamatavians belong to Protestant churches like the FJKM (Fiangonan'i Jesoa Kristy eto Madagasikara, Church of Jesus Christ in Madagascar), the Malagasy church founded in 1986 that represents a coalition of the major protestant missions to Madagascar.

Historically, Catholic doctrine encouraged Malagasy to incorporate their beliefs about ancestors into their practice of Christianity. As a result, many Malagasy Catholics argue that the ancestors are just like saints. Whether this association has anything to do with the Catholic practice of preserving relics is difficult to know. But many Tamatavians say that just as one supplicates saints in the Catholic Church, so too one supplicates ancestors in Malagasy religion. One young woman's discussion of her family's religious practice illustrates this point:

> We are Catholic, but we still do our ancestral customs, like the *tsaboraha* [a kind of cattle sacrifice]. I've already attended three: twice for my mother's family and once for my father's family. Often they are to announce a new tomb. We call the family together and kill a cow and invoke the ancestors. Ancestors for us, they are intermediaries between God and the living. The reason we honor them is that they bring our requests to God.

Despite Catholic doctrine's general tolerance for local beliefs, Catholic practice nevertheless contributes to the more general disembedding visible in Tamatave. Much as just sending money for ceremonies eliminates a range of actions, so likening ancestors to saints simplifies a complicated arena of ancestral practice in relation to land and kinship. After all, ancestral practices are always partly political claims about who farmed which land first, and who can therefore claim it. Christian interpretations and practice alter the meanings associated with land and kinship woven into the fabric of daily life, creating a disjointed religion akin to Christianity.[16] To say ancestors are just like saints and relegate them to a separate religious domain is a way of Christianizing them.

The growing number of Pentecostal churches that have come to Tamatave in the 1990s accelerates and intensifies this process. Madagascar has seen many people leave the traditional churches, sometimes referred to as "ancestral churches" (*fiangonana razana*) because of their deep roots in Malagasy history, to take up Pentecostal practice.[17] In 1961 there was only one Pentecostal church in all of Madagascar. By 2000, ten could be found in Tamatave alone. Jesosy Mamonjy (Joining Jesus), Pentekotista Afaka (Pentecostals Saved), and the Rhema (Revelation) are the largest, but there are also many small ones, including the Assemblée de Dieu (Assembly of God) and Herin'ny Finoana (Power of Faith church). Some have existed in Madagascar since the 1960s, but others such as the Assembly of God or the Arapilazantsara (the Good Word) appeared only in the early 1990s.[18] Many of the Malagasy Pentecostal churches have links to Pentecostal churches in the United States and South Africa. Of the six provincial capitals in Madagascar, Tamatave had the highest rate of adherence to new evangelical churches (INSTAT 2001).[19] Though exact statistics on the number of converts are hard to obtain, in the past ten years the development has been important enough that in 1997 the Catholic Church organized a weeklong conference devoted to its relationship with the new churches. Their main goal was to lessen the numbers of congregants lost to Pentecostalism. Every family I knew had someone who had joined one of the new sects, as they are pejoratively called by those not affiliated with them.

From the perspective of Malagasy ancestral practice, the most radical requirement of these churches is that they forbid adherents to engage in sacrifice or tomb building, rituals closely associated with the maintenance of ancestral power. Instead, much as Birgit Meyer (1999) has described for Pentecostals in Ghana, they argue that ancestors are a manifestation of the devil. Noela, a young woman who attended Jesosy Mamonjy, explained, "The ways of God and the ancestors are contrary because God says not to worship anyone but him. He says, 'I am the one God who made all things on this earth.' So you should not worship idols [*sampy*]. The ancestral custom of going to the tombs and bowing to the dead, they are all against the word of God." Pentecostal practice also forbids adherents to consult diviners or use medicines made from bark, beads, and leaves. Julie, a fifteen-year-old girl, observed, "For me there isn't a dead person who can help you. When I passed my CEPE [certificate of primary school] there was someone in my class who went to Be L'assietty and begged to do well on the exam and they passed.[20] I didn't go there, but I also passed. There are those ancestors who make you dream, but what people don't realize is that good things on this earth come only from God. Ancestors can't move [because they are dead]; it is the devil that takes the face of others in order to trick you."

By demonizing the ancestors and forbidding the practices that build people's connections with them, membership in these churches accelerates the process that is begun when people leave their rural homelands to come to Tamatave and is further promoted by older forms of Christianity like Catholicism. Church membership contributes to disarticulating ancestral practice from daily life. But it also offers alternative rituals and forms of community for binding people to one another, as we shall see later.

Modernization Discourse, the Creation of Ancestral Tradition, and Wanting Progress

The ideology of modernization, present throughout the colonial period, and now adopted by Tamatavians to explain their everyday circumstances, further contributes to Tamatavians' movement away from the ancestrally based rituals that organized social life and toward a new social order based on monetary exchange and conspicuous consumption. In the logic of modernization, ancestors are simply the dead weight of tradition: investing money in them prevents people from spending money on the living and hence contributes to Madagascar's underdevelopment. Zeulhan, a sixteen-year-old, clearly expressed this logic when I asked if he ever went to family ceremonies:

> Youth in the city hardly know about what people do in the countryside! For me, ancestral customs aren't true. Where I come from there is something called a *rasatsiny*—you pay money, and if you don't pay then you get blame [*tsiny*], so you won't be blessed. For me that is wrong. And at the cattle sacrifice, you don't just kill a cow. You're also supposed to buy clothing for the dead! It's ridiculous. But there is no story that I've ever heard that says that ancestors are real. I don't worry my head about them too much.

Likewise, Noelphine, a young woman whose parents were Catholic, complained that her family spent too much money on the *fête de morts*, when people travel out to clean the ancestral tombs. Rather than being wasted on the dead, she suggested money would be better spent fixing up her house.

As Noelphine's remark suggests, the ideology of modernization brings with it a host of new goals, many of them captured in the concept of *fivoarana*, meaning "evolution" or "progress."[21] Although *fivoarana* and *fandro-*

soana have slightly different connotations, in their current usage both imply evolution according to a modernization narrative that constructs Western Europe as the apex of civilization, in which all who have not yet achieved a Western standard of living are "behind" and need to "catch up." One young man I knew made the equation of progress with European modernity perfectly clear: "You know the proverb, 'When the land becomes vazaha, that is progress.'" Or as Claudia, a young woman at the university, explained, "The way I see it, the reason young people here want to show off and make themselves 'on top' [*ambony*] is because Madagascar is still a developing country. We want to be like youth in countries that are developed. We want to be civilized." Much as James Ferguson (2006) has described for the Zambian Copperbelt, Tamatavians have also adopted, as native categories for interpreting historical experience, ideas about modernity, tradition, and progress that were once part of now outmoded scholarly theories of modernization. They inhabit a structure of feeling that has been described in many other postcolonial contexts, where the former metropolitan power becomes the standard against which those living in the former colony are measured (Bhabha 1994; Gupta 1998).

This notion of progress has an important spatial component in which Tamatave figures as "ahead" of the countryside but "behind" Europe. These coordinates are in turn mapped onto another spatial hierarchy of higher and lower. Nathalie, a young woman who earned her living by selling used clothes but also got financial support as the mistress of a local politician, exemplified this spatial dimension of fivoarana when she observed, "Fivoarana means that you desire to move toward a higher place than what you have in order to live a peaceful life. You need evolution in life, and what I have desired since I was little is to go overseas. If I have good luck perhaps I will get there. There they have many more things than we do, and [if you moved there] you would become the pride of your family." Alternatively, Tamatavians also draw on a discourse of lightness versus darkness and talk about the town as "clear" and "light" (*mazava*) in contrast with the ignorant darkness of the countryside, a discourse Christian missionaries also used during the nineteenth and twentieth centuries (Raison-Jourde 1991).

Consistent with the long-standing emphasis on social change emerging from movement beyond ancestors, Tamatavians argue that change comes from foreign sources, especially the arrival of foreigners in Madagascar bringing novel goods and practices. Like the colonial administrators in the early twentieth century and the policymakers who embraced economic liberalization in the early 1990s, they share the idea that a broader and more rapid inflow of outside modernity creates progress. Mamitiana, a fifteen-year-old girl from the local junior high school, expressed a widely shared opinion when she remarked,

> For me liberalization is a good thing because it helps Malagasy to progress. The economy depends on many foreigners coming here, not just the French. For example, cell phones. If the Europeans hadn't brought cell phones we wouldn't have known about them. There are things that are good that come from colonization because our way of thinking wouldn't have changed if the French hadn't come here. The arrival of the French made it possible to make this building, the streets, and the train.

For many Tamatavians, Madagascar's ability to progress depends on connecting with the world beyond the island.

If progress comes from incorporating foreign practices and ideas, Tamatavians insist that Western commodities or Western technologies reveal its presence. Maman'i Claire, a middle-aged woman I had lived with for many years, delightedly explained as she led me through the pet food aisle of Champion when I first returned to Madagascar after economic reforms: "Malagasy are no longer behind." (*Gasy tsy tara!*) Olivier, a university student, also articulated the close connection between Western material and technological knowledge and modern progress when he commented, "The people who have evolved [mivoatra], they are people who follow all new progress. For example, if the telephone comes out they should have one of those, because you really need them. In other words, you should follow all the new technological advances and your social standing will become higher than it was before. And if you are a student who doesn't follow progress, it makes you deeply ashamed. Like if you don't know how to use a computer, it makes you ashamed."

Olivier was hardly the only one to link modern commodities with social competition and shame. When she explained to me about how Europeans brought cell phones, Mamitiana also remarked that "While we need cell phones, we shouldn't *show off with them.*" If one reads Mamitiana and Olivier's remarks in light of long-standing ideas about how one builds social power through exchange, and how east coasters signal their power by displaying the latest foreign goods, one can understand how deeply humiliating, how malahelo-making, it must feel not to be able to partake in these symbols of progress. One can also appreciate that those who value social harmony should not "show off with them" because to do so humiliates others. For many Tamatavians, their desire to acquire commodities has "as much to do with aspirations for particular kinds of personhood as with specific material goals" (Mills 1997, 39). Though these young people were students, and hence comparatively elite, Tamatavians of all social classes echo their views. People might have had different access to the ideal of progress, but the content of that ideal was widely shared.

These ideas about modernity and tradition, progress and backwardness correspond to two contrasting bodily states. Tamatavians frequently use expressions like "to spread one's wings" (*mivelatra*) or "to move" (*mietsika*), words that convey a moving forward and outward in space to capture desired physical properties associated with being modern. The meanings of these words contrast with the idea of being constrained or, worse, crushed (*voasindry*—a word that refers to the tremendous humiliation suffered when others succeed in your place). Olivier explained, "To me being crushed means you have an inferiority complex. For example, if there is a person who really cares about clothes, then they feel at ease when they are well dressed, but if there is someone who dresses better than they do then they would feel crushed." Being crushed, being ashamed, and being held in place so that one cannot move forward are all negative dimensions of social experience. By contrast, Tamatavians imagine progress as a liberating movement, allowing one to take flight into a realm beyond the island of Madagascar. Insofar as traditional power operates through restraint (as opposed to movement) and concentration (as opposed to dispersal), Tamatavians conceptualize modern power as its exact inverse. In their imaginings, the embedding created by ancestors and the disembedding that takes place when people settle in Tamatave are mirror images: perfect continuity in one version, endless rupture in the other.

Consequences of Disembedding: Anxieties of Modernity, Tradition, and Money

And yet change, and creating a new future, is never so simple. To be sure, the decreased role of ancestors in Tamatavians' everyday lives does free them up to seek new goals and undertake new activities. It means that the fundamental mode of figuring the future in terms of the past as it was lived by the ancestors is no longer relevant. But the ancestors never just organized people's relation to the past. The beliefs and practices relating to ancestors always also mediated relationships in the present, and it was always the present competition that led people to negotiate with the past as embodied in ancestors. Given that the practices creating ancestors mediate relations not only between the living and the dead but also among the living, disembedding does not just change people's relations with their ancestors. It means that urbanites do not have the same kin-based networks as people who continue to live in rural areas. They have also lost many of the ritual occasions when they might otherwise have positively renegotiated their relationships among both neighbors and kin, softening the competitive interactions that are an ever-present part of social life on the east coast.

In the sand paths of Tamatave, people continue to live in close quarters and to watch one another's every move. They continue to believe that to be a valued person is to be at the center of a network of fitiavana, although, given the different political economy of Tamatave, the way they build those networks has radically changed. Money—who has it and who does not—is a crucial part of how people achieve these desired forms of modern power.[22] As I mentioned in chapter 2, and as Mamitiana explained above, the liberalization of the economy in the 1990s has meant that the inflow of outside goods and images has converged with a highly unstable economy, bringing growing social inequalities within the city of Tamatave and between Tamatave and the surrounding countryside. The difficulty of finding jobs within the formal economy means that in an increasing number of families, more and more dependents cling to one person who has a stable salaried job. The rest struggle in the highly volatile informal economy. The close connection people make between progress, the exchange of resources, and intimate forms of care, the profound sense of pleasure and satisfaction people gain from them, and the ways not-having is tied to feelings of inferiority intensify the competition and concern over who has and who does not have. Tamatavians experience this set of circumstances as an excruciating anxiety about how to get money.

The intense monetization and consumerism that currently characterize life in Tamatave make the meaning of relationships among the living even more unstable. Sometimes receiving money can create the illusion of fitiavana, lulling people into a sense of comfort and happiness, only to have the financial and emotional protection ripped away in sudden betrayals. Recounting her experiences with her latest boyfriend, a man who got her pregnant and then left her, Njira, a woman I introduce more fully in the next chapter, commented, "At first fitiavana shows itself as desire, and you think that the man is well-behaved and that you will search [for money] together, but in the end it isn't as you hoped. . . . At first you get small gifts [tsara tambitamby] and you are tricked." Or as Florence discovered when no one attended her wedding to a poor man, fitiavana existed only in moments of wealth.

Yet in Tamatave the kinds of gossip that in the rural context might give rise to sacrifices, which would in turn slow the fission that is integral to change, does not have the same effect. The ancestors who might overhear people's envious remarks remain in their rural homelands and do not usually wander the sand paths of Tamatave. Ancestors intervene only in their descendants' lives, so they are unlikely to be provoked by the gossip of jealous neighbors who are brought together by locality and the goal of searching for a livelihood rather than by shared kinship. Consequently, many of the checks rural contexts place on the social competition that may lead to social transformation fall away. This creates an ambiance of anxiety about social mobility. Increasing material insecurity heightens these concerns.

The urgency associated with acquiring money is closely connected to how monetization and commodification have become intertwined with long-standing ideas about how people build themselves up through networks of fitiavana and exchange, propelling them into the future in ways that are nevertheless connected to the past. Ideas about what it means to be a modern person have converged with older ideas that portray valued personhood as emerging from one's position in a network of exchange. Being poor is now about much more than not having resources. Ideas about modernity, tradition, personhood, and exchange converge so that to be poor is to be triply damned: it is to be perceived as someone who is unloved, unmodern, and inferior, a perpetual child who cannot pull the past into the future and hence cannot generate new life.

FOUR

The Changing Social Economy of the Female Life Course

The intensified importance of money as a means of achieving respected social adulthood has changed the social economy of Tamatavian life. Someone with money to share has *hasina*, or generative, life-giving potential.
Someone without such resources is a social nonentity. Most people in Tamatave struggle constantly to attain and maintain the respectable status
of a person with hasina. Many urbanites see themselves as having barely
achieved a modern identity, and they stake all their dignity in their effort
to become someone who is "considered" (*consideré*). Understanding what
it means to be a woman with particular aged and gendered capacities and
how the political economy of Tamatave affects women's choices is central to
illuminating this quest.

Tamatavian Variations

The way aspiring urban Tamatavians move through life modifies, but does
not entirely displace, the conception and practices of social maturation
through exchange I have sketched out so far. Whereas in the country from
the age of five children contribute to the family's well-being by doing small
jobs, urban youngsters are much more likely to attend school, and they will
do so for more years than their rural counterparts. Spending time in school
profoundly changes the manner of growing up; children are still supposed
to help around the house, but in general young urbanites consume their
parents' wealth (in the form of school fees, school supplies, and money for
school lunches and snacks) rather than contributing to it through household production. Young people who attend school in Tamatave remain dependent on their parents much longer than children in the countryside.
Ideally, this prolonged dependency means they defer adult responsibilities

in order to obtain the skills needed for certain jobs. In theory, when they do reach adulthood they should achieve a higher social status, and have more economic resources, than rural members of their family, although contemporary conditions make this comparison and assumed trajectory less likely than it might have been in the recent past.

Likewise, urban youth also "seek," though differently than their rural counterparts. Where a rural young man might go out to farm fields that have not yet been cultivated, a newcomer to the city might go to work unloading ships at the port and an educated urbanite might form a connection with a local political deputy in hopes of acquiring a well-paid job. There is wide variation in how urbanites seek resources. Nevertheless, no matter how a young person searches, the basic assumption is that because attaining adulthood requires amassing resources, and because opportunities to obtain them depend on historical (and geographical) circumstances, this moment in the life course is a fulcrum, delicately balancing the reproduction of existing social arrangements with their possible transformation into new patterns.

Marriage, Sexuality, Labor, and Consumption: Rural and Urban Patterns

Getting married, forming a household, and raising children epitomize respectable adulthood in Tamatave. One young man who was both unemployed and unmarried regretfully remarked, "To me, boys who are not married are always considered troublemakers by others, and they aren't respected by either their families or the wider society." A Tamatavian woman I knew echoed his comments when she observed that, now that she was married and her sister wasn't, her mother respected her more. Examining local conceptions and practices of marriage and intimate relations between men and women enables us to explore in more detail the ways that women in particular are most likely to become integrated into the networks of exchange that confer adulthood in Tamatave.

Repeatedly, men and women emphasized that marriage requires compatibility to "know how to get along" (*mahay mifanaraka*) and to "respect one another" (*mifanaja*). Both rural and urban inhabitants imagine marriage as a generative pairing capable of producing children and wealth, although there is also a more sentimental dimension (see also Bloch 1998b; Thomas 1996). Part of the reason sexual experimentation is permitted in many contexts is that it helps a young person find a compatible partner, and compatibility is highly prized. Both how people talk about those they would like to marry and how they judge marriages retrospectively reveal this criterion. I often heard people evaluate their own marriages in terms of the wealth (and children) they had produced as a couple. Generativity, then, is both a value during courtship and an ex post facto sign of compatibility and a successful marriage.

Not only are husbands and wives supposed to be compatible, they are also supposed to enter into reciprocal exchange in order to build a household. Although today east coasters do not always complete the marriage ritual, it nevertheless embodies widely shared precepts of what marriage *should* be like. During the ceremony, the man's kin go to the woman's kin and engage in competitive oratory during which his kin must ritually prove that he is able to care for her in his house (see also Keenan 1974). They also give the woman bridewealth, which she controls. During the speech, the speechmaker, who is ideally a kinsman of the groom but may also be a hired orator, often says that the families are "exchanging a boy crab for a girl crab," implying that each family is benefiting equally from the arrangement. In practice, however, such exchanges are always ambiguous (Bloch 1989). Another proverb, one that the woman's kin always repeat to the man's kin as they hand over their daughter, underscores this ambiguity: "Look at our daughter. Her eyes are not damaged, her hands are not broken. If you decide that you no longer want her, give her back to us in the condition in which you received her."[1] The proverb acknowledges first that men are more capable of physically harming women than women are of harming men and second that the girl is ultimately on loan, never fully alienated from her own family or incorporated into her husband's. Despite these caveats and tensions, negotiated equality within exchange remains the unattainable ideal.

Ultimately, the set of exchanges referred to in the marriage ceremony produces a new household. In fact, one way to ask if people are married, as many other scholars of Madagascar have also noted, is to ask if they already "have a house" (Feeley-Harnik 1991; Bloch 1998a; Thomas 1996). The house is the ultimate symbol of marriage. But building a house—like building a marriage—involves human action that can be made and unmade over time. It is a process that starts in courtship, with the giving and taking of small gifts like clothing, long before people inhabit an actual structure, and continues once a couple has rented, built, or bought a house together. The changing contributions men and women make to creating a household and how they are valued provide a powerful lens for examining women's life trajectories and gives insight into some of the choices they make.

East coasters often insist that whether a man marries a woman or remains her more casual lover, "men make women living" (*lehilahy mahamelona ve-*

hivavy), meaning that men are supposed to earn the money to support their wives or lovers. They also sometimes say that "girls are soft movable goods," an expression used to justify women's moving into their husbands' houses rather than the reverse.[2] What these expressions do not make explicit, but everybody knows, is that men support women in exchange for their sexual, reproductive, and caring attentions. Sex, the ability to bear children, and caring consideration are the most evident proof of a woman's hasina that, while different than men's, also requires recognition. The widespread practice of men's giving their lovers gifts or money makes the relation between exchange and respected forms of personhood even more explicit. Material resources, emotional attachments, and social power are in this way profoundly, albeit unevenly, intertwined in what I call a sexual economy (see Cole 2009). All women must learn to navigate this economy in order to succeed in life.

Given these ideas, women expect gifts or money from lovers as recognition of their general female generative capacities. Both my ethnographic and historical sources suggest this has long been the case. The explorer G. Grandidier (1913, 11) described how "Malagasy use the same word, *'mitangy'* to say [to] work for wages as a domestic or to have intimate relations with a lover, because it is not only foreigners who give gifts to their Malagasy concubines; the indigenous men must also give them some small present, which can't be compared to what Europeans normally offer but nonetheless is a remuneration for their services."

Although Grandidier vulgarized the issue by using the word remuneration, he nevertheless exposes the basic assumption that men are supposed to acknowledge women's generative capacities through such gifts.[3] Similar assumptions guided the lives of many rural women I knew. For example, Ramarie, who was by then in her late sixties, who died in 2003, recounted how in her youth she was "free and wanted to live." So she left her daughter by her divorced first husband with her mother and became mistress of a chef de canton who would pass through the village where she worked on his rounds of the district. "He taught me how to count the days so I wouldn't get pregnant. We'd go to Mahanoro [the nearby town] and stay in a hotel. And we'd walk into the Arab merchants' store, and I'd say, 'Oh, I like that fabric over there.' And he'd buy it for me. And then later he left and I became the mistress to another chef de canton."

Ramarie's dalliance with the chef de canton did not prevent her from later remarrying. During their courtship, her third husband, Ravanona, would load his dugout canoe with pineapples and sugarcane from his fields and come calling. Ramarie interpreted Ravanona's gifts as both proof of his ability to care for her and recognition of her feminine capacities and worth. Women younger than Ramarie operated with many of the same assumptions.[4] Generally, women revel in their ability to get things from men. Their sexuality and caring capacities are an important part of what they offer in this system of exchange. Just as the life course is often imagined as a movement from soft to hard, movement to fixity, so women move from exchanges built through soft, ephemeral cloth to the more enduring sign of the house, a structure most new brides hope will be a long-lasting symbol of their ability to generate life and weave kin networks together.

While the bodily, sexual, and caring dimensions of women's labor contribute to making and sustaining families, rural women always also work outside the home and usually have access to other forms of capital, especially land. The resources women inherit, and their ability to labor in the fields, can make a material difference to a family's well-being. A family is just as likely to farm the wife's land as the husband's; pragmatic concerns determine which field a family works. Men and women explicitly recognize the importance of women's labor in making and sustaining households. Men never remain alone for long, not only because they believe they require women's caring attention to flourish, but also because they need their wives to work the fields with them. Women's productive labor may be less valued than men's, but it is still important.

Respectable Marriage in Tamatave

Some women who lived in Tamatave probably had intimate lives very similar to what Ramarie described. Yet at least during the colonial period, and even throughout the early independence period in the 1960s, young women from families who aspired to modern, socially prestigious forms of marriage were more constrained in their sexuality. Institutions like school or the church gave youth more opportunities to meet potential lovers and spouses away from the prying eyes of parents. Nevertheless parents often did exercise control over whom their children married and, in some cases, over their daughters' sexuality before marriage.[5] Their attitudes reflect both the influence of missionary Christianity and a concern for consolidating or improving their class position by adopting French practices.

Jacqueline's story of how she met her husband, and of their marriage more generally, reveals how new ways of earning a livelihood and new ideas about respectability altered intimate relations. Jacqueline's father was the schoolteacher in their village near Mahanoro. Jacqueline and her older sister had the same name (a practice that is not uncommon—middle names would have distinguished the two girls). At that time Philibert, Jacqueline's husband-to-be, had already gone off to the regional school in Tamatave to study law. While on vacation, he returned to his natal village, where he met Jacqueline the elder and started to flirt with her. Jacqueline the younger continued her story:

> I don't know what happened between them [her older sister and the man who would later be her own husband], but after the holidays were over, our father took us up to live in Fandriana [a town on the high plateau]. Then the 1947 rebellion came, and we stayed there. My older sister met a man there and married him and stayed on. But I came back and started to go to school in Mahanoro. I didn't know it, but Philibert's friend wrote to him and said, "That girl you like, she's come back to school in Mahanoro." But of course the friend didn't know that Philibert really liked my sister with the same name. So Philibert wrote to me at school, through his friend, thinking he was writing to my older sister. The teacher gave me the letter, and I was so embarrassed I just ripped it up. But after two weeks he wrote again. I took that letter, and I hid it in my clothes, and when I went out to wash dishes by the sea I took it and read it. It said, "Do you remember that time at the fête? I hear you've come to school in Mahanoro." And I wrote back and said, "I'm not who you think I am. I'm her younger sister. The one you liked has gotten married in Fandriana."

Philibert wrote again to announce he was coming home on vacation. Jacqueline continued her story: "And I don't know what happened, but I guess he was my fate [anjara]. I accepted him. He did not want me to work, and Maman almost forbade us from getting married since he didn't have a job yet. But he started working as a secretary while waiting for his post, and she let us do a simple marriage." Jacqueline's husband went on to become a functionary with a position fairly high up in the colonial administration, and they lived in Tamatave for years before retiring and moving back home to Mahanoro. The entire time, Jacqueline took care of their many children, and the family lived on her husband's salary. When he died many years later she continued to live on his pension.

Jacqueline had a proper marriage. The structure of the marriage and its expectations illustrate how changes in the economy, and particularly the growth of the state bureaucracy, contributed to the reorganization of production and consumption within the intimate domain. The great majority of Tamatavians do not rely on cultivating land for their livelihood. Rather, they tend to work in the government bureaucracy, in service industries, in commerce, or at the port. Women often stay at home, supplementing household income by selling cooked food, sewing, and the like. Historically, men have disproportionately obtained those jobs that are a more stable and better paid part of the formal economy. The French favored men over women for employment in the colonial administration, a pattern that continued in the postcolonial period. Although, compared with many parts of the world, Tamatavian women enjoy relative equality with men in access to education or the proportion of resources parents invest in female versus male children, they are nevertheless at a disadvantage in the formal economic sector compared with Malagasy men. The missionaries, who deliberately sought to reshape the modern urban intimate sphere, reinforced these tendencies by elevating the importance of women's appropriate care of the home and children.

Where before in the ideal marriage the couple grew rice together with their children, in the urban context it became somewhat more common for men aspiring to middle-class status to earn wages and then turn them over to the women. Women are supposed to use the money their husbands give them for the family's material and social advancement—improving the house, caring for children, and generally investing wealth in long-term household reproduction. Many people I spoke with assumed that, without wives to discipline them, men are incapable of managing resources to fulfill household needs because they will naturally spend their money on drink, women, and other short-term pleasures. The proper economic relationships in marriage hopefully ensure the maintenance and reproduction of families (see Cole 2005). Several older men who had successful and enduring marriages even told me with pride that they had never once bought their own shirts, as evidence of how completely they trusted their spouses to manage the resources they brought home to the benefit of the household. Such comments are boasts about a highly valued form of marriage. When a woman achieves such a marriage, she can become a pivotal, honored member of her natal family as well as her affinal family. Her ability to create and sustain the networks that knit families together earns her the love and respect of those around her.

Tensions in Marriage

But this desired state is both difficult to achieve and precarious to maintain. Although men in these marriages become respected elders in their communities, competing demands on men contribute to the instability and vulnerability women endure in marriage. While local gender ideals enjoin women to be faithful to their husbands, men face less moral pressure. Local conceptions of masculinity hold that men *should* have many lovers, because it proves their potency. The proverb "men with money make rivals" (have many lovers who compete with one another) encapsulates this idea.[6] So widely accepted is the idea that men have more than one lover that one woman told me "men can't cheat," using a grammatical formulation implying that no matter how many women other than his wife a man had sex with, it did not constitute cheating. By contrast, if a woman is caught cheating on her husband, he can turn her out of his house and keep their shared property. If the marriage breaks up for other reasons, she is entitled to one-third of their shared wealth.

The expectation that men will support their wives exists in great practical tension with the expectation that men with money will naturally drink and spend their money on other women. Women are neither passive nor blameless in the face of these circumstances.[7] The marriage ceremony makes explicit the different ways that both men and women, in their gender-specific ways, can threaten the joint project of creating and maintaining a household. At a certain point in the ceremony, the couple publicly discuss what they will tolerate in the marriage. The widespread acceptance of male philandering notwithstanding, women frequently say they do not want their men to sleep with other women. The couple may also state the conditions under which either member can attend balls, widely understood to be places where philandering is likely. For their part, men frequently say they do not "want the woman to leave the door white" (that is, closed), meaning they do not want their wives wandering around outside the house and neglecting their domestic duties.[8] The implicit subtext to this statement is that women who do "wander around" are more likely to take lovers and possibly break up the household. Although women are ideally expected to be faithful to their husbands, and though the consequences of cheating are potentially much greater for them, nevertheless they do occasionally form extramarital liaisons. They are especially likely to do so when they are traders who travel to other parts of Madagascar to sell their goods. However, they also sometimes do so at home, in front of all their kin, despite their disapproval. During my rural fieldwork I heard as many stories about unruly women as I did about unfaithful men.

Although the structurally produced tensions created by competing gendered norms exist in both rural and urban contexts, their distinctive political economies powerfully mediate the effects of these tensions in different ways. In rural villages, a woman who is angered by her husband's philandering is not entirely dependent on him. Although she may not have a lot of resources, she can usually return to her kin, and she usually has access to family-owned land. No woman ever *wants* to be in this position. Women who stay married and build up networks of dependents according to the ideal always garner more social respect. Nevertheless, when their husbands create hardship, these women have options. Since women are never fully alienated from their natal kin and have a right to inherit land from their fathers' and mothers' families, they usually have other resources and other people they can rely on when a husband proves particularly disappointing. They rarely are truly without recourse.

By contrast, the nature of the economy and new patterns of residence in Tamatave intersect with the local ideas about growth, marriage, and men's responsibility to "make women living" so that urban women can become more vulnerable than their rural counterparts. When women move from country to city, a crucial piece of their productive and reproductive capacity drops away: they lose their control over land and with it the concrete ability to feed their families. This means that whereas in the countryside women are valued both through their connections to land and through their sexual and caring capacities, in the city a young woman's body may be her most valued productive asset. Of course, some educated women do work as teachers, secretaries, doctors, or businesswomen, but they are in the minority. Even when women gain access to money and can engage in trading, which many women do, the money is often given to them either by family members or by the men they are linked to, and to whom their sexual/caring services in a sense belong.

Not only do urban women lose access to land, but they are also less densely integrated into kin networks. More often than not, their family members live in other parts of Madagascar. Consequently they have fewer people they can turn to for succor if their relationship with their husband breaks down. If their family in rural areas happens to have resources, they may be able to turn to them for help. In one case, for example, a young woman I knew got pregnant in Tamatave, and when her family back in the village heard what had happened, they came and took her home. But such a scenario requires money. Many families are too poor to save their own kin. The nature of the urban economy inadvertently strips women of some of the ways they accrue social value in rural contexts.

The Opportunities and Constraints of the
Urban Female Life Course

Any young woman in Tamatave knows that to build up a respectable position in society, she must acquire money, food, clothes, even housing in part
through her relationships with men. Likewise, parents hope their daughters
will find men to support them, and they are generally pleased when they
do. From early on, girls learn to exercise their powers of seduction, and as
Ramarie's narrative implies, they are proud that they can do so. Women's
ability to earn money and obtain resources protects them. Sometimes it can
be even more important than contracting a proper marriage.

Cathy's narrative illustrates the mundane interactions through which
women learn how to "get things" (*mahazo raha*) from men. When Cathy
was fifteen, her father worked as a stevedore at the port, and her mother sold
cooked food by the side of the road.

When I was still little, I already loved money [*tia vola*]. But my parents could
hardly afford to support that. There was a boy who was the child of a merchant here [thus by implication wealthier than she was] in the neighborhood. Each time I would see him I would ask him for things. At that time
I was already very flirtatious; I loved every boy I saw! And I saw my older
sister having many boyfriends, and I wanted to do that too. Often, that boy,
he would give me chewing gum, or a bit of money, and I'd be overjoyed. In
the end, Independence Day celebration came. The boy's parents had gone
up to Tana [Antananarivo] for a funeral, and the boy was home alone. It was
evening, around four o'clock, and my mother asked me to buy some salt.
When I got there, the store was closed. He was sitting out in front and called
to me, "Come here. Let's take a walk tonight." "Won't you be scolded by your
parents?" I asked. "My parents aren't home," he replied. "I'll be there soon,"
I said, "I just have to change clothes." I ran home and changed . . . and ran
back to his house. He was very surprised to see that I'd returned so quickly.
"Come in for a little while," he said, "we'll go out to stroll when it gets dark."
I went into the house, and we drank cocoa and ate cookies. And we ate rice,
and there was meat for our sauce. I looked at him and he was getting closer
and closer to me, staring at my breasts. He said, "I love you" [*tiako anao*].
Then we started caressing each other. That was the first time I went with a
man. At eleven o'clock that night I went home to sleep. The next day there
was a party for Independence Day, but I was sick. And my mother asked me,
"Why are you sick?" "Malaria," I answered. But it wasn't that at all; I was

lying. Starting then, I really loved men [*tia lehilahy*]. And I wasn't afraid of them. (Cited in Cole 2009, 122)

Although Cathy's narrative is a story of fickle young attraction, as they grow older many young women forge relationships with men in which they are deeply invested and that ultimately lead to marriage. They usually also give birth to children. Their husbands may support them, or they may also work to supplement their husbands' incomes. In this way they embed themselves within networks of exchange. Such women achieve valued forms of personhood. But this status can easily be undermined if a husband takes a lover. Whereas a wealthy man might have enough resources to support two or more households, wealthy men are hard to come by. Much more commonly, a man earns a bit of money that might just be enough to support his wife and children but then starts supporting another woman, decreasing the resources available to the first family. Marriages frequently end in divorce, with men displacing the first wife and her children by bringing their lovers into the house.[9]

When a wife becomes pitted against her husband's unmarried lover, the latter is more at liberty than the wife to manipulate this arrangement to her own ends. Less constrained by responsibility, she can, for example, have more than one lover at a time. She is also free to seek other opportunities. Stelline's account of how her lovers divert income from their households to support her illustrates younger women's (temporary) freedom. It also reflects a dynamic in which men marry and have children, then betray their wives and children with other women. Later the daughters, who have usually witnessed their mothers' suffering most closely, in turn take up the position of the mistress or "little wife" (*vady kely*). Although Stelline's response, and particularly her remarks about her own father, makes clear the anger and moral opprobrium directed at men who leave their families, such disapproval does not appear to make the practice less common:

The reason I live off of my lovers is that my father was a rich man, yet he cheated. His cheating killed my mother [the implication is that she died either from heartbreak, anxiety, or witchcraft]. I had to leave school early because my father just paid attention to my stepmother [and not our material and emotional needs]. Yet I did not want to work as a maid, because I knew I was so beautiful that my boss would inevitably want to sleep with me. So instead I have boyfriends. There are three men who go with me: Maxime, Gerard, and Paul. Maxime has a jewelry store at the Big Bazaar, but I won't tell you its name. He comes twice a week, on Saturdays and Tuesdays. He brings my food for the week (*mitondra bazary*), and he gives me about 125,000 fmg (about thirty dollars at that time). Gerard is his chauffeur, and one day he brought me home and *wasn't* content just to drop me off [laughs]. He pays my rent and my water and electric bill. And then there is Paul; he's a truck driver who carries goods to Tulear.

Those who believe a young urban woman should move from school to marriage, becoming dependent on a single man within a housed, married relationship, do not respect women like Stelline. While it would be tempting to argue that those who criticize her strategy are more middle class, and while such an assessment might have been true throughout the colonial and early postindependence period, today it is harder to map class position onto the approval or rejection of such strategies. Suffice it to say that, ideally, most parents probably want their daughters to find husbands and stay married to them, since this is generally considered more respectable feminine behavior. But because fewer people can obtain the resources to marry, more people are forced to adopt these strategies than in the recent past (see also Hunter 2002; Nyamnjoh 2005).

Stelline and others like her know that while married women occupy a more respected position, that position can be a vulnerable one, particularly if they do not work. This risk appears to be built into the nature of east coast families and marriages. In the best of times women depend on their husbands' support to foster the well-being of the household, and they use their relations in marriage to establish a sense of self-worth within a network of kin. Their children both rely on them for support and feel themselves similarly bound within a network of exchange so that they give back to their mothers and help secure their welfare. True, some husbands take lovers, and not all children reciprocate as they should. Ideally, however, there are enough resources that husbands' affairs do not completely undermine the well-being of the household, and the many children who do reciprocate make up for the occasional child who does not.

In contemporary Tamatave, however, these tensions have sharpened. A married woman should not take lovers, as we have seen. If she has children, it is harder for her to work. And if a woman does not work, she becomes increasingly dependent on her husband's income. This financial dependence becomes a problem if her husband decides to give his resources to someone else. When women do not receive income from their husbands, they cannot give it to their children, weakening their control over them and unraveling the network of exchange. Mothers require resources like food, medicine, or household goods to express their care. A woman's ability to bear children, so celebrated in the rural context, becomes yet another potential liability when money is scarce.

Young women see that older women who become trapped by their husbands' lack of attention, their lack of resources, and the need to care for dependent children find these circumstances both painful and difficult to escape. The competitive dynamics of display and disgrace that are such an important part of how Tamatavians evaluate themselves magnify and exacerbate their humiliation, sense of loss, frustration, and anger. So common is this scenario that the mortification from a man's investing his resources elsewhere is widely perceived as part of marriage. Another often quoted proverb reminds brides, "Marriage is like a chicken's house. Smells good? There you are. Smells rank, there you [still] are." In the rural areas and in Tamatave, women are supposed to endure their husbands' behavior to ensure proper social reproduction. It often seems like a thankless, lonely task. It certainly makes some women angry or emotional, as local cultural discourse about women implies. And at a certain point it may not seem worth undertaking, especially if other options come along, as they do in Tamatave.

The Challenges of Women's Lives

Clearly, conceptions of gender, family, and marriage converge with the unstable political economy of Tamatave to make women's daily lives a constant struggle to obtain the resources that signal respected adulthood. But it is one thing to understand these ideas abstractly and another to see in intimate detail how people live. There are many kinds of families in Tamatave, and many ways of cobbling together a life and making ends meet—or not. Nevertheless, I want to give some idea of the households people live in and how they came to be. The sketches I provide are situated along several axes of difference. These include a woman who has a stable relationship with a man versus one who does not, a woman who has access to forms of capital that enable her to run a business, and one who has access to a regular salary through her husband. These differences in status and wealth are crosscut by people's various relationships to the rural worlds they often hail from. I start with the most successful case in local terms, a woman who maintained her marriage to a functionary who receives a regular salary, and then go on to consider several comparatively less successful cases.

Maman'i Noelphine's Courtyard: One Man, Many Dependents

Maman'i Noelphine is a forty-nine-year-old Betsimisaraka woman whose parents were farmers in the southern part of Tamatave province, where she spent part of her youth. When her father died, relatives divided up the siblings and she went to live with her mother's brother, who worked as a chauffeur for the customs office at the port. She and her two cousins stayed with him, helping him cook and clean until he married; she also briefly studied sewing before she got married. As she described his financial situation, "You wouldn't have said that he was rich, but nor was he poor: we had enough to eat." Maman'i Noelphine married at seventeen. Her husband, to whom she had stayed married for more than thirty years at the time of our conversation, was a low-level bureaucrat in the municipal office. Since Maman'i Noelphine did not have a formal job, she supplemented the family income by buying things like used clothing to resell at a profit. She and her husband had nine children. Despite her many children, Maman'i Noelphine seemed surprisingly young; she had me take her picture, which I was supposed to use to find an American man who would marry her. She complained that her husband had girlfriends and cheated on her, so she too wanted to find a new lover. Yet despite her husband's dalliances, it was clear from the family's circumstances that his actions had never seriously damaged their welfare. Nor do I think Maman'i Noelphine really wanted to run off with an American, although I don't know what she would have done had I actually found her a suitor.

By local standards, Maman'i Noelphine's household lived fairly well. Nevertheless the problem of scarcity, of managing too many children—who in turn kept producing children of their own—with too few resources, was still acutely felt. Of Maman'i Noelphine's nine children, several had grown up and gone away. One adult son, however, had fathered a child and then divorced his wife, and she had left the child, Kala Rosa, at Maman'i Noelphine's house so she could work. It wasn't clear that her son was contributing money to the child's upkeep. Kala Rose's aunties would sit in the family courtyard and dandle the little girl on their laps or pick the fleas out of her toes, showering her with affection. Still, it was hard to tell, given the household resources, how long that little girl would be allowed to stay in school. Another son who was only sixteen had gotten the maid pregnant. Though she'd gone home to the country to give birth, she too had brought the child back to his paternal grandparents. Yet a third son—in his late twenties—was not yet married, in part because he did not have consistent employment and was therefore unable to organize a virilocal marriage. Of two daughters,

Figure 4.1. Maman'i Noelphine and her children, 2003.

also in their early twenties, Noelphine was married and had set up house on the edge of the property, while a boyfriend covered her younger sister's expenses, which her parents encouraged. Maman'i Noelphine summed up the situation when I asked who controlled money in the house: "I do. But we [her husband] only receive very small wages, even if he works for the government. Since there are so many people in the house we have to get people to sell things to make enough money; my children who already have households, they support themselves, but the rest of them live here, and we support them." There were indeed a lot of mouths to feed.

Maman'i Haja: A Widow and Her Children

Like Maman'i Noelphine's, Maman'i Haja's household exemplifies the lives of many people Tamatavians refer to as "middling" (*antonitony*) and whom I would describe as petit bourgeois.[10] However, whereas Maman'i Noelphine is married to a functionary, Maman'i Haja had always worked in business, and by the time I knew her she had been widowed for several years. I first met Maman'i Haja through her son, Haja. Because the house was on my way back to the university, where I stayed, I would often stop by to chat.

Maman'i Haja was a fifty-year-old Merina, and she had lived in Tamatave since 1959. She had even lived for many years in Morarano, a neighborhood inhabited by immigrants from the southeast of Madagascar, who speak a markedly different dialect, though she never lost her Merina accent. Her father had moved from Antananarivo to Tamatave in 1959 to teach at the Catholic mission, while her mother traded in bananas. They had eight children, of whom Maman'i Haja was the eldest. After she received her grammar school diploma, she left school to help her mother. When she was eighteen, Maman'i Haja became involved with a man whom she almost married. She got pregnant during the courtship, but only a month before the ceremony her husband went off with her best friend, leaving her to bear the child on her own. Shortly thereafter, her brother was killed in an automobile accident. Her parents, too grief-stricken to remain in Tamatave, returned to Antananarivo. By that time, however, Maman'i Haja was selling rum at a local company to support herself and her child, and she did not want to leave Tamatave. She sold rice for the local government council (*fokontany*). As she described it, "It was there—working at the council—that I met Papan'i Haja. There were no ceremonies, nothing. He was Merina, and we loved each other and moved in together." After living with him for a year, Maman'i Haja went back to school to get a technical high school diploma and started selling concrete while he worked as a chauffeur. Only much later did they legalize their marriage with the state; she agreed to do so only after he had broken up with another woman.

Besides her son from her first marriage, Maman'i Haja had three children: Landy (twenty), Haja (eighteen), and Vola (fifteen). By the time I met them, however, her husband had died of a heart attack while on a business trip to Antananarivo and had been buried there. Maman'i Haja had spent an enormous amount of money and effort to rebuild his tomb and to perform the famadihana, or second burial, an event that had been enormously meaningful to Haja, as I described in chapter 3. Maman'i Haja remained in the house they had purchased together and sold various baked goods, juice, and confections. No matter what time of day I stopped by, I would find her installed in the storefront of their house, cigarette in one side of her mouth, busily working over new techniques for making brioche or preparing tamarind or passion fruit juice. Maman'i Haja also employed several young men to help her with the time-consuming work of sealing the small packets of peanuts and other snacks with wax.

Maman'i Haja worked constantly, often staying up until two or three o'clock in the morning, working by candlelight. Her children never helped. It appeared that the entire family had accepted the idea that children should go to school rather than contribute their labor to the household. Haja's time was completely taken up with school and his new church. Landy had quit school and was learning to sew, and Vola was still in school and spent most of her time with Julie, a girl who lived a few houses down and whom everyone identified as "going with men" and thus possibly entering the slippery slope that might lead her toward prostitution. In the many conversations I had with Maman'i Haja and her children, it was evident that the household structure had fallen apart since their father's death. Maman'i Haja's eldest son, the one she had before marrying Haja's father, spent most of his time out drinking and smoking hemp. His mother feared he would either steal from her or attack her, and she often asked me if I knew some way to help him. He would blow into the house while everyone else was gathered there, then quickly leave. Haja himself often recounted how when Papan'i Haja was alive the household had been more disciplined. Now, however, he didn't respect (*tsy matohatra*) his mother and did more or less what he pleased; his sisters behaved the same way. The father's death had weakened the web of exchanges and responsibility. Haja and his sisters and brother had enough food and were able to attend school. But the loss of their father, combined with difficult financial circumstances, left their mother struggling to stay afloat. She had less time, fewer resources, and lacked authority to structure her children's activities.

Njira: A Rural to Urban Trajectory

Njira was the youngest daughter of Ramarie, whose narratives I cited earlier. Although Maman'i Noelphine and Maman'i Haja struggled to make ends meet, they nevertheless supported many children and had attained successful adult womanhood in Tamatave. By contrast, Njira's story offers a glimpse of someone who comes from the countryside and, through a combination of little education, bad luck with men, and unwanted children, is slotted into the lowest rung of the Tamatavian economy. Although she is by now adult in years, she has never really attained the marks of social adulthood. Some young women who come to Tamatave do fare much better than Njira, but her story gives some sense of one possible outcome of the rural-to-urban trajectory.

When she was eighteen and attending school in the neighboring town of Mahanoro, Njira became pregnant. She wanted to abort the baby and even found someone who "gave shots," but it cost 20,000 fmg (about ten dollars at the time), and she didn't have enough money. She tried various methods to get rid of the child, but nothing worked and she eventually gave birth to a little girl. Njira cultivated rice the year after Kamarie was born. When the harvest was in, she took her rice to market in Mahanoro. She left that weekend to follow her new boyfriend north to Tamatave, leaving a note and the rest of her rice for her parents and asking them to take care of Kamarie.

Like many girls who come from the countryside to live in Tamatave, Njira's first job was working as a maid for a wealthier family for 7,000 fmg a month (approximately two dollars at the time). Though her wages were small and the work was hard, she had few expenses and would spend what little she earned on clothes and shoes—"things to make me clean." As she became more integrated into the city, she soon learned of better-paying work and left the first family to work for a woman who was *métisse*, Malagasy and European. Her new job paid 10,000 fmg a month (about three dollars at that time). Her new employer earned her living by selling baked goods and getting money from her lover, who worked at the Neptune, the fanciest hotel and nightclub in Tamatave. She regularly took Njira to nightclubs. Eventually the woman married an Italian and moved to Italy, but by this time Njira had herself "gotten married" (*manambady*), by which she meant she moved in with a man. Within a few years she gave birth to a boy, Rolfe, and a girl, Nellie.

Though her rural kin had told me stories about Njira in 1992, and though I knew her daughter, Kamarie, I first met Njira in 1999. By that time she was twenty-nine and the poorest of Ramarie's four children living in the city. She lived in a tiny shack in Anzoma, one of the poorer neighborhoods in Tamatave, where many of the people from the southern region of Tamatave province gather. Her house was divided into four sections and shared by several single women and their children. Njira's room contained only a double bed, a dresser, and a couple of small stools. There was hardly room to move. There was no electricity, and they had to walk out to the pump to get water for cooking and washing dishes. I never figured out where the outhouse was.

One of the first things Njira asked when I met her was whether I could help her find a European boyfriend. By my return trip in 2000 she had already found a Malagasy boyfriend, whom I discovered by accident, much to her embarrassment, when I walked in to find him sleeping on her bed. The man worked for a while, then lost his job when he was wrongly accused, according to Njira, of stealing from his employer. Meanwhile, Njira worked to support herself and her daughter (her son had gone to live with his father) by selling cooked food by the side of the road. Though they had enough to eat, and in fact she and Nellie ate meat and vegetables more frequently than people I knew in the countryside, she rarely had money to buy the worm medicine Nellie so evidently needed, though she did manage to send her to school for a while. She found herself pregnant again and kept the child, but her relationship with the father soon ended when she caught him cheating with another woman. When I saw her in 2002, she was forced to leave the newborn alone with six-year-old Nellie to go sell food. By late 2003, however, her fortunes had taken a turn for the better as she had moved in with an older man who apparently—at least according to her brother—had money and was invested enough in her and the children's well-being that he had contributed money on her behalf for her mother's funeral sacrifice.[11] Though she often reminisced fondly about her natal village, she didn't seem very interested in returning there. In the meantime, Njira's daughter, Kamarie, now fourteen, had moved to Tamatave and was working as a maid as her mother had before her.

Julie: Depending on Others

The households of Njira, Maman'i Haja, and Maman'i Noelphine give some sense of how women in Tamatave live and the profound sense of stretched resources, and too many demands, that most families face. Yet with the exception of Njira, these women are relatively fortunate: although they struggle, they do not experience the intense shame, powerlessness, and anger that others feel when they become entirely dependent. Many young people, however, live as vulnerable dependents. The girls like Njira who come to work as maids and inevitably drift from one employer to the next, seeking an environment they can bear, illustrate one kind of vulnerability. The tensions within families that I have just examined, and the fact that many parents divorce and remarry, create another kind of pressure when young people live with stepparents where they often feel unwanted and unloved. Alternatively, families sometimes send their children to live with wealthier kin as a way to ease the household burden. Often, though not always, these situations entail a rural to urban shift as well, so that poor rural kin become dependent on sometimes only slightly wealthier urban relatives. When poor children go to live with richer families, or when children live with stepparents, they often feel exploited, forced to constrain their desires (*miafy*) and fulfill the demands of others.

Julie, for example, was a girl of sixteen who lived only a few houses from Maman'i Haja and had joined the Assembly of God church. Over the years I worked in Tamatave I watched as she moved from the Assembly of God to the Power of Faith church. Despite her enthusiasm for these churches, which strongly oppose premarital sex, much of what concerned Julie when I knew her were her adventures and misadventures with wayward men and her problems and disputes living with her mother and stepfather. Julie had long ago quit school, and she helped out in her mother's house. Though she did considerable housework, her stepfather continued to oppose her church activities, picking fights with her whenever he was drunk. When they fought over who would do the housework, her mother accused her of working as a prostitute while she claimed to be in church. During one of our discussions, Julie recounted an incident that encapsulated her lack of choices and lack of resources, providing a glimpse into her daily circumstances:

> One of our beds was broken, and the three of us [she and her half siblings] had to sleep together in one bed. We were squeezed together, and my step-father told me to get off the bed because my little sister was too squished. I would sleep on a mat on the floor, but then they told me to get back in bed, and I just stayed on the floor. There are four of us children who have the same mother and father, but two of my siblings are from my mother with my stepfather. My stepfather really hates me—he won't buy me even a dress, but he has lived with us for five years. He works at the port, and my mother sells. My older sister loves me and wants to take me to live with her, but my mother won't let me go. My mother sometimes says to me, "Go live with your father, even though they don't want you." My father also works at the port, but we don't see each other very much.

By the time I returned to Tamatave in 2003, Julie lived alone with her siblings in a small house near the church; I never learned where her parents had gone. It was not clear whether she would ever be able to improve her circumstances, but it was obvious that she desperately wanted to.

Conclusion

I often asked Tamatavians what it meant to be "comfortable" (*miadana*)—the word people use to mean the opposite of "struggling" (*sahirana*). Men and women, old and young, responded by talking about a household that is "complete" (using the French *complet*), which they opposed to "not enough" (*tsy ampy*) or "lacking" (*misy banga*). What counted as "complete" included employment, money to buy necessities including food, clothes, and school supplies, and—a ubiquitous, slippery phrase I encountered again and again—enough "so that you could be like your friends."[12]

Tamatavians have good reason to want to "be like their friends." "Not having" suggests one does not have hasina or generative potential—the basic prerequisite for being a valued human being. The close connection people make between affective attachments, the exchange of resources, and intimate forms of care sharpens these feelings of inferiority and unhappiness. Yet, as we have seen, how Tamatavians obtain the resources to achieve valued forms of personhood differs profoundly both by gender and over the life course. It also differs in rural and urban circumstances. In both cases, young women deploy their sexuality and caring services in ways that older women cannot, but in rural villages women are more likely to have access to land, a material resource that contributes to their value. They also have a wider network of kin who may be able to help them if their relationships with men fail.

By contrast, the contemporary political economy of Tamatave gives women less access to resources than men have. Combined with the reduction and fragmentation of kin networks that takes place in the city, this situation can makes urban women more vulnerable. This vulnerability emerges in different ways at different points in the life course. Young women like Stelline who use their relationships with multiple men to obtain resources can create a life that may be far preferable to being trapped in a marriage with many dependents and few resources. But they may also risk their reputations. Women who get married according to local norms are more respected, but their respectability comes at the cost of vulnerability later in life, should their husbands choose to share their resources with others. Ultimately, whether they are young and old, such precariousness leads women to want to make money of their own, using whatever resources are available to them.

Consider Maman'i Noelphine, Maman'i Haja, Njira, and Julie. Maman'i Noelphine and Maman'i Haja are roughly the same age. Both have built stable marriages to men with whom they bore and raised children, although Maman'i Haja also had a child from a previous relationship, as is common. Both have achieved widely shared east coast norms about how women should grow up, get married, have many children, and support them. Both have achieved what in Tamatave is perceived as middle-class status. Yet both are struggling. These women have reached a point in life when, ideally, they should receive at least some acknowledgment and support from their children, even if only small gifts. Instead, both of them have children who remain dependent on them. Maman'i Haja's children also lack respect for her. Meanwhile, Maman'i Noelphine's husband continues to take lovers. These are the kinds of women who, if things go wrong or if they suffer too greatly, may find Pentecostal churches and the new futures they offer appealing.

Njira, on the other hand, has been unable to find a Malagasy man to support her, yet she has continued to bear children, slipping increasingly into a hand-to-mouth existence that may lead her toward dependence in old age rather than the reciprocal interdependence she aspires to. Julie is a little younger. She is still dependent on her parents, but whereas no one would question a child's right to be dependent, Julie is now almost adult in years, though not in social accomplishments. Julie resents this situation. She wants a way out so that she can "be like her friends" and have the things that signal successful adulthood. That women can get money from men and that they can use their charms to insert themselves into networks of exchange constitute part of the possibilities she imagines for carving out the life she so desires. She is at that crucial phase when searching is very likely to lead her deeper into the sexual economy. She is also at that moment of seeking when maybe, just maybe, her fortunes will turn.

FIVE

Jeunes: The Future in the Present

Think of your future [*avenir*]! Don't you want to become someone?

Aren't you young? Don't you *want* things? What are you doing? Do you want to be left behind?"

—Words of encouragement and competitive teasing frequently heard among young people in Tamatave

I don't remember when I first heard a Tamatavian use the word *jeune* or *jeunes* (from the French word *jeune,* meaning young).[1] It might have been in early October 2001, when I was visiting with Josephine, a young woman in her early twenties. We were sitting outside her small shop at the edge of one of the sand paths as dusk settled on the town. Another friend, Tania, joined us wearing a fashionable tiny top cut off at the midriff and even tinier shorts. Tania talked to us as she danced seductively to the music drifting out from Josephine's shop. In hear early twenties, Tania had a child while she was still in high school, but she had left the baby with her mother so she could be free to pursue her "avenir"—her future. She had a steady boyfriend, but as the conversation continued, it became clear she also had a lover on the side. When I asked her why, she just laughed, danced harder and said, "My lover fulfills me. After all, I'm jeune."

Or perhaps the first time I heard the term was when Stefan, a young man in his early twenties, was describing what life was like for young people. He explained,

Jeunes think only of progress [*fivoarana*]—they all follow the new things from the outside [outside Madagascar], and that way they won't be late [*tsy tara*] but will make good progress. For example, if there is a new song that comes from overseas, jeunes run to turn on the television, or even to the Internet. That way they know the songs that are famous overseas. It's from watching those video clips that the young people take their fashions. For example, in terms of how they dress, pants that are inside out, baseball caps turned backward, long T-shirts and short jackets on the outside. The reason? That is how they believe they keep up with progress.

Whenever it was, it soon became clear to me that jeunes was an important Malagasy category that both young people themselves and older people used for youth who behaved in the manner described by Stefan and exemplified by Tania. To be jeune was to follow the fashions and to know the latest "new things." It was to be sophisticated and worldly and to have watched the latest Britney Spears video or know about the latest platform shoes. To be jeune was also to have lovers in addition to boyfriends and to have watched the latest porn videos and learned new sexual techniques— tabooed by the ancestors—so that you really knew how to make your partner "dream" (mirevy, from the French rêver). And it meant to know how to access abortion and birth control to avert an unwanted child and a truncated future. Tamatavians did not use jeunes to index the same idea as tanora, the local Malagasy word traditionally used for youth.[2] Indeed, urbanites sometimes said that young people in the countryside had no youth, bound as they were (in the eyes of my urban informants) to a miserable life of planting rice, with nothing else to do and no knowledge of progress. They even sometimes paternalistically asserted that rural people do not *know* enough to desire. Only young urbanites who self-identified as sophisticated consumers of sex, fashion, or the latest Internet site were truly jeunes.

As Stefan's remark suggests, jeunes represent a way of being young, and a way of seeking progress (fivoarana), that has accompanied the goods and images economic liberalization brought to Madagascar; it is most closely associated with the children of the aspiring middle class. By the 1990s the ideal life course for individuals, in which the journey from childhood to adulthood moved from rural to urban and traditional to modern, was becoming more chimera than reality (see also Comaroff and Comaroff 1999, 2000, 2005; Hansen 2005; Jeffrey, Jeffrey, and Jeffrey 2008; Lukose 2009; Mains 2007; Masquelier 2005; Weiss 2004, 2009; Zhen 2000). Nowhere was this shift more visible for young urbanites than in that quintessentially modern institution, the school. Not only did most schools lack books and other resources, but many teachers had begun to moonlight, needing extra income. Families experiencing the inflation and devaluation of the currency resulting from the economic policies of the IMF and the World Bank struggled to buy even the minimum school supplies or pay fees required to keep their children in school.[3] As the schools became literally impoverished, and diplomas no longer guaranteed employment, education also came to be understood as an ineffective strategy for finding one's way to productive adulthood. These circumstances produced disaffection with school among many young urbanites, just as they also began to be caught up in globalized consumer youth culture transmitted via television, videos, and the Internet. Although many Tamatavians lamented these changes, most agreed that these urban, consumer-oriented young people were at the forefront of change.

This interpretation of jeunes as a unified group that embodies the future direction of Tamatavian society creates a "synoptic illusion," a selective representation whereby a few individuals at a particular time come to stand in for a more complex, changing whole. Barrie Thorne's (1993) work on gender stereotypes illuminates this process in a different empirical context. Drawing on her ethnography in a grammar school in Southern California, Thorne demonstrates how stereotypes about gender and the subgroup of young women who embody those stereotypes obscure heterogeneity in boys' and girls' actual behavior. By simplifying a complex range of practice, a few girls come to symbolize all female gendered behavior. Similarly, when Tamatavians talk about jeunes they often speak as if all young people behaved like Stefan or Tania, but they really have in mind a particular subset of consumer-oriented young people. East coasters interpret jeunes in this way because their own theories of change emphasize that young people are supposed to go out and "seek" the resources needed for the appropriate reciprocal interdependence that signals adulthood. Moreover, they have a long-standing belief that when seeking new practices to adopt, it is foreigners, not fellow Malagasy, who offer the most useful models. Over the past century, urban youth, who have come to see themselves as the vanguard of modernity and new ways of incorporating the resources that come from external connections, have embodied this more general pattern. This select group of consumer-oriented youth becomes iconic of new ways of being that stand out against the wider background of life in Tamatave.

Yet as my choice of the word "illusion" implies, this representation bears a complicated relation to reality. Not only are those perceived as jeunes only one small part of the wide variety of ways of being young that includes maids from the countryside and men who do day labor, but even among those who do attend school, some belong to the category of jeunes, some do not, and some fit it only some of the time. Jeunes is both a mobile and a performative category. The term refers to a set of culturally marked behaviors that some young people adopt some of the time, and a model other young people aspire to. Much as a process of contingent negotiation shapes how individuals become associated with particular social categories (Johnson-Hanks 2006, 112) so being a jeune is an outcome of adopting certain performative practices and ways of engaging the world. Moreover, jeunes is not a coherent category. When one starts to unravel it and explore young people's concerns in detail, there is far more ambivalence and self-critique, not to mention reliance on older ways of understanding, than the traditional emphasis on newness implies. Newness, is, to be sure, essential to "being jeunes." But when "newness" is relied on exclusively, it implies a homogenization that occludes the complex dynamics at work. Any analysis that talks categorically about a generational crisis brought on by recent economic changes implies too clean, too homogeneous a break between one generation's ascension to adulthood and that of the next. As a result, it obscures the complex social and cultural interactions and reconfigurations through which "newness" is made.

Nevertheless, this illusion has effects. Even as the complex heterogeneity of young people's lives far exceeds the category of jeunes and has many more links with past practices, the crystallization of a generational dilemma contributes to new ways of conceiving social life. Jeunes do not just symbolize the direction of contemporary change. The category of jeunes has force in the world. Tamatavians, both young and old, talk about jeunes as an important way of being and see it as relevant to their own lives. They constantly criticize young people who behave in this manner: recall the young man's somewhat bitter comments in chapter 1, that "girls used to follow you if you have cattle, but these days they only want you if you have a television," or another young man's remark in chapter 3 that it was shameful for young people not to know how to use computers. The behaviors associated with being jeunes are both despised and admired at the same time. By seizing on new kinds of practices and enacting them in ways that all can see, jeunes make these ways of being more available to others to integrate into their worlds, albeit in highly uneven, partial ways. Representations of the life course, of particular moments within it, are part of how history happens because they make certain paths and certain trajectories more imaginable than others. By adopting new kinds of practices associated with economic liberalization and the opportunities of the present moment and enacting them publicly for all to see, jeunes embody the path to a simultaneously desired and feared future for many Tamatavians.

Jeunes' Predicament: The Haves, the Have-Nots and Consumer Youth Culture

The young people who see themselves as jeunes revivify dilemmas that have faced generations of urban Malagasy since the mid-nineteenth century, while giving old questions renewed relevance. As each generation confronts enduring questions of how to "make themselves living" (*mahamelona tena*) in ways that enable them to achieve valued forms of personhood, they do so under historical conditions different from the past. Consequently, young people evaluate the practices through which generations of Malagasy achieved these goals. When these fail, they seek new ways to succeed—to create their own avenirs. This process of seeking resources and extending themselves in new ways goes beyond the conceptual, ideological, or practical. It is infused with affect every step of the way. As one girl tartly remarked to me, "Everyone wants to become someone," meaning that everyone wants to grow (up), progress, and flourish.[4]

Many difficulties stand in the way of jeunes' ability to fulfill their desires. Although a few may come from somewhat wealthier families, where the father can try to guarantee his children a future, for most the question of who has sufficient resources and who does not, and how this status will translate into future prospects, constantly weighs on them. The material conditions they live in make it hard to achieve their goals of acquiring money and goods. Like Tamatavian adults, young people too worry that their peers will mock them. The condition of "not having" can lead others to make fun of you behind your back, or, most cruelly, just near enough to ensure your humiliation.

Young people's fear of not keeping up and their obsession with commodities is more than simple social competition among peers. Knowing that others watch you in a particularly fashionable dress, bicycling casually past your friends as they trudge through town in the heat, or proudly answering a glossy new cell phone—using these commodities is partly about the satisfactions gained from social recognition in the moment. But young people also imply there is a correlation between their present success as jeunes and their future success as modern, respected adults. Jeunes believe that if they achieve the same status as their peers in Western countries, they may achieve a similarly modern future. They take their social status as "ahead" and "behind" so seriously because they see themselves at a fork in the road and fear they are in danger of being left behind forever. Cell phones and stylish clothes are about social competition among young people in the present, to be sure. But they are also about seeking to build particular kinds of relationships that they hope will bring the adulthood they desire.

As a result of these competing demands, jeunes face a further dilemma: they must take commodities and practices that in other sociocultural contexts are part of a present-oriented youth culture and convert them into the tools for reaching longer-term goals. To do so, they try to use the consumption of certain commodities to position themselves within broader networks of exchange, thereby creating the identity they aspire to. Their attempts to transform the commodities associated with an ephemeral culture into more enduring relationships create ongoing contradictions between short-term and long-term goals and cycles of material support. They constantly need additional current resources to create the future relationships that will in turn provide still more resources. The cycle cannot continue indefinitely, because at some point consumption requires labor and income to sustain it. Moreover, jeunes' positioning within these networks through which commodities and resources circulate depends in part on biological youth, leaving a comparatively small window of opportunity. These contradictions eventually drive jeunes to seek still other options, as we will see in the next chapter.

The Dilemmas of Progress

Despite the repeated assertions that those who see themselves as jeunes make about the profound divide between country and city, traditional and modern, and their efforts to situate themselves on the modern side of these dichotomies, their day-to-day experience unsettles such divisions. After all, most Tamatavians have contact with their kin in the countryside in some form, whether because they house younger relatives while they attend school or because they are asked to contribute to ceremonies or other ancestor-related projects. Constraining aspects of what jeunes perceive to be traditional life are all around them, eliding the sharp divisions between them and their less desirable counterparts that their discourse creates.

At the same time, they remain troubled by the moral implications of their desire to shake off the past. Far from embodying a coherent and carefree movement toward the future, they are profoundly ambivalent about the consequences of their quest for modern adulthood. They are torn between their desire to adopt what they see as foreign practices, perhaps losing a Malagasy identity, and their fear of failure, which will forever mark them as "late." The tension between the past and future, between a local tradition and a global modernity, has similarly confronted earlier generations of elite Malagasy. Like their predecessors, these aspiring young urbanites generate a discourse about the perils of change and what it means to become modern, particularly when becoming modern implies adopting practices that are culturally marked as foreign.[5]

Recall that during the nineteenth century the Merina king Radama I (r. 1810–1828) sought to incorporate the technological and organization skills offered by LMS missionaries into his kingdom to help him conquer other parts of Madagascar. Ideally, he wanted to modernize the bureaucracy and the army without risking either his political control or his cultural sovereignty. His successor, the Merina queen Ranavalona (r. 1828–1861), reversed many of his policies, banishing the missionaries. She was followed by Radama II, who reopened the kingdom to innovations brought by foreign missionaries. So abrupt were Radama II's efforts to embrace foreign practices that they provoked a reactionary religious movement in which Merina commoners became possessed by ancestral spirits and began to enact the return of the now-dead traditionalist queen (Bloch 1971, 22, citing Sibree 1870, 561–564). Radama II's rule, and the reactions it sparked, embodied the tension between innovation and the reproduction of traditional practices that continued to inform elite Malagasy cultural politics in subsequent decades.

Likewise, during the early decades of the twentieth century an elite group of Merina students organized the VVS (Vy Vato Sakelika, or Iron, Stone, Branches), a secret society that the colonial administration accused of plotting to overthrow the French administration. The members of the association sought to adopt Western innovations while nevertheless retaining a Malagasy cultural identity. As part of their ritual incorporation into the society, members had to swear to "love and defend their country and inspire their compatriots to achieve progress and civilization" (Esoavelomandroso 1981, 102). Members of the association explicitly invoked Japan, which had recently resisted Russian imperial encroachments, as a country that had successfully managed to incorporate foreign practices without sacrificing national unity. They held it up as a model for Madagascar (Esoavelomandroso 1981, 107). Here, too, elites found themselves torn between the desire to emulate more modern others and the desire to maintain cultural continuity.

Like their predecessors in the VVS, jeunes often worry that material progress will inevitably lead to the loss and corruption of what they perceive as essential to Malagasy culture. The examples are many: not only the young man who lamented that control of cattle was no longer a valued part of masculinity and prestige as it had been in the past, or his friend who argued that Malagasy ways had been "ruined" by colonization, but others who claimed that young women's pursuit of sexy clothes destroyed local notions of modesty. In response to these fears, many high school– and college-educated jeunes, men in particular, similarly argued that it was important to attain technological progress without cultural loss. Stefan, whom I cited in the beginning of this chapter, argued that "evolution [*fivoarana*] is about good things. That is to say, you go from the bad to the good. But now we are going downhill—the things that young people do are shameful. But for me good progress [*fivoarana tsara*] would be to bring back Malagasy ancestral customs. Malagasy have been cursed by colonization, and we'll never get rid of it. They want to be European but can't keep up with European practice."[6]

Yet another young man, a musician, similarly suggested blending ancestral practice with modern knowledge to create what he saw as true progress: "Fivoarana is the knowledge that makes you you, that you keep, and then you know how to select things from the outside. So the customs you take up from the outside should be good practices. What that means is that you take good things from the outside and use them to improve your ancestral customs. And you combine those two things and that brings you progress."

Young people who adopted this position argued that, ideally, it was important to incorporate outside elements in such a way that they amplified and improved, but did not lose, what they perceive as Malagasy culture. That these young people were usually men seems fitting given that nationalism historically was a largely male project in Madagascar and that today men do not always have the same opportunities as women, as I discuss in the next chapter.

The Spiritual Perils of Modernity and the Church

Just as the church has long provided an alternative path to social mobility for some east coasters, it offers a parallel discourse lamenting the spiritual emptiness that accompanies modernity. This discourse implies that modern practices and increasing technological and material sophistication lead to spiritual impoverishment. Such concerns threaded through the VVS organization, which remained deeply committed to Protestant Christianity and feared the anticlerical tendencies in the French administration. They also motivated the missionaries of the 1920s and 1930s who sought to ensure that young urbanites were not so seduced by the glitter of civilization that they ignored their spiritual well-being. In the past, members of the Catholic Church and traditional Protestant churches were most likely to elaborate this critique. Today, however, the voices taking this position arise primarily from evangelical churches.

Participants in these churches decry the nature of contemporary social and economic change, arguing that what most people define as progress, including fashionable, sexy clothes and large numbers of material possessions, is really a temptation to forget God in favor of worldly pleasures. Clotilde, a young woman who belonged to one of the larger Pentecostal churches, expressed a fairly typical view when she complained, "TV brings bad changes. Before, when people were fourteen years old, they just played. But now, they think only of sex. It is because of the films and songs on television. Because seeing people behave that way makes people feel desire. And the devil loves to use sex to trick Christians." Many further argue that the changes taking place in Tamatave are not evidence of progress but proof of the devil's power. They stress the nature of fivoarana as spiritual rather than material progress and emphasize that progress in the material domain should be tempered by increasing Christian devotion. For this group, progress means moving away from sin and toward a more Christian lifestyle. Comparatively few jeunes identify with this perspective—in fact, they mock it. Nevertheless, it remains an important part of the context in which they operate and against which they sometimes define themselves.

The Figure of the Métis

Much as jeunes' dilemmas echo those faced by earlier generations of urban Malagasy, so the images through which they elaborate these anxieties have a long history. Both colonial officials and Malagasy nationalists deployed the figure of the métis to problematize and sometimes to police the changing relations of colonizer and colonized. Today those young people who identify as jeunes often deploy the image of the métis or métisse, the person born of a mixed cultural and racial heritage. Here métissage is not simply about intermarriage, though actual intermarriage and the birth of mixed children remains the iconic example. Rather métissage becomes a powerful metaphor to capture the pleasures and perils of cultural mixing.

Early colonial administrators encouraged French settlers to take Malagasy wives. Over the course of the colonial period, however, as the numbers of métis children increased, it became more common to invoke the term métis to highlight the dangers of such intermarriage. During the 1920s and 1930s, for example, French authorities feared that, once they grew up, métis would become a restless group of déclassés, torn between their European

12. MADAGASCAR — Types Malgaches - Métisse Behimisaraka

4 a — *Comptoir photographique, G, Bodemer*

Figure 5.1. Both colonial officials and contemporary Tamatavian jeunes
continue to use the image of the métisse to debate cultural
change. Courtesy of Dominique Bois.

and Malagasy heritage (see Rajaonah 2001; Saada 2007; Stoler 2002; Tisseau
2007; White 2000). Colonial officials especially feared métis men and concentrated on finding them jobs to keep them out of trouble. Métisse women
more easily incorporated themselves into European society by marrying European men, as Violaine Tisseau (2007) has argued with respect to the high
plateau. Tisseau further shows that many métis chose to retain their French

names rather than adopting their mothers' names, to signal their inclusion in colonial society.

In the 1940s, Malagasy nationalists adopted the mirror image of this position to defend the integrity of Malagasy national culture, partly by warning young Malagasy women about the dangers of intermarriage. During a political speech on the east coast in 1947, at the height of nationalist fervor that preceded the 1947 rebellion, Alexis Bezaka, regional director of the MDRM (Mouvement de la Rénovation Malgache), the party that campaigned for independence after World War II, declared that "the massive waves of French, Europeans, Asians and Indians are going to ensure the disappearance of our Malagasy race . . . because our daughters couple with foreigners. These unions give rise to métis who are no longer Malagasy. They seek our disappearance. Young girls, you work against your Nation when you unite with foreigners. Young men, guard the integrity of our race" (cited in Randrianja 2001, 29).

Young people who see themselves as jeunes similarly invoke the image of the métis to emphasize the perils of mixing. They do so in debates with each other about the morality of their own actions rather than at political rallies or in declarations about government policy. Listen to Céline as she explains why métissage is potentially annihilating:

> Métissage is very dangerous for the *races d'hommes*. Because métissage is very strong. And then little by little what makes Malagasy Malagasy [*maha gasy ny gasy*] will disappear. After a century, it will be very difficult to see someone who is pure Malagasy. The thing that happens is this: If there is a French man who married a Malagasy and they have a child, then it is obvious that the child is métis French, so if the child marries a *karana* (Pakistani/South Asian), and then they have a baby, then the child is métis *français*, Malagasy, karana. And so if they then marry an Englishman, then what makes you Malagasy will all be lost; the Malagasy ancestral customs will be lost little by little.

While Céline's comment implies that repeated intermarriage causes cultural dissipation, Tamatavians also commonly use métissage to evoke uncontrolled hybridization and sterile forms of mixing. In Malagasy, one of the terms used for the mingling of types is *safiotra*, meaning the crossing of two biological species that renders the offspring sterile—the prototype being the mule. Safiotra carries strong negative connotations, and mid-twentieth-century Malagasy nationalists occasionally used that term rather than métis to refer to those whose allegiance was suspect (Rajaonah 2001).

Whether and how much young people knew about these older discourses is hard to tell. What is clear is that many used the figure of the métis as a person of mixed ancestry to debate the nature of cultural borrowing more generally. They frequently expressed the fear that inappropriate mixing would hinder their ability to create a future. The very same young people who expressed the vision of felicitous combination that I explored in the last section also voiced enormous fear about the unruly ways change was occurring. Again and again self-identified jeunes told me that young people in Tamatave "wanted to become vazaha" but "could not keep up with it" or could not get it right. Phrasing the dilemma with particular poignancy, one young man explained, "Malagasy these days they aren't on the bed and they aren't on the floor [and thus are stuck somewhere uncomfortably in the middle].[7] They want to keep their customs, but they also want to take on foreign ways. It is bad because you no longer know what makes you you." Another young man who came from a town in the north to attend university in Tamatave remarked, "We are like the offspring of a duck and a *dokitra* [a ducklike Malagasy bird]. That produces a *sadoko*. Do you know what a *sadoko* does? He wants to fly, but he can't get off the ground."

So resonant is the symbol of the métis that even Tamatavians who are deeply involved in the new churches, who argue that they need to renew their spiritual purity rather than pursue greater material advancement, use the métis to talk about contemporary spiritual perils and the necessity of religious commitment. During Sunday services at the Power of Faith church, Pastor Aimé, a man of twenty-five who led the congregation with gusto, used the following image in his sermon: "God does not like métis Christians. He wants you to be pure Christians. People who are métis are like this—their father is Japanese and their mother is Congolese. The Christians who don't truly believe or stay with one church, they are like métis as well. They are like a girl who cleans the house, washes the clothes and cooks, and makes the bed, but when the night falls she doesn't sleep with her husband but at some other place." Whereas jeunes use the image of the métis to reflect on the dangers of a too-rapid modernization that results in cultural loss, Pastor Aimé uses the same image to remind his flock about the importance of pure and undivided religious commitment.

Jeunes' use of the métis embodies a curious historical irony. French administrators and Malagasy nationalists, who were primarily though not exclusively Merina, may have tried to impose an exclusionary nationalist logic on local Tamatavian practice, disparaging east coasters' eagerness for relationships with Europeans. Historically, however, most inhabitants of this port town valued métis highly. After all, intermarriage with foreigners, and the offspring these unions produce, enabled east coast women and their families to forge valued social connections, as we will see in more detail in the next chapter. Tamatavians often remark that whether they are of mixed European and Malagasy descent or Malagasy mixed with either Chinese or South Asian, métis are more beautiful than ordinary Malagasy: they naturalize the benefits of having children from mixed unions. Both métis Chinese-Malagasy and métis Indian-Malagasy men are said to have more lovers because they are *bôgôsy* (beautiful boys). The same is also said of métisse women. One young man I knew whose sister had married a European said he too wanted nothing more than to marry a European because he had "always desired métis children."

Perhaps the young people who use the image of the métis in their discourse have inherited the views of Malagasy nationalists who believed in the importance of establishing the value of Malagasy culture in relation to the outside world. Certainly jeunes have been incorporated into a state system that espouses nationalism and teaches nationalist values in schools, so they are familiar with this way of thinking. However, jeunes' behavior bears a contradictory relation to this discourse. They are pragmatically oriented, and when they critically invoke the figure of the métis they distance themselves from the very practices they otherwise engage in. This is true symbolically, as I show over the course of this chapter by examining their engagement in new commodity practices. But it is also true literally, since so many young women pursue European husbands and give birth to métis children. Invoking the dangers of métissage is a form of ground clearing that enables the speaker to establish his or her moral value as a Malagasy who simultaneously is modern *and* cares about the continuity of an idealized Malagasy identity. Such performances of ambivalence, however, are usually temporary and situational. Jeunes may share dilemmas with previous generations of Malagasy who have confronted postcolonial modernity, but they are nonetheless faced with the pragmatic problem of achieving adulthood under contemporary conditions. They are not idealists. They lament the choices they face and engage in them ambivalently, but they engage in them nevertheless.

Alternative Strategies: Put-Downs

One of the ways young urbanites distance themselves from the social status they reject, and shore up their own position as successful modern people, is by making fun of others as part of their self-presentation (Goffman 1963). Although these put-downs resemble the practices of humiliation and exclusion I discussed earlier, they also differ insofar as they draw on well-known cultural types to build social distinctions. For example, jeunes frequently invoke the personages of the diviner (*mpisikidy* or *mpanajary*) and the *ambassady*, the young woman who works as a maid in other people's homes, either to mark their distance from, or express their ambivalence toward, what they perceive as the traditional past (see Pigg 1996). They also make fun of those invested in what they see as the now outmoded route to adulthood: schooling. These practices exemplify the more general tendency for those living in former colonial empires to require a double distancing in their efforts to establish their own modern status. People seeking to achieve modernity require, as Holly Wardlow notes, "the ability to look out and not only see 'others' behind [them] on the teleological line between tradition and modernity, but also the ability to look within and see internal 'others' always in the past, enacting the 'traditional,' [and thereby] demonstrating how far [they] have come" (Wardlow 2002, 162).

The diviner is a figure of tremendous mockery and ambivalence among young urbanites. In both rural and urban contexts diviners heal people by using seeds to determine whether particular ancestors, spirits, or problems with social relations are making their patients sick. Many people of all social classes visit diviners to find the cause of their ills. When Ramarie's widower from the countryside came to spend time with his children in Tamatave after she died, his divining services were so much in demand among the neighbors that he quickly earned enough money to buy a little radio to take back to the village (to "keep him company," he said). He was able to do so even though in keeping with rural mores he only asked clients for what they felt like giving *after* they had been cured rather than trying to extract payment in advance. Clearly, a great many Tamatavians embraced his services. But despite people's actual use of these healers, much public culture and everyday discourse in Tamatave mocks the diviner. One comedy skit that aired on national television featured a drunken diviner who carried out his divination in the rice fields (yet another indicator of rural, traditional culture) and squeaked idiocies at his foolish clients, who paid him amply. In such reified representations of rural culture, the diviner embodies all that is backward, superstitious, and ridiculous.

Those young people who see themselves as jeunes similarly make the ambassady, the maids who come from the surrounding countryside to work in Tamatave, the butt of their jokes.[8] These young women, usually somewhere between fourteen and twenty-five years old, work very long hours. They clean people's houses, wash their laundry, cook their food, and do other jobs people consider demeaning. They are usually paid very low wages, about 50,000 to 75,000 fmg a month (ten to fifteen dollars, circa 2004). On

Sunday afternoons, however, ambassady get a few hours off. Typically they dress in their best clothes and go down to the beachfront to strut their stuff and pick up boys. But people who live in the city know that their employers' castoffs constitute these girls' Sunday best, and they mock the way they proudly wear their hand-me-down clothes. Moreover, more sophisticated, long-standing urbanites inevitably comment on the way ambassady get the fashions wrong. They seek to achieve modern styles but only end up looking ridiculous. Gilda, an eighteen-year-old girl who had grown up in Tamatave, observed,

> Ambassady are people who come from deep in the countryside and move to town. There is a new fashion that comes out, and they want to follow it, but they don't know how to do it. They never learn because they don't talk to other people and get their opinions, but just talk among themselves. There are those who wear denim overalls and they put on a belt, but the fashion is to wear it loose! They don't get enough progress [tsy misy fivoarana] because they work in houses and don't go out. They only get to go out one day a week, so their thinking is really behind.

So scorned are the ambassady that the narrator in one popular song, who also wanted to go for a Sunday afternoon promenade, sought to distinguish himself from the maids strolling alongside: "I'm *not* an ambassady, I just want to go out strolling Sunday with my friends." I even heard people of roughly the same social class—for example, the children of pousse-pousse pullers, who lived in a part of Tamatave that looked much like a rural village—make fun of the ambassady as a way of claiming urban sophistication. Yet even as jeunes laugh at the ambassady in their ill-fitting clothes or point at them behind their backs, exchanging knowing glances with their friends, their laughter is always uneasy. While it is unlikely, though not impossible, for ambassady to ascend the social ladder and become jeunes, jeunes are also vulnerable. They know that just as they laugh at certain rural practices and seek urban sophistication, so their Western peers might well laugh at them.

Young people who aspire to the status of jeunes also make fun of schooling or of those who invest too much time in schooling, even when they sometimes continue their own studies. Eric, a nineteen-year-old man who was just finishing high school, pithily summarized jeunes' mistrust of schooling: "Jeunes have seen that it is not necessarily people who have learning who have money. But if you go to school it costs your parents.

And so you are not respected [*tsy consideré*] if you have learning. You are mocked because you have wasted both time and money." Again and again young people who self-identified as jeunes emphasized that schooling was a waste of time because some with lots of schooling ended up pulling rickshaws or generally working in jobs that did not match their level of education. Flechard, a junior high school student from a modest background, observed:

> The people who really study have a harder time, because they are choosier about their work; but what makes people rich is that they start with low work and move up. You need to study a trade so you can earn money. But if you study for too long you spend money without earning it. Our teacher even told us it was a waste for him to have studied for so long because some of his fellow students only received their CEP [certificate of primary school], but they already manage factories. But he just grows old holding the chalk at the chalkboard. My teacher was right, because his friend really succeeded—maybe his parents found work for him after he quit school.

Both these young men implicitly reveal what they think the contemporary alternatives to schooling are: Flechard refers to the personal connections one needs to be successful in business, while Eric notes the importance of "making do" (*débrouiller*). But they agree that acquiring money, rather than academic knowledge, is truly necessary in order to be perceived as a valued human being. Régis, a young man who said he wanted to be a journalist and who was studying at the university, summed up this idea: "The way I see it, everyone wants to show that they have money because in Malagasy society it is people who have money who are more respected than those who have learning. That is what is happening these days."

To be sure, young people also emphasized that one learned important skills in school. Some said schooling, and book learning in particular, made it harder for others to trick you, a quality most people valued. Others remarked on the importance of becoming adept at new technology like computers and the Internet. Nevertheless, Flechard's and Eric's comments capture how many high school– and college-age young people felt about school. Perhaps they viewed school ambivalently because their families' financial difficulties had forced them to quit. Perhaps it was because they knew their families could not pay for them to continue, so they dismissed schooling rather than face the pain of being forced to give it up. Perhaps it was sour grapes because they saw that schooling could no longer guarantee employment as it once had. I suspect all these factors were important to different degrees in different cases. What is certain is that many young people weighed current privation against an uncertain future and questioned whether schooling was truly worth the bother.

Making Do in Tamatave: Fashion and New Ways of Making Value

At the same time that jeunes try to distance themselves from stigmatized social positions such as the diviner and the ambassady, they also use commodities to build connections that can be used in the future. Drawing on John Berger, David Graeber (2001, 104) distinguishes two kinds of social power: "The power to act directly on others, and the power to define oneself in such a way as to convince others how they should act towards you." Those who identify as jeunes try to achieve this latter goal. They seek to parlay many of the commodities associated with competitive consumer youth culture into longer-term opportunities. Nowhere are these processes more visible than in the changing use of fashion.

There are many commodities that signal progress—cell phones, computers, foam mattresses (as opposed to old-fashioned mattresses stuffed with raffia), mountain bicycles. Nevertheless, like the famous *sapeurs* of Congo, young men who travel to Paris to acquire fancy brand-name clothing, jeunes covet fashion: fashionable clothing is the most widely shared domain of competitive consumption. In keeping with their desire to obtain the same status as peers in Europe and the United States, jeunes take their ideas about what is fashionable from foreign places, particularly American popular culture. They try to emulate looks created by pop stars such as Celine Dion, the Spice Girls, Britney Spears, and the Backstreet Boys, whom they either see in music videos on television or read about in teen magazines like *OK Podium*. Many of the words used to describe what it means to be well dressed—*mikata*, from the French *catalogue; miposiposy*, from the French *poser* (to pose); and *migenty*, from the English "gentlemen"—reveal the channels through which young people learn about fashion. At the turn of the millennium and the years immediately following, fashionable clothing for young men consisted of a T-shirt, jeans, and Pistons, thick-soled shoes that resemble Dr. Martens. Young women had more styles to choose from, although some were highly contested. Young men and women widely agreed that "sexy clothes"—those that show off a girl's thighs, breasts, or navel—are most fashionable in Tamatave, precisely because they are revealing. Such clothes include the tiny *je m'en fou* ("I don't care") top that shows one's belly; the "Marimar," a backless halter dress named for the heroine of the soap opera; and the *maladià legon* ("come quickly, boys"), a form-fitting dress that buttons all the way down the front, so named because it implies easy sexual access. One young woman explained, "Girls like fashions that really cling to their bodies! That way, people can really see your figure. The objective is to seduce men to look at you."

Many aspiring jeunes further imply that dress reveals a person's status. This idea has a long pedigree in Madagascar, as elsewhere (Lepovetsky 1994). In the past a person who knew the social context could tell men's or women's social caste by the way they were dressed; only nobles could carry an umbrella, for example, or wear red (Ellis 1838). Jeunes give these older ideas a new twist by arguing that today older social distinctions based on caste, ancestry, or even educational level are not as important as how much money one has. Veblen's (1992 [1899], 118–119) observation that "expenditure on dress has this advantage over others: that our apparel is always in evidence and affords an indication of our pecuniary standing to all observers at first glance" captures this attitude. Veblen further notes: "Since the consumption of these more excellent goods is an evidence of wealth, it becomes honorific; and conversely the failure to consume in due quantity and quality becomes a mark of inferiority and demerit" (Veblen 1992 [1899], 64). Economic worth constitutes personal value; fashion publicly announces one's status in this hierarchy (Simmel 1971 [1904]).

Jeunes constantly seek to interpret other people's clothes to learn how much money they have. They repeatedly described meeting others and mentally totaling up the worth of their clothing to learn what economic power they possess. Young men, especially, described with considerable resentment how young women size them up, carefully considering the price of each item of clothing before deciding to pursue a social interaction. Eric remarked bitterly to me, "Girls start at your shoes, and if you're wearing flip-flops, they won't even bother to look further." Jean Aimé, a high school student who was quite fashionably dressed, noted, "It is mainly girls who compete over *lamaody* [from the French *la mode*, or fashion]. The way I see it, they want to show people that they have money, that they can buy many things that are expensive. Here, only people who have money have weight or importance. The old proverb 'Better to lose money than friendship' no longer holds. Now it is the reverse." Haja, the young man whose family I discussed in chapter 4, supported Jean Aimé's perspective, though he distinguished it from his own deeply Christian approach. He remarked, "For youth who don't pray, they like shirts that have a picture of things that scare you and shoes that are very expensive. They think that if something is expensive it is good, but if it is cheap, then it has to be bad. And they pursue everything that is expensive and do whatever they can to get that."

Yet what jeunes *do* with clothing undermines the relation of fashion to enduring forms of social status that they verbally espouse. After all, clothing conceals as much as it reveals, letting people appear richer than they really are. Consequently, jeunes manipulate fashion to suggest how they *want* to be treated in order to generate new opportunities and new social networks. They do not have many resources, but what little they do acquire they deploy to make future social investments possible. Like the sapeurs, young urbanites "dress precisely in order to blur social lines and make class values and status illegible" (Gondola 1999, 31).

There are several gender-specific ways that jeunes employ these strategies of proleptic, wealth-inducing display. Young men regularly use clothes to give the impression of wealth. This impression may then let them attract women. It also allows them to ingratiate themselves with particular social networks and thus form connections with more powerful men who may give them still further access to resources. Perhaps the best-known example of this strategy is the *chomeur luxe*, or "luxury unemployed," a young man who puts together a stylish wardrobe despite his lack of formal employment, then constantly uses his social connections to generate further opportunities. Meanwhile, young women use clothing to attract the men who embody the futures they aspire to. Ultimately, jeunes reconfigure the relation between the commodities one controls and more enduring forms of social status derived from the kind of labor one does in the economy.

Whereas in the past, having certain commodities signaled a social and economic status already acquired by farming, trading, or working one's way up through the government administration, today jeunes apply an anticipatory calculus. A young man or woman may use commodities to project the status they aspire to while not actually having access to a sustained or stable flow of resources. "The display of goods," as Julie Livingston (2009, 662) notes of consumer practice in Botswana, "is more than the aesthetic and utilitarian pleasure consumers derive from these goods." Rather, "there is an anticipatory calculus here in the particular form of building that such wealth is meant to engender." This anticipatory calculus creates an unstable cycle in which young people engage in short-term practices that help them get commodities. They hope to transform these commodities into further opportunities that will have a more enduring transformative capacity—a well-paid job, a wealthy husband—enabling them to achieve the adult personhood they so desire. This is a risky endeavor, because consumption cannot take place ex nihilo. At some point jeunes must find a steady income so they can rent a house, buy food, or pay a doctor. Their ability to transform the present into the future depends on transcending the vicious cycle they are caught in.

Seeking Resources: *Biznesy* and Entry into the Sexual Economy

Given their frustration with the opportunities provided by schooling, many jeunes seek alternative paths to get what they want. Some young people stay in school even as they seek better ways to support themselves. Others leave school and try to patch together various kinds of employment. A tiny minority of such young people find work in the NGOs that have come to Madagascar in increasing numbers or work as cashiers or clerks in the new large supermarkets or import-export stores in the area. Generally, however, jeunes tend to take on various ephemeral jobs that depend on opportunities that arise, then quickly dissipate. These jobs rarely provide enough of an income to support the status they desire. Yet jeunes passionately want to succeed. Humiliation, anger, and hurt pride may lead young men to attach themselves to older patrons or try out *biznesy*. These sentiments of anger and frustration are also a prominent part of what leads women deeper and deeper into the sexual economy, as we shall see.

Young Men

Young men engage in a variety of practices to acquire resources. Some earn money during the lychee season, when they work long night shifts packing lychees in boxes for export to France. Others, with minimal education, try to get low-level jobs at the port unloading ships or work in manual day jobs as mechanics or handymen. However, by virtue of their aspirations and their years in school, those who see themselves as jeunes also believe they are above such types of labor. They prefer to embrace two options: undertaking what they call biznesy or finding powerful political patrons.

Many young men claim the only way to get money is from biznesy, or any kind of illegal traffic you can get your hands on. The term refers to obtaining goods that others want and turning them over for a profit. Young men engage in many ventures they define as biznesy. Perhaps one of the most popular is to break into the containers at the port, then sell the goods they steal. Others said they stole gasoline out of the trucks parked along the road during the night and resold it for a profit. And still others claimed they sold bones—part of the rash of tomb raiding that has been taking place along the coast since the early 1990s. Anything that could be bought or sold to turn a quick profit comes under the rubric of biznesy.

Before the 2001 elections, young men also joined political associations connected to particular political parties and particular deputies. The deputies would then pay them to work as personal aides and carry out the small jobs of a right-hand man, procuring services and smoothing their way during the election period. Such biznesy could also entail spreading propaganda, for example, by paying other young people to vote for their deputies or by driving around town blaring their political messages from speakers perched in the bed of a pickup truck. Some young men were also paid to tear down the opposition party's political posters, usually at night. Generally, male jeunes agree that the only way to succeed is to become a more powerful man's dependent and client.

Young Women

Meanwhile, the tension between the desire to project the identity they aspire to and the reality of scarce resources leads some young women to enter the sexual economy. Women start to rely on their relationships with men to obtain resources through a variety of paths. Very often they begin to get money and gifts from their boyfriends, since it is normative practice for men to support them and pay for their material needs. They may tell their Malagasy boyfriends that they need money for a variety of purposes. Consider how in chapter 4 Cathy happily recounted the small gifts she received from the merchant's son.

Female jeunes who embrace such strategies are called vehivavy mietsiketsika (girls who move), a term widely used for young women who enter the sexual economy with an eye to earning a livelihood from men. In the context of wider Malagasy ideas, motion is part of being young, implicitly opposed to the stillness associated with ancestors. When young women refer to themselves or others as "girls who move," they use the term positively to mean someone who follows the latest fashions and knows how to search for money. My conversations with underemployed and unemployed young men suggest a similar interpretation. Like women, they define a "girl who moves" as a girl who dresses well in order to establish alliances with men and so obtain resources and possibly marriage. One young man remarked, "Those girls who move, it is to seduce men's eyes. When the man is seduced, he might marry her if he really likes the girl." Still others say that a girl who moves is responsible and knows how to search for money. If such women find a Malagasy man who gives them what they want, they may form an attachment that transcends the need to obtain resources, as jeunes argue that true love implies (see Cole 2009).

Several factors, however, make this romantic ending unlikely. Most young men have trouble earning enough to support a family. Moreover, they are rewarded by peers for having more than one lover. Very often young women find themselves with young men who cannot fulfill their needs. Where men complain that women *manataka*, a pejorative word meaning they try to extract resources from men, women often accuse men of distancing themselves from their girlfriends and playing with their affections (*mampifilafila*). When girlfriends try to extract too much, young men break off the relationship, violating the norms of reciprocity that ideally guide such interactions. Or they may simply not have the resources that make them attractive; young women often seek older men who have more. As one young woman remarked to me, "Everyone wants to have a manager at the port." Others play several men off against each other. Recall how Stelline, whom I described in chapter 4, had relationships with three men and used their resources to forge a life for herself.

What is certain is that the woman who suffers at men's hands, and who fails to obtain the resources and the social status she covets, will seek solutions. When she does obtain the goods and resources that mark her as a powerful person, she may even seek revenge by flaunting them in front of the man who spurned her (see also Gregg 2006). One young woman who worked at the port married a wealthy man after her previous boyfriend, and first great love, rejected her by running off with another woman. She recounted with delight her visit to the town where she used to live. She showed off her new husband and her improved social status, hoping to make the man who had rejected her jealous. Like the *pasinja meri* of New Guinea who take up sex work because they are angry with their male kin's refusal to honor the bridewealth system (Wardlow 2004), these young Tamatavian women often pursue other men because they are angry at the way their Malagasy boyfriends treat them. The powerful and hurtful sentiments of malahelo and the desire to escape humiliation motivate them. Friends often encourage each other to refuse to let men mistreat them. After all, jeunes see themselves as a resourceful lot. In the chapter epigraph I cited how jeunes encourage each other to go out and get things by saying, "Aren't you young? Don't you want things?" Another comment girls make to one another is more explicit: "Are you going to just leave your vagina to *rot*?" At the heart of this statement is the idea that young women *must* use their sexuality to achieve social success and social mobility. They must try to build their futures using existing gendered norms. When a young woman is angry or disappointed, she may partly abandon the search for Malagasy men. Yet as a young woman I cited earlier remarked, "Everyone wants to become someone." And as we have seen, everyone acutely feels the pain of "not having." So while young women may partly turn away from Malagasy men, they usually seek other ways to achieve the relationships through which they can make themselves living and become respected, as they so dearly want to be.

Conclusion

Like their counterpart "youth" in recent Euro-American theorizations of youth and globalization, jeunes are a synoptic illusion in which the whole is mistaken for its parts. A few iconic sets of behaviors and ways of thinking that some young people engage in some of the time stand in for what *all* young people are doing. Insofar as my analysis focuses on jeunes, it too is necessarily partial. There is more synchronic heterogeneity among Malagasy youth than is implied by the category of jeunes, which Tamatavians highlight in their theories of change. There is also significant heterogeneity *within* the category of jeunes, both male and female.

Yet the content of this synoptic illusion is an important part of how jeunes contribute to change, because the illusion of coherence makes certain dilemmas and their solutions more visible and available for others to grasp. Young people who adopt the ways of being marked as jeunes stand out against the backdrop of Tamatavian life because others see them as on the leading edge of social change. With their conspicuous use of commodities, their visible engagement in politics, their use of biznesy, and above all young women's participation in the sexual economy, jeunes enact change for all to see.

At another level, however, Tamatavians' focus on jeunes obscures some of the processes that contribute to social change. Treating jeunes as a homogeneous category exaggerates the importance of rupture to generational change. Many of the dilemmas facing jeunes today are the very same ones that faced earlier generations of urban Malagasy who wanted simultaneously to adopt modern, Western practices and to retain an autonomous Malagasy identity. The idioms and practices they engage in—young women's pursuit of fashionable clothes, or jeunes' anxieties regarding métissage—are recognizably particular to the east coast. Consequently, while their solutions are partly novel, they are never entirely so. Their need to deal with dilemmas common to their past suggests they will likely be led to adopt well-worn paths to the future.

In the next chapter I trace the fate of young women—some who embody what it means to be jeunes, some who have followed other paths—when they decide they can no longer arrive at a satisfactory future using only local resources or local men. By following female jeunes and their contemporaries as they take hold of various opportunities provided by the globalized social context, we can begin to see the differences that emerge only with time. We will see that even when people start out with shared visions of how to create a new future, their actions have unpredictable effects.

SIX

Finding Vazaha?
Navigating the Sexual Economy

These days things are different. Before, it was only prostitutes who tried to marry Europeans. But these days, even girls who completed quite a lot of schooling look for European husbands.

—Glwadys

The young women who see themselves as jeunes face a predicament. Like previous generations of Tamatavian women, they want to build futures that include marriage and children. They want a future in which others recognize them as *considerées* ("considered"). Yet no matter how successfully they engage in the practices that mark them as jeunes, no matter how fashionable and sexy they are, if they do not find a stable source of income they may eventually be trapped as social juniors and face social opprobrium, their exploits in the sexual economy no longer lucrative. No one can remain forever jeune.

In this chapter I examine young women's efforts to resolve this predicament and attain the futures they so desire by marrying vazaha, Europeans. At the time of my fieldwork, young women's desire to marry European men was on everyone's lips, not only young women but older people and young men too. Some older women wanted me to find vazaha husbands for their daughters, while others disapproved, in part because pursuit of vazaha is closely associated with prostitution. Young men unanimously shared this disapproval and felt women's preference for vazaha threatened their manhood.

Although interest in vazaha husbands was ubiquitous in Tamatave, it was by no means unique to urban Tamatavians. From what east coasters said, and given the relatively rural origins of many of my informants, it

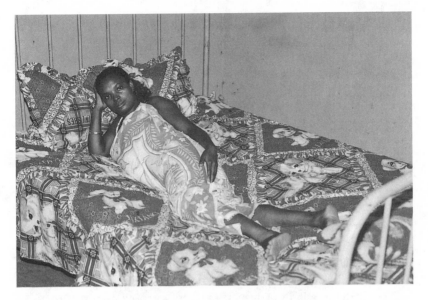

Figure 6.1. Fanja seeks a kind husband. Hotel Pangalanes, Mahanoro, 510. Madagascar.

appears that young women throughout the small towns to the north of Tamatave province seek out relationships with Europeans. Pursuing vazaha lovers and husbands is also hugely popular among women in the northern port city of Diego Suarez.[1] The practice is also being taken up in areas south of Tamatave. When, in 2007, I went back to Mahanoro, the small town near where I had done my earlier fieldwork, I encountered young girls from the surrounding villages who had come to work in the hotels, largely to meet vazaha. When I casually mentioned the topic of my new research to the seventy-year-old mother of the household where I stayed, she responded (somewhat puzzled by the ways of current youth), "Everyone was doing that Internet-Internety thing." This woman's granddaughter, who had gone to college in Tamatave and whom I had met when she was a little girl, had found a foreign husband on the Internet while she was away at school.

It might be tempting to think young women's quest for vazaha is historically new. After all, sex tourism has increased in many parts of the world, and Internet-mediated marriages between women in East Asia, Africa, and Latin America and men in the United States and Europe are on the rise (Brennan 2004; Constable 2003, 2005; Farrer 2002; Johnson-Hanks 2007; Kelsky 2001; Luhermann 2004; Schaeffer-Grabiel 2004, 2005). But unlike many prominent examples from other parts of the world where transnational, interracial marriages are a relatively recent development, largely associated with modern forms of globalization, on the east coast of Madagascar women's use of sex to build lasting alliances with Europeans has deep historical roots. Nonetheless, the current historical conjuncture has changed the scope and significance of these practices, offering a striking example of how the confluence of a new generation with existing social, cultural, and economic conditions creates novel patterns. The disillusionment many young people feel about school and the difficulty young women have in finding stable employment, paired with the fact that most young Malagasy men lack a stable income, making them less appealing partners, have converged to make marrying a vazaha an increasingly popular solution to the problem of attaining modern adulthood. Also important to this convergence is that more Europeans now come to Tamatave, making this idealized solution at least a little more likely. Young women draw from traditional ideas about their sexuality, as well as the value of international marriage, but they also enact these conceptions of gender, family, race, and sexuality in a new historical context, with different effects.

Despite the popularity of the practice, there are enormous risks to navigating the sexual economy. Tamatavians trying to explain the sexual economy to an outsider usually describe ranked categories. Florien, for example, delightedly recounted, "There are three categories of prostitutes [*makorelina*]"— and he went on to detail the "first category," the "second category," and the "high-quality" category. He also described the techniques each used for finding and seducing men, including their social networks and the types of self-presentation they preferred. Likewise, an older woman who had set up an association to help other women leave prostitution explained, "Young girls just learning how to work, they go in the sand paths. Then when they graduate they work their way up to the truck stop. From there, they seek to study foreign languages and work their way over to the big boulevards near the hotels [where they can meet vazaha]. And from there they end up at the Neptune [the fanciest hotel in Tamatave]." What these observers do not say, because they take it for granted, is that if young women make it into the "high-quality" category, and if from this position they succeed in marrying a vazaha, they become a *vadimbazaha* (spouse of a European). This is not stigmatized—quite the contrary. The term and the category date back to the eighteenth century, and marriages between Malagasy women and Europeans or other foreigners have long been valorized on the east coast. When young women working in the sexual economy fail to find an economically stable future, however, they risk falling into the category of sand path prostitute, which has a history almost as long but much more stigmatized.

Following jeunes into the sexual economy allows me to elaborate my argument about the nature of generational change in two respects. First, though jeunes, as young people who embody the future and have developed a distinctive style associated with the contemporary moment, enact newness across a broad spectrum of domains, female jeunes' encounter with the sexual economy is the most visible way they meet an existing social field and, in many ways, transform it. The young women seen as jeunes do this by taking a very old practice that was, at least in the recent past, much more closely associated with prostitution—as the epigraph to this chapter implies—popularizing and diffusing it well beyond the boundaries of formal prostitution. As young women who have acquired certain fashions, knowledge, and skills associated with globalization, by example jeunes teach others how to succeed. Although many women from many social backgrounds seek vazaha in the sexual economy, jeunes lead the charge.

Following young women as they navigate the sexual economy further reveals how generational change occurs through an uneven dialectic between an image created through certain shared cultural representations deployed in social discourse and the actions young women take. Tamatavians from different social backgrounds sometimes implied that, with the option of finding a vazaha, "all our young girls are becoming prostitutes." Others complained that soon all young women would marry vazaha and, following the local logic of how métissage leads to cultural loss, "there would be no more Malagasy." Still others talked about how young women's ability to obtain resources through European men changed generational and gendered relationships, undermining the established social order. They also complained that their pursuit of vazaha, and their strategic use of the sexual economy, meant true love no longer existed, so overshadowed had it become by the need to find money. All of these narratives converged with their preconceptions of the life course to create new horizons both feared and hoped for. Yet when we examine the consequences of young women's relationships with Europeans, it becomes clear that they are far more subtle and complex than popular discourse suggests. Young women contribute to changes in generational and gendered relations as well as to local conceptions of love, but not exactly in the ways much local commentary implies. There is a gap between the image of the future that people present through their representations of the changing life course and the actual life course they help to create.

Historical Conjunctures, Convergent Fantasies

Although the ways and means are often new, some old reasons, including the desire for adventure and the need to make their fortunes, continue to draw French men to Madagascar. The liberalization of the media and the government's new economic policies make young Malagasy women more aware of life in France. Meanwhile, images of available foreign women increasingly saturate France, making European men more aware of Malagasy women. In some cases, French men who have difficulty finding wives in France turn to Madagascar instead. Rural-to-urban migration has made it hard for men with less glamorous, rural jobs to find wives, so some have sought women in the former French colonies. Such transnational marriages between French men and Malagasy women have even helped to repopulate and reanimate economically depressed French villages (Burley 2004; Cole 2008b).

In most cases, however, men meet women when they come to Madagascar for other reasons, not because they are actively seeking lovers. Statistics from the Ministry of Tourism show a massive increase in foreigners coming to Madagascar in recent years. Although I was unable to trace the numbers back to the early 1990s, statistics available in 1999 suggest a sharp upswing. Between 2005 and 2006 alone, the number of visitors increased by over 120,000. In addition to men who initially come as tourists, others work as *coopérants* sent by the French government either to teach French or to offer technical assistance in the former French colonies. Others are businessmen, and still others come through the ports, whether as sailors on shore leave or because they work there. Often, what begins as a short-term adventure becomes a long-term plan to remain in Madagascar.

Colonial connections between France, Madagascar, and Réunion also make Madagascar a likely destination for Francophone men. During Marc Ravalomanana's presidency, the government made it easier for foreigners both to own land and to start businesses. Though the historical circumstances are different, the freedoms and privilege these men enjoy are similar to what Albert Memmi described for the French colonial period: "He finds himself on one side of a scale, the other side of which bears the colonized man. If his living standards are high it is because those of the colonized are low; if he can benefit from plentiful and undemanding labor and servants, it is because the colonized can be exploited" (1966, 8). Memmi goes on to note other advantages colonizers enjoyed, including better treatment by administrators. Although Memmi was writing about a time when colonial relationships placed European men in a position of legally guaranteed privilege, now foreigners gain privileges primarily from their economic power. When these men come to Madagascar, they often find they can attain a lifestyle they could never achieve in France or other parts of Europe—such as living in large villas with servants to attend to their needs. Moreover, because many of the old colonial assumptions about white men still operate, they may also be treated with a respect and deference they could never command at home.

These men also bring a long tradition of French colonial fantasizing about Malagasy women. Even the briefest perusal of the French literature on Madagascar, in books ranging from Vicomte Évariste de Parny's *Chansons madécasses* (1787) through Charles Renel's *Le décivilisé* (1998 [1923] and Robert Mallet's *Région inhabitée* (1964), reveals the recurrent theme of the French man who comes to Madagascar and takes a local woman as a concubine. These Malagasy women are often portrayed as beautiful and sensual (Andrianjafy 1990). Mallet's description of Kitany, his protagonist's love interest, is fairly typical: "She walked straight, her legs, bare to the knee, were long and fine, and with each step she bore her weight like a dancer . . . the rough cloth she wore molded her breasts. . . . She had a way of looking at you with the tranquil assurance of an animal more used to caresses than violence. Villers found her beautiful" (Mallet 1964, 52). Malagasy women are also portrayed as sensitive to men's needs and ready to help them with their business endeavors in Madagascar, as when one man's Malagasy concubine helps him recruit labor for his plantation (Mathiau 1930, cited in Andrianjafy 1990, 140). These examples all date from the colonial period. Nevertheless, many of the reasons contemporary men give for finding Malagasy women appealing are strikingly similar—for example, finding a spouse who is not "demanding" or who "respects her husband" (see Cole 2008b).

The men who come to Madagascar with their economic wealth and their ideas about exotic Malagasy women encounter the situation I have depicted: a large population of young people who feel frustrated because they cannot find a stable source of income that will allow them to create families and maintain them in the modern conditions they aspire to. On the one hand, comparatively few young Tamatavian men have stable incomes, so many live on various kinds of biznesy. As we have seen, this is a highly undependable way to earn a livelihood, usually characterized by rare periods of abundance and much more common penury, so young men have a hard time consistently supporting a family. The cultural expectation that men with money make rivals (*lehilahy manambola mampirafy*), and that men who do have resources will share them with more than one woman, exacerbates this situation. But young women want to build relationships through which they can succeed; they look around them and see that this is harder to do with a Tamatavian man. As I heard many young women cynically remark (both those who saw themselves as jeunes and those who did not), all men cheat. Since total fidelity is unlikely, it is better to marry a man who has resources and may be able to support more than one woman. Still other young women insisted they had been too wounded in the past to continue investing in Malagasy men. They wanted something different. They saw relationships with vazaha as enabling more equitable, loving interactions within the household. Just as some Japanese women seek out foreign men to escape Japanese patriarchy (Kelsky 2001), so women in Tamatave often believe European men will treat them in a more egalitarian matter.

The confluence of these factors means more young women seek to marry vazaha than in the recent past. Statistics from the French consulate give some sense of the increase in such marriages. While in 1992 only 210 marriages were performed for French men and Malagasy women, by 2006 that number had jumped to 914, and in June 2007—just halfway through the year in terms of statistics—the number was already 537, heading toward an increase of almost 20 percent in one year.[2] These statistics tell an even more compelling story when one considers that French is only the majority nationality among vazaha; marriages with men of other nationalities would be recorded elsewhere. Many women also forge relationships with Belgians, Germans, Swiss, and Italians. The marriages reported at the consulate also probably represent a very small portion of actual Malagasy-vazaha relationships, since many do not end in formal marriage. Marriage remains the gold standard, in that it opens up possibilities for formal inheritance, citizenship, and migration, significantly increasing the benefits local women can offer their kin. Nevertheless, many more young women are in liaisons with vazaha than formal marriage statistics represent. Yet despite this very real increase in numbers, for most young women the hope of finding a vazaha remains a fantasy: those women who succeed are only a tiny proportion of all women who live in Tamatave. That many young women will not find vazaha to marry does not deter them. Rather, those who succeed become a lure—a beacon of possibility and a concrete image of the good life and how to achieve it.

Vadimbazaha or Makorelina?

Young women who seek vazaha in the sexual economy move uneasily between two positions: the *vadimbazaha* (spouse of a European) and the *makorelina* (prostitute).[3] During the nineteenth century, and even earlier, it was common for Europeans who came to the east coast to take local concubines.[4] So popular was the practice—and so appreciated not only by the foreigners but also by Malagasy—that the eighteenth-century French explorer and slave trader Mayeur reported that parents would come forward and offer their daughters to visiting Europeans (Rantoandro 2001, 109 citing J. Valette). A sailor who stopped on the east coast in the mid-nineteenth century remarked that "these relations are maintained with the greatest devotion until the departure of the European. The girl protects his interests and directs his affairs. And it is through her that all commercial transactions with the locals take place. A European would have tremendous difficulty in conducting his business without the aid of his faithful companion" (Valette 1967, 51). The women who established these enduring liaisons came to be referred to locally as vadimbazaha, a highly coveted role.

Women who created liaisons with foreigners occupied a prominent position in late nineteenth-century Tamatave. In 1861, when the Jesuits arrived in the town, they remarked that "women play a huge role [in social life]. It appears that it is only their advice and arrangements that work" (cited in Bois 1997, 61). Women who lived as concubines with Creole settlers often eventually inherited capital or other valuables amassed during the relationship. When their inheritance rights were challenged, the Merina state courts protected them as Malagasy citizens. When their European partners succumbed to malaria and they were widowed, some women married still other vazaha, gaining access to still more wealth. So well respected were the vadimbazaha during the nineteenth century that they played an important role in representing Merina state power to the soon-to-be French colonizers. They formed a part of formal processions of state during which they were allowed to carry the Merina flag as a symbol of their privileged connection to the Merina monarchy (Bois 1997).

With the formal establishment of colonial rule, the French colonial government became less sanguine about French settlers' marrying local women and more concerned with the problems created by the mushrooming population of métis children, as I discussed in the previous chapter.[5] East coast women, however, still viewed marrying vazaha as a desirable strategy for achieving social mobility. One inhabitant of the east coast made the point clearly when she told the colonial commission on métis children, "To have a child by a white man is a precious advantage, because it allows the woman to hold onto her man whether he wants her to or not. When that child turns out to be a girl, if she is beautiful, when she is older she too will find a European to marry, and continue to help her mother" (Decary 1938). If the woman bore a child and the French man recognized his paternity, the child could, after a lengthy procedure, acquire French citizenship and privileges otherwise difficult to obtain, including more generous pensions, more and better schools, and exemption from forced labor.

Even when the state did not formally recognize métis as citizens, the bonds of kinship created between French or Creole men and local women often offered advantages to the woman's kin, including a place to hide when the labor recruiters or tax collectors came around. Rural east coast inhabitants often complained to me that the families who became connected with these French and Creole men through the intermarriage of sisters and daughters had more resources than others. Such inequalities could cause jealousy and conflict within families, and they occasionally divided relatives, counter to local ideals of family unity. Acknowledging that intermarriage with Creoles brought both opportunities and disadvantages, one elderly man who had lived through the colonial period wryly remarked, "We used to long to marry our daughters off to foreigners, but it would only get us into trouble." This old man was unusual, however, in mentioning the negative effects of marrying vazaha. From the perspective of most east coast women and their kin, a foreign husband or father was and is a mark of social distinction, one that carries very practical benefits.

The institution of the vadimbazaha has long coexisted with shorter-term sex-for-money exchanges that, from the perspective of a Euro-American observer, look like prostitution. Over the nineteenth century, Tamatave earned a reputation for immorality and debauchery because so many women went out to spend the night on European ships anchored in the harbor. The traveler Louis Simonin (1867, 295) described how one ship captain who plied the trade between Tamatave and what was then Bourbon (now Isle de la Réunion) took such good care of his crew that "he never hired a man without promising him the *simirires*, Malagasy girls who were registered with customs at Tamatave, and who fought to get into the little boats sent to shore, that then ferried the women back to the ships where they would spend the night."[6] As early as 1906 the French governor-general Victor Augagneur, who had formerly worked as a syphilis doctor, wrote that prostitution was to be legal in Madagascar. He justified his decision by arguing that prohibiting it created more problems and abuses of power than the practice itself. He decreed that women could do as they pleased, but that solicitation would remain illegal (Centre d'Archives d'Outre Mer/MAD/PT194 1938; see also Stoebenau 2006).[7] Casual forms of what the French defined as prostitution continued throughout the colonial period, particularly near the ports or close to where soldiers were garrisoned. The legacy of these practices is visible in many of the words used for women who exchange sex for money, like *makorelina*, probably derived from *la maquerelle*, or madam, referring to a time when Réunionnais women worked as madams (Solofo Randrianja, personal communication, February 7, 2002).

Whether Tamatavians in the nineteenth century and early colonial period interpreted such short-term sex-for-money exchange as prostitution is difficult to say. What is clear is that while the historical lineage of the powerful and respectable vadimbazaha is important for illuminating current practice, the legacy of prostitution looms large in the popular imagination—and not only that of the foreigners who travel to Madagascar.[8] Close to two centuries of Christianity as well as interaction with French settlers and colonial officials has left its mark. Ideas about female sexuality derived from Christian theology and practice have intertwined with, and been imposed on, local ideologies with markedly different interpretations of women's deployment of their sexual and reproductive capacities. The interaction between these diverse ways of approaching female sexuality has made prostitution a locally meaningful category with a decidedly familiar, moralistic tenor. Indeed, in Tamatave one hears the terms for prostitute (*makorelina, mpivaro tena*) used regularly. When young women use these terms to describe either themselves or their friends, they have fairly neutral connotations, indicating one way of making a living. For others, however, these words may serve as epithets to mark disreputable sexuality.[9] To describe a social scene (or even occasionally a person) as *bordel be* (literally, "big bordello," from the French expression *Quel bordel*—What chaos!) implies that it is sleazy.

When young women enter the sexual economy to seek vazaha, they often risk their reputations. If they are successful and marry a vazaha or otherwise amass the resources to establish new networks of their own, they can accede to a valued form of adult status. It is precisely the allure of becoming somebody who is "considered" that draws young women in. At least some women have long followed this path. In fact, several middle-aged women I knew had set themselves up in business with money earned, so people claimed, from prostitution. While they were mocked as young women just starting out, once they gained money they also gained status. Their neighbors knew where the money came from but did not dare comment on it to their faces in the teasing interactions through which Tamatavians shame one another. Likely the neighbors feared that any critical comments they made now might be turned against them in the future. The acquisition of wealth whitewashed its provenance. Young women balance precariously between a basic cultural acceptance of youthful sexuality and a strong sense that only women who can use their sexuality to amass resources and build long-term family networks accrue respect and value over time.

Jeunes Engage the Sexual Economy

When female jeunes move from seeking support from boyfriends to exploiting the sexual economy more consistently, they enter an existing social field, as is clear from the quotation early in this chapter describing "three categories of prostitutes," or the movement from "sand paths to the truck stop to the Neptune Hotel." These informants imply that every young woman starts at the "bottom" (the sand path, or *première catégorie*), then works her way up to nightclubs and "high-quality" status, from which they can seek vazaha. They also imply that all these young women fall unproblematically into the category of "prostitute." Although I have already suggested that this is a highly unstable classification, the young women who perceive themselves as jeunes further contribute to its instability by helping to popularize a set of practices associated with prostitution well beyond the "sand path," "truck stop," and "high-quality" categories. They also add to the repertoire of practices through which young women seek vazaha, particularly by introducing Internet-based dating. As young women who pride themselves on knowing the "latest new things," they bring new kinds of savoir faire to the sexual economy.

Based on my interviews with women who had found vazaha, the four most likely ways include working in places like hotels or restaurants that are likely to bring them into contact with such men, attending nightclubs, finding a man on the Internet, or occasionally being introduced by family or friends. Whether they are physical spaces like hotels or new social networks, these pathways are closely linked to the changes in Madagascar's economy and its relation to the rest of the world since liberalization in the mid-1990s. These include the growth of tourism, and with it the creation of new businesses that cater to tourists, and an increase in people who have moved to France. In addition, the spread of the Internet makes it easier for women to pursue vazaha. Young women have increasingly begun to put their profiles on matchmaking sites in order to find foreigners. They pay a minimal fee, submit a photograph, and an agency then acts as middleman. Young women may also place ads in the personal sections of magazines like *AMINA*, or occasionally they may send their profiles to newspapers in Réunion. Formal marriage agencies have also opened up in Tamatave. One of these, on the rue de Commerce, was run by a Réunionnais woman. In another case a young Malagasy woman ran an agency in partnership with her older sisters-in-law who lived in France. Her agency found its clients in Tamatave by word of mouth.

Figure 6.2. Many young women frequent the Queens Nightclub in their search
for vazaha, 2009. Courtesy of Laura Tilghman.

Since young women explicitly seek to adopt the models that will enable
them to find vazaha, jeunes' social networks as well as their knowledge of
new fashions, new technologies, and foreign tastes give them an advantage
in the sexual economy. In part, their knowledge helps them know where
to go. For example, marriage agencies and Internet sites can be ephemeral,
existing for a few months and then closing down; the clientele of hotels
or nightclubs can change, underscoring the need to be up-to-date with the
expertise jeunes excel at. Jeunes who are familiar with the urban spaces of
Tamatave are also likely to know other people who inhabit these spaces.
Access to these different ways of meeting Europeans also depends on being
part of the right social networks, since most young women rely on their
friends or family members to get them jobs in the first place, and most
feel comfortable frequenting certain nightclubs only when they know their
friends will be there.

Meeting a vazaha is not merely a question of knowing which clubs to go
to or which Internet sites to use and the technicalities of how to use them.
Jeunes also excel at the all-important techniques of self-presentation. In

their online presentation, young women must know how to appeal to men without implying that they are prostitutes, an impression that is unlikely to attract the response they want. In one Internet ad on Madalove.com, for example, a young woman from Tamatave described herself in the following terms: "I am a young Malagasy woman aged 19, seeking a foreign man who is serious for a serious relationship" (http://www.madalove.com/p.php?id =9599 accessed May 26, 2008). By describing the kind of man and relationship she sought as "serious," this girl clearly hopes to find someone who wants more than sex. In most Internet ads, women describe themselves as "modest" (*tsotra*) and "romantic," implying that they are out for love, not money.[10] In the bars as well, women constantly trade information about what vazaha like, how to seduce them, or even which diviners have the most powerful love magic. Francine, a young woman whose story I give in more detail below, explained,

> The other girls taught me how to take a pencil and outline my lips before putting on lipstick, and how to dress fashionably so that the other women wouldn't mock me. And they taught me how to get clients. Some men hate it if you just go up to them and ask them to go with you. They want you to make small talk, like "Is this the first time you've come to Tamatave?" But other men, if you just go up to them and start kissing them, they'll go with you. You can always tell the best approach by looking at the man.

The importance of savoir faire in self-presentation is well illustrated by an experience I had with my son's nanny, Anastasie. Though Anastasie came from a modest rural background, she had long worked as a maid for Europeans. Consequently, though she did not consider herself jeune, nor was she considered so by others, she had been well integrated into many of the same social circuits and had acquired much of their know-how. One day I accompanied her on an errand to take her friend's photo to a local marriage agency that coordinated meetings between local women and European men. Although Anastasie was savvy in city ways, her friend had only recently arrived from the countryside. The photo showed a young girl dressed in white ruffles—the poor country girl's Sunday best—and clearly startled by the camera. Anastasie and another young woman who was with us commented repeatedly on how inappropriate the photo was, and how it would not please men. The girl's self-presentation betrayed the fact that she had not yet been integrated into the jeunes' urban networks or acquired their self-presentation skills.

Although young women who see themselves as jeunes often have skills and social networks that enable them to enter the sexual economy at a higher level, the sharing of knowledge and expertise, as well as the way networks cut across different groups, may let them move in several directions at once. In some cases jeunes may enter a scene already dominated by women who consider themselves prostitutes and who teach them specialized knowledge, reinforcing older categories. In other cases jeunes teach others their new knowledge and expertise in ways that cut across rural/urban divisions and unsettle received social hierarchies. A young woman with very little schooling may arrive from the countryside and, because she has a friend who works in the nightclub, quickly acquire the social know-how needed in this setting. She may "jump categories"—a term Florien used—and end up at the Neptune, where she finds a vazaha. But a young woman who tries this route may also fail, ending up either settling down with a Malagasy or slipping into the stigmatized category of sand path prostitute.

Finding Vazaha: Eudoxie, Noelline, Mamitiana, and Francine

With this background in mind, I want to examine more closely four cases of women who succeeded in creating long-term bonds with vazaha. The first three offer examples of the various ways jeunes participate in the sexual economy. The college-educated Eudoxie is the epitome of the jeune. Her case illustrates how some young women seen as jeunes use nightclubs to meet European men and so adopt paths that were in the recent past more closely associated with prostitution, as the epigraph implies. Noelline, the second case, also saw herself, and would have been seen by others, as jeune. But her story reveals how even those who symbolize generational change sometimes reproduce existing patterns rather than transforming them: Noelline follows in her mother's footsteps. Mamitiana, the daughter of a functionary who frequents nightclubs, is also a jeune, but she has far fewer material resources than the other two. It is not her fellow students who ease her entry into the nightclubs, but other young women who define themselves as prostitutes. Finally, Francine offers an example of how young women who would not be considered jeunes also enter the sexual economy, and sometimes succeed.

Eudoxie

A college-educated girl who frequented nightclubs and kept up with the fashions, Eudoxie, originally from the northern town of Diego Suarez (Ma-

lagasy, Antsiranana), is the epitome of the jeune. Her father was a civil ser-
vant who had retired, and her mother looked after the house. There were
three girls in her family and one boy; all the girls had married Europeans.
Her oldest sister had gone to France on a fellowship and married there. Her
second sister had married a vazaha friend of her brother's. Eudoxie's story,
however, was different. She went to the university in Tamatave, and every
weekend she would hit the discos with her girlfriends. She recounted, "I
found my [vazaha] husband from playing around. A big group of us from
school went out to a nightclub in town. Our tables at the club were pushed
up close to one another. I saw he kept staring at me. I was drinking beer. Not
drunk, just tipsy. Eventually I went outside to cool down, and he followed
me out. 'So what is your name,' he asked. And I told him. And he told me
his name was Paul."

Eudoxie told this foreign man that she and all her friends were students.
In turn, Paul said his parents had a shop in town and had moved to Madagascar for work. They enjoyed living there and decided to stay. He asked if
he could come to the university to see her again. Sure enough, he turned
up two days later and took her to a restaurant. Later that day he said he was
attracted to her. Eudoxie continued:

> When he confessed his attraction to me, I just laughed. But it was as if there
> was something hot within my heart, as if I was carried away by fitiavana [love].
> You know, the first time I'd seen him, I wanted him. I said to myself, "I dream
> of a vazaha boy like that!" When I went back home, everyone was teasing
> me—saying how I'd gotten a vazaha. All the other kids remarked, "Well, it
> has been a long time, but *finally* Eudoxie has found her vazaha, always hang-
> ing out at the nightclubs." Before I went with him, I checked to see if he had
> a wife, and he said no. He took me back to his parents' house. I was so shy,
> eating in the house of a vazaha! But I saw his parents were so happy to see
> me. Before he'd been so wild, and he's calmed down since going with me.
> Over time, as I was with him, I grew less interested in my studies, and finally,
> I had to bribe one of my professors so I could pass my exams. I quit school
> and went to live with him. Eventually he took me back to Diego. My parents
> were so happy! My mother said, "So who is this famous son-in-law of mine?"
> We got married, and his parents set us up in business here in Tamatave selling
> automotive parts.

Eudoxie offers the perfect example of a young woman who frequents
nightclubs, and trades on her sexuality, without ever really risking her reputation. She is lucky: she finds a vazaha while she is still, in effect, jeune and

can opt out of the schooling to which she was only half-heartedly committed.

Noelline

Not all jeunes, however, meet vazaha because they frequent the nightclubs or the Internet. In about a quarter of the cases I encountered, women met their vazaha husbands through family networks established when their mothers or aunts married vazaha years earlier. Noelline was thirty at the time of our interview, though she met the vazaha she married when she was only eighteen. She was originally from the island of Sainte-Marie, a popular tourist destination, but she lived in Tamatave because she and her husband were building a house there. Her mother had married a vazaha when she was still small. She recounted,

> As I understand it, it was my mother who left my father because she found a vazaha. This is the short version of their story. My father was a teacher, and he went to teach in Mahajanga. My mother, she was a *vehivavy mietsiketsika* [girl who moved], and so she didn't just sit but started selling things moving back and forth to Antananarivo. That's where she met the vazaha. The vazaha wanted to marry her, even though he knew she was already married. When the vacation came, Mama came and took us to her sister's in Sainte-Marie and left us with our aunt. She went to France. She lived there for two years, then she came back and found a lawyer to divorce Papa. We were so sad for him, but there was nothing we could do. And she married the vazaha.

Noelline grew up in Sainte-Marie, where her mother and her stepfather had opened a hotel. She was free in her youth, she said (*tena libre!*)—an expression Tamatavians use to imply that a girl can do what she pleases with regard to men and money.

> When I was just thirteen I already started going with Mama to the nightclubs. And at fifteen years old I was already cheating on men. There was one man, who had a lot of money, métis Chinese, whom I really liked. But Mama hated him. And finally I learned they had been lovers in the past. But I still wouldn't give him up. Finally, she threatened to send me to Tamatave, to boarding school with the nuns. The family warned her that would make me even naughtier; I warned her too. "You think I'm bad now," I said, "just wait till you see what I can do if you send me to the nuns." So she acquiesced and let me stay at my aunt's house.

She continued to have many lovers in Tamatave, some who were wealthy Malagasy, others who were vazaha. Eventually she fell in love with a Malagasy—the son of someone with money. Even though the man came from a wealthy family, her mother was furious, scolding her, "What are you doing with one of these Malagasy men who make women suffer?" True to her mother's prediction, the man kept taking lovers. He and Noelline fought. Eventually, two years later, she went home to Sainte-Marie on vacation. Her stepfather's friend, a Swiss man, came to stay for three months. "We fell in love. Mama was happy that he was with me. He loves me so much. I was just eighteen years old, but Mama had already had my passport done. I went with him, and I didn't want to come home, but I called Mama and she asked me to do the *mariazy* [church wedding] here." Like Eudoxie, Noelline is jeune, or at least she was at the time she met her vazaha. Her mother's situation enabled her to find a vazaha, along with her frequenting a tourist-oriented milieu where many vazaha circulate.

Mamitiana

Mamitiana was twenty-six, a slight, pretty women who loved to wear high heels, straighten her hair, and smoke cigarettes—slightly risqué for a Malagasy woman. Although her family was much poorer than either Eudoxie's or Noelline's and had less cultural capital, Mamitiana was still the daughter of a government functionary. However, she never benefited from her father's status. When Mamitiana was twelve her parents separated, and her mother was left caring for ten children.

During this time her mother lived off the "beauty of her face," an expression Mamitiana used to indicate that she relied on men, and the expectation that men give their lovers money, to "make herself living." She even became the mistress of a married man, a practice that public discourse decries but that many women continue. Nevertheless, her mother wasn't able to earn enough money to support all the children, and so, Mamitiana remarked dryly, her brothers were all wastrels, thieves, and drunks. Mamitiana's fate was different, however. Eventually her mother told her to find a man who could support her directly. Mamitiana was more than ready. She started going to nightclubs, sleeping at her boyfriends' houses, drinking. When her mother scolded her, she retorted, "What? *You* told me to get boyfriends. Why are you mad at me now?"

Over time, Mamitiana's friends started taking her to nightclubs. Since she was the youngest, the older girls took her under their wing as a little sister (*zandry*). They would sneak her into the Queens, a notorious spot in Tamatave for trolling for vazaha. Mamitiana remarked with admiration and gratitude,

> My friends were really professional *makorelina* [prostitutes], and I wanted to be like them, because they all had money. They explained to me, "If you go out at night as a prostitute, you have to make it like your work, and then you can really support yourself." And my mom was so happy. Not that I gave her all my money, of course. I had to keep some for myself. Eventually I met a vazaha, a German who had come to Madagascar to trade in medicinal plants. I don't know why he loved me, but he did, and he wanted to marry me. We went to Germany for five years, but his family does not really like me, and now we've come back here to live. My sisters worked as prostitutes too, but one of them, she married a Malagasy man and moved to Mananjary. I guess it wasn't her lot [*anjara*] to find a vazaha.

Mamitiana explained how marrying the German had transformed her life. Her mother, she said, was enormously proud of her daughter's accomplishment and treated her with new respect. Her father, she remarked with bitterness, had suddenly made an appearance—having left her years before—and wanted to reestablish the relationship he had abandoned. She took her revenge by ignoring him. She continued,

> We all know that if you marry a Malagasy you'll suffer, unless maybe you both have big diplomas and great work. But I only have my CEPE [primary school] diploma, so it is better for me to marry a European and leave my suffering. I look at my friends who've been married to Malagasy men for years, and I outstrip them in terms of possessions: none of them have cars, and I have one. I've been overseas, and they haven't. I know how to speak German, and they don't know any language but Malagasy.

Mamitiana's relationship with the vazaha gave her tremendous social mobility. Moreover, because they were legally married, her new status could be formally transmitted to her children.

Francine

Although jeunes have more cultural capital than newcomers to the city, other young women also succeed in the sexual economy. Francine was also twenty-six, and she originally came from a small town to the north of Tama-tave. She recounted how since she was little she had loved going to night-clubs:

> I don't know why but I loved going to nightclubs; I used to admire the pros-titutes [makorelina]. When I didn't pass my BEPC [the exam taken at the end of middle school], I decided I would quit school. I loved to do sports and had many friends. Each Saturday we would all go to the nightclubs. I had a boyfriend then, but I caught him cheating, and we broke up. I was looking for a new nightclub and would go with my friends. At the end of it, I would just look for clients along the roads [she solicited]. My mom was mad at me, but she could not control me. My parents had divorced years ago, and she lived alone. When she would yell at me, I would tell her I was going to live at Papa's, that she was too strict. She never knew, because they didn't speak much, but I went with my friends [instead of to her father's]. When I was tired or had had a bad time, I would come home, and she would always take me back because I was her child.

Francine went on to tell how she met the man she was still with at the nightclub "the way all prostitutes do." They bargained and eventually agreed that she would spend the night with him for 100,000 fmg (about twenty dollars at the time):

> We went to stay at the hotel, and I asked him what had brought him to Ta-matave. He explained how he was terribly disappointed because he had met a girl on the Internet. They had planned to meet in person, but when he saw her she was not at all like the picture she sent. Instead, she was much older and not as attractive. Well, when I heard that, I started to cosset him in case he became my spouse. I explained, "Oh, I've been looking for someone on the Internet, but I haven't found anyone yet." He asked me what Web site I used, and I responded, "Affection." "I don't know that site," he said, "but if you'd been on my site, perhaps I would have found you before, for you are just the kind of girl I'm looking for. Maybe then I wouldn't have been as disappointed as I am now." And I responded, "I'm looking for someone like you too." And he said, "Then why don't we be together seriously, as I was planning with the girl who disappointed me?" And I agreed. And he asked me to bring him to my parents.

Although the man asked to meet Francine's parents, a sure sign the re-lationship was heading in the right direction, things did not go exactly as she had hoped. Her fiancé returned to France, and he continued to regularly send her large sums of money—about 1,000,000 fmg, which at the time was about five hundred U.S. dollars. When she asked if they would get married when he returned to Madagascar, however, he revealed that he was still legally married in France. Francine was disappointed, but she kept the secret to herself, too ashamed to tell her family what was going on. After all, the man promised to marry her eventually, and he still sent money regularly and returned for visits.

She lived off the money he sent. But at the same time she continued to frequent the nightclubs. It was there she met a young Malagasy man who became her lover:

> He was very beautiful and had a beautiful body! Each time I would see him I would be in wonder. He knew I liked him, and he started to flirt with me. And I said to him, "If you go with me, I won't ask you for money and I'll treat you as my spouse, for I do not want someone else to get you." And he agreed. And that day we were already together: I took him home and made love to him. He was amazed, and he stayed.

Describing a second relationship with another Malagasy man after the first one had failed, she said that the young man had walked into her house and "was astonished to see how many things she owned in her house." She continued her relationship with her second Malagasy lover and the vazaha at the same time.

Lasa Maodely and the Intimate Politics of Social Change

Eudoxie, Francine, Noelline, and Mamitiana have become models presenting more or less desirable situations that others aspire to. As Tamatavians say, they have *lasa maodely,* an expression east coast Malagasy use to describe how new practices gain popularity. Although this phrase was used in many circumstances (see chapter 3) and long predates the emergence of jeunes, during my fieldwork it was most likely to be applied to building relationships with vazaha. I first learned about it in that context when a college student who had come to Tamatave from the north used lasa maodely to describe what happens when girls come from other east coast towns to look for vazaha in Tamatave. She remarked, "All the young girls in Maroansetra make vows to their ancestors' tombs that if they marry a vazaha, they'll come home and hold a cattle sacrifice. And when they are successful and come back home with their [vazaha] men, all the other girls want to be like

Figure 6.3. This young couple was married in Tamatave, which will make it easier for the bride to get an entry visa for France. Courtesy of Raissa Zénaide.

them—they've lasa maodely." Lasa maodely was also used by the singer Mamy Gotso in a different, but related context. The popular song "Jaloky" recounts the story of a man who lives off his wife's earnings from prostitution. He sings, "These days, there are very strange customs. It has *lasa maodely* for young men to marry prostitutes."

Stories like Eudoxie's, Francine's, Noelline's, and Mamitiana's are recounted endlessly in Tamatave among neighbors at the water pump, among friends at church, or between parents of girls under the mosquito net at night. These stories illustrate the subtle ways that young women draw on the older meanings and the practices associated with the vadimbazaha and the prostitute, splicing them together in new ways to confront current circumstances, much as studies of culture and history, like those offered by Sahlins and Sewell, imply. They also reveal the importance of the resources that vazaha bring in this process—resources that are structured as much by global inequalities as by local cultural meanings. But these stories do not simply indicate cultural transformations taking place in the present. They are also part of how people create a future. These stories hold out a positive model of the future and how to attain it, prompting other young women to act. Such narratives have consequences in the world, contributing to an increase in these practices. Their circulation makes it easier for other young women to imagine similar futures or to try out similar paths—by getting an Internet account so they can search for vazaha online or by frequenting the Queens nightclub. Yet even as these stores circulate throughout the sand paths, markets, nightclubs, and restaurants of Tamatave, the consequences of adopting this model are not easy to predict or control. The effects of the relationships that develop are far more heterogeneous, subtle, and contradictory than people's perceptions of change make them appear.

Recrafting Families and Generational Relations

When women craft enduring alliances with vazaha, they tend to acquire resources their family members do not have, changing their position not only within the sexual economy, but within family economies as well.[11] An apocryphal story I heard repeatedly during my time in Tamatave illustrates one prominent interpretation of the ways young women's participation in the sexual economy transforms relations between parents and children by inducing parents to exploit their daughters. According to the story, the parents had a pretty daughter who loved a Malagasy boy. They wanted to capitalize on their daughter's beauty by forcing her to marry a vazaha, but the vazaha used the girl for his sexual pleasure and then discarded her. One young man who told me the story commented that it was the parents' fault this girl had been ruined (simba), a term he used to mean she lost her virginity but that also implied she had been morally compromised by those around her. Other versions of the story ended up with the use of love magic to bind the vazaha to the girl and keep the money flowing to her parents. Though most people expect daughters to contribute some material support to their natal households, they also believe girls have a right to choose their lovers. The use of love magic to enslave one's own child cogently bespeaks young people's fears about how sex and marriage for money could undermine family life, allowing parents to exploit their adult children.

My own initial expectation about the impact women's connections with vazaha would have on intergenerational relationships was the inverse: I presumed that young women's acquiring substantial resources would overturn parental authority within households. This conclusion seemed plausible, because poverty makes it difficult for parents to exert the authority that comes from resources, weakening their control over children. Moreover, a great deal of historical work in Africa has shown that the money earned through labor migration let young men challenge gerontocratic authority (Lindsay and Meischer 2003). Whereas before labor migration they had relied on their fathers to provide the livestock to pay bridewealth, their more recent acquisition of cash meant they no longer needed their fathers' help to get married, undermining traditional authority. There are, of course, significant differences between contemporary Madagascar and colonial southern Africa. Nevertheless, it seemed plausible that analogous transformations might be taking place in Tamatave: that the resources women acquire from vazaha men would free them from dependence on their parents so they could pursue their own desires and ignore their parents' preferences.

Women's accounts and my own observations, however, belie both of these alternatives. Rather than greedy parents' feeding off their children or children's seizing authority and turning it against their parents, acquiring resources through vazaha often reproduces and even strengthens daughters' bonds with their mothers. In many of the cases I encountered, the girl's mother had also either been the mistress of a Malagasy man (recall Mamitiana's recounting that her mother lived off the "beauty of her face") or had married strategically, like Noelline's mother, who left her Malagasy father and took up with a vazaha. When the daughter formed a liaison with a vazaha, she often followed her mother's path but was even more successful. These mothers encouraged their daughters' efforts. Mamitiana's mother, for example, counseled her to support herself that way. Although married to a Malagasy man and apparently in a fairly comfortable and respectable position, Eudoxie's mother was thrilled when her daughter brought home yet another vazaha son-in-law, following in the footsteps of her older sisters. Finally, Noelline knew her mother had abandoned her father for a vazaha and had caused her own father great pain. She had also taken Noelline to nightclubs as a young girl, dragging her along as she pursued vazaha, a child-rearing practice most urbanites would not condone. Her mother even actively sabotaged Noelline's relationships with Malagasy men, seeking to ensure that she would end up with a European. But far from the cautionary tale of forced liaisons above, Noelline's eventual successful alliance with her vazaha husband proved her mother had been right all along.

Of course, these young women sometimes do fight with their parents. Parents often feel ashamed when their daughters' active pursuit of vazaha men draws them dangerously close to prostitution. Francine's mother, for example, disapproved of her daughter's behavior, but she lacked the authority to stop her. Another young woman, Marriette, who came from a similar background, encountered parental resistance when she quit her job as a maid and began working as a prostitute. Her parents were furious, scolding that no matter how much she hated working as a maid, she should stick with it. In response, friends who already worked the nightclubs urged her to move in with them. Her parents scolded her further: "What, you're going off to be a prostitute with your friends, and *that* is why you left work? You're a terribly behaved child!" Marriette, however, continued to flaunt her clubbing and to bring home vazaha men. She remarked, "My parents were so angry with me! They claimed it was shameful to have a daughter who was a prostitute. But I didn't want to listen. I had tried to help them before [as a maid], and it was as if it had no meaning."

But parental embarrassment often dissipates when success whitewashes the daughter's reputation. A successful marriage makes them not the parents of a prostitute, but the in-laws of a European. Both Francine's and Marriette's parents' views of their daughters' behavior changed radically when they formed liaisons with vazaha. Francine's mother was "incredibly proud of her," while Marriette remarked, with some satisfaction, "That was when my parents *finally* realized. I didn't reject them, for I could see that they regretted their behavior. My mother even told me not to be offended by my father's harsh words, but to continue to help them and give them money." In all of these scenarios, the women's connections with vazaha enable them to fulfill an idealized vision of intergenerational reciprocity, forcing parents to revise their views of their daughters' behavior. Perhaps Lala summed it up best:

> You get a lot of respect when you marry a vazaha! And sometimes your family starts to treat *you* like a vazaha! For example, if I put on clothes that are just a little bit dirty, my mother tells me to change my clothes for fear that I'll develop bad habits, and then, when I go overseas, I'll be ashamed. When my vazaha came here, he was treated like a king because they were so respectful of him. Since I have been with the vazaha, no one has scolded me at home, for my parents fear and respect me now. But before, just the littlest thing would make them mad at me.

For most young women, acquiring resources enables an idealized form of reciprocity with their parents that they would otherwise be unlikely to achieve. There are tensions involved, to be sure. Nevertheless, the material ability to reweave lines of interdependence, and the respect young women can gain as they achieve the goal of becoming a "considered" person, dominates their experience.

Though young women's associations with Europeans often strengthen mother-daughter bonds, they tend to sharpen cleavages within extended families. A story Maman Pasy told me exemplifies this effect. Maman Pasy owned a hairdressing salon, and her two younger sisters had fulfilled the dream and married Belgians they met through a *koresy* (correspondence, usually through a marriage agency or other intermediary). A fourth sister was married to a local man. Owing in part to the unequal distribution of wealth within the extended family, there were persistent tensions among the sisters. Nevertheless, the sisters and their husbands cooperated. The Malagasy brother-in-law drove a truck owned by the Belgian brothers-in-law. Eventually the Malagasy man lost a huge sum of money; the sisters married to the Belgians accused their brother-in-law of theft and took him to court. When the case was tried, he was eventually proved innocent. In the meantime, however, family and neighborhood opinion sided with the sisters married to the Belgians, assuming the Malagasy brother-in-law's guilt. Remarking on the way popular opinion had taken the vadimbazahas' side against the poorer Malagasy, Maman Pasy concluded, "People here, you know they like money, they like vazaha, so if the spouse of the vazaha does something wrong [like wrongly accusing her brother-in-law of theft], people protect her, because she has money. It makes me really sad to think they no longer have what makes us kin because they are only thinking about money." Notice the direction of the split in this example: within the extended family, relatives side with the sisters who have European husbands, against the sister who has married a Malagasy man. Or to put it bluntly, they follow existing lines of alliance and cleavage, which in turn line up with which members of the family have more access to resources. More often than not, over time a young woman's ability to get resources from European men deepened existing cleavages.

Gendered Inversions

The figure of the *jaombilo*,[12] the young Malagasy man supported by the money a Malagasy woman earns through her connection with a vazaha, and the stories that circulate about these men, brings into sharp relief how women's liaisons with vazaha affect relations between Tamatavian men and women. Claudin explained the jaombilo like this:

> A jaombilo is when the European supports the Malagasy girl, and the Malagasy girl then supports the Malagasy man. That is to say, there is a parallel finance system going on [*financement parallel*]. The way I see it, the Malagasy man is doing *l'amour par intérêt* ("love for self-interest"—a line from a celebrated song) to the Malagasy girl. Because he too has another girlfriend he really likes somewhere else. For example, there is an old Australian man who is married to my cousin. And I see that my cousin only loves him for his money, for my cousin, she has a Malagasy boyfriend hidden away, but the old

vazaha he doesn't know. Often I joke around with the old man, "You know my cousin, she is just using you for money," and he just laughs and says, "That is true." People who do jaombilo, they are people who are very *bôgôsy* [handsome], and they really follow the fashions. They are people you just support but they don't work—they don't want low wages. For example, the song by Mamy Gotso says, "Has money—full; doesn't have money? Still full." You see, jaombilo are full whether they work or not.

Though there is a good deal of humor, and perhaps a bit of admiration, in Claudin's description, many Tamatavians argue that women's acquiring wealth from Europeans and using it to support young men signals the perversion of local gender norms. Many people emphasized that jaombilo who enjoyed not working because women supported them bargained away their manhood. The jaombilo accompanies his girlfriend to nightclubs, then leaves her there to look for vazaha or other wealthy men. He fetches her when she calls him, washes her underwear that has been soiled with other men's sexual fluids, and massages her tired feet after she has been dancing. He even wears the clothes the woman has bought him, the ultimate sign of dependence. From the point of view of most men, these things are profoundly humiliating, and some insist that "jaombilo don't deserve to go by the name of men."

Young women, however, view the situation differently. For many who have liaisons with vazaha or who frequent the nightclubs, having a jaombilo signals their growing power to care for dependents. They take enormous pleasure and pride in being able to seduce and maintain young men. Young women with jaombilo emphasize that they "raised them" (*mitaiza*—the same word used for caring for a child) out of love and sexual desire: the jaombilo attracted them because of their youth and beauty. They also clearly enjoyed exercising their seductive powers. These women represent themselves as obtaining money from their vazaha but loving their jaombilo. Because they love their jaombilo they spend their money on them, a gesture taken as the ultimate sign of love and commitment. Francine, the young woman who was married to a European but still maintained a jaombilo relationship with a young man, explained, "If it were my own choice I'd go with a Malagasy, but since they have no money I'm married to a vazaha. But I really love my Malagasy boyfriend. He's younger than me, and he's my jaombilo. I'm very jealous of that boy. I buy his clothes, I pay for everything. He's tall, dark, and well-muscled; my European spouse is fat, but at least he's gentle and easygoing."

Not surprisingly, given how central having a house is to local conceptions of feminine adulthood, many young women's stories about their jaombilo, as well as young men's stories about becoming jaombilo, revolve around movement in and out of houses. Florien told the following story:

I was with a girl who came to Tamatave to work as a maid in someone's house, and she earned 30,000 a month [about five dollars]. On Sundays she would go out with her friends to the beach, and her friends were all working as prostitutes. She went with them and got a man, and that night she earned 30,000—what she'd usually earn in one month. And so she decided to work as a prostitute. I saw her first on the Avenue of Independence, and I called to her. I was twenty-two at the time. At that moment I didn't have a penny in my pocket, and I said to her, I don't have any money right now, but I like you. Would you go with me? She wasn't difficult, and said, "Let's go home together." And we got to her house, and she fed me, and there was already rice and sauce, and I didn't hesitate but ate. And we slept together. And when the morning came I woke up to leave, and she said, "Don't leave now." Well, I didn't have anywhere to go, so I stayed. But I went home the day after that. *But she said to me, "Why don't you live with me?" To keep me she told me to go get my clothes and to bring them to her [house] to wash them, and I just stayed.* And I became her jaombilo, for I did not have work at that time. I would sit there and she would bring money home, and I would do things around the house.

Consider also that Francine recounted how "I took him home and made love to him. He was amazed, and he stayed." In both cases the women try to consolidate their power over the young men by making them into household dependents. Young men were always uncomfortable when I made the comparison, but they agreed that jaombilo did bear similarities to local conceptions of what makes a slave.

Although both young men's and young women's narratives imply that jaombilo relationships invert local gender norms, albeit from contrasting gendered perspectives, their actual negotiation belies the image of a total reversal. Within the jaombilo-woman relationship, the power dynamics oscillate. Young women try to seduce young men to live in their houses, setting them up as dependents. Yet they can never force a jaombilo to stay. Moreover, the combination of a woman's love for her jaombilo and her reliance on him to do little services for her means she also becomes dependent on him. Such dependence may enable the jaombilo, because of his physical strength and attractiveness, to recuperate a dominant masculine position. Occasionally jaombilo control the woman by violence, a tactic that appeared more likely when they worked as her bodyguard, collecting outstanding debts and physically protecting her.[13] More frequently the jaombilo recuperates a dominant subject position by taking the money from the woman and spending it on short-term pleasures with his friends, or on other girlfriends he keeps hidden away. Neighbors who know about the jaombilo and his circumstances encourage him, goading him on by saying that if his girlfriend can sleep with whomever she wants, he too should have his pleasures. But jaombilo who have other girlfriends risk the wrath of the women who support them. One young woman recounted angrily, "He saw that I loved him, and he wanted to take advantage of me. If they see you are weak, they do what pleases them. At that time, I almost ripped off all his clothes that I had bought for him, but I thought about the fact that I too have a brother, and I took pity on him."

The constantly shifting links among a woman, her vazaha lover, and her jaombilo illustrate how partial, unstable, and contingent the changes in gender relations enabled by young women's control over resources really are. Women who can establish liaisons with Europeans acquire resources that enable them to better negotiate their relations with Malagasy men. But not all of these women have jaombilo. Nor are all young men destined to become jaombilo. And nobody is a jaombilo for life. Usually it is a temporary solution that young men engage in for a short time. There is not one sudden, total transformation in gender relations that takes place as increasing numbers of young women manage to form liaisons with Europeans. Rather, their connections with vazaha have contingent effects on local gender relations: between women and their jaombilo the dynamics of gendered power shift constantly. These dynamics illustrate how gendered social change takes place not only through definitive changes in positions within a system, but also through tiny oscillations made possible in part by the acquisition of new resources. The popularity of the jaombilo role helps tip these oscillations ever so slightly in women's favor, but only some of the time and in specific contexts.

Reimagining Fitiavana: Tensions and Displacements

Much Tamatavian discourse also holds that women's ability to gain resources through vazaha and in the sexual economy has changed the very meaning of fitiavana, the local word for love. Recall that historically, and in many situations today, east coasters constitute and express fitiavana, the word the missionaries later translated as love, through the exchange of material resources. Giving goods or money to a friend, brother, or lover signals one's affective commitment (chapter 3; see also Cole 2009). Ideally, fitiavana fuses the material and the ideal dimensions of attachment into a single set of practices through which people build what are supposed to be ongoing reciprocal relationships.

Undoubtedly east coasters always struggled to create such reciprocity: discussions about stepmothers who cruelly extract resources from husbands to the detriment of the first wife's children, or philandering men who abandon their wives, and the wives who suffer yet remain loyal, are frequent topics of conversation in Tamatave. Nonetheless, one of the most common anxieties I heard expressed with respect to young women's pursuit of vazaha was that nowadays there was no such thing as "love" because urbanites were so obsessed with obtaining money. Such complaints presented a sharp opposition between "fitiavana" and "money," implying a dichotomy that had been less sharply pronounced in the recent past. Consider how in rural areas fitiavana was defined in terms of the exchange of labor and resources. Recall, too, how even twenty-five years ago, some women in Tamatave might ask cheating husbands for material compensation as proof of love and commitment.

Although women and men use different examples to illustrate their points, they tend to imply that women's increased use of men to gain money means that now fitiavana exists only where women give *without* expecting material support. The jaombilo relationships depicted above clearly illustrate how this works. When Tamatavians discuss women who form associations with both vazaha and jaombilo, they imply that these women take the affective and the material dimensions of fitiavana, which are usually intertwined within one relationship, and map them onto two separate ones. Women like Francine were quite explicit about this separation. Recall how she remarked, "If it were my own choice I'd go with a Malagasy, but since they have no money I'm married to a vazaha. But I really love my Malagasy boyfriend." Francine has one relationship for money and one for love, differing considerably from the idea that fitiavana is defined in terms of material *and* affective exchange.

I also heard young men assert that fitiavana existed only in relationships where women not only did *not* receive material support, but sacrificed themselves. One young man, for example, talked about the idea of *fitiavana madio* (clean love). Its meaning became clear when, after expatiating on the nature of love, he remarked: "But clean love *still* exists. My neighbor, she goes out with this boy, and that boy he doesn't give her any money, and he makes her suffer. Yet she never breaks up with him, even when he hits her on occasion. For me, that means she really loves that man with a clean heart." In both of these examples, a bifurcated notion of fitiavana, which has very little to do with older notions in which the material and ideal dimensions of attachment were intertwined, is taken to an extreme: the Malagasy woman uses the vazaha man for his money, while she loves her Malagasy boyfriend so much that she allows him to beat her. One scenario demonizes the woman, while the other justifies her suffering. So sure is this young man with his emphatic insistence that "clean love *still* exists" that he cannot imagine it any other way.

Yet the realities of young women's simultaneous links with both vazaha and Malagasy men complicate these stark divisions. Although Francine talked about her Malagasy boyfriend in ways that implied a conception of love unfettered by material demands, in practice complex exchanges of goods and services characterize women's relations with their jaombilo. After all, the women give their jaombilo goods and money that they receive from their vazaha, but they also expect him to perform certain services. Moreover, and despite what Malagasy men like to claim, not all liaisons with vazaha are made entirely for material reasons. Many vadimbazaha do love their vazaha husbands. Eudoxie, who mentioned how love pierced her heart when Paul declared his attraction, explained when I asked her about why she didn't have a jaombilo:

> Well, I have a friend who does that, but I just don't get it. She always tells me it's because she doesn't love her vazaha spouse. But as I told you just now, I have a lot of love in me. I love my husband, and I don't need anyone else. It's truly about love, our story, not money. That's why my [Malagasy] spouse made me suffer before: he saw that I loved him too much, and so he made me suffer. But God isn't crazy, and he gave me another spouse, and he's given me someone I truly love. I will always thank God for that.

But what that "love" looks like is often a combination of affective attachment and material support. In speaking to me, Eudoxie carefully distinguished between those who love and those who only want money. But in the myriad ways she described her relationship with her present husband and how it unfolded, it was clear that material exchanges were also a part of how she conceptualized and practiced fitiavana. Young women's use of relationships to obtain resources means that some people, in some contexts, reconceptualize fitiavana according to a more idealist conception of love. But these same practices also reassert and recreate the older meanings of fitiavana as a form of attachment that combined material and ideal dimensions.

Failure: Social Juniors

Despite the prominence of these women who become *maodely*, many young women fail to succeed in the sexual economy. A wide variety of mishaps may impede success. Not only is there enormous competition, but many things can go wrong along the way. It takes very little to knock someone from the status of getting by to really struggling. Reasons for failure include proximate events like having a baby and being abandoned or having a sick baby and not being able to pay the hospital bill. But insofar as women rely on men for their income, they are also vulnerable to wider political and economic circumstances. During the political unrest in 2002, not only did men have fewer resources to spare, but the turmoil meant fewer vazaha came to Tamatave. Women who earned their livelihoods from them suffered as a result. The distance between comparative wealth and terrible poverty—the line between success and failure—can be treacherously narrow.

Flavienne

Flavienne's narrative illustrates what may happen to a woman who never successfully acquires the habits and style associated with jeunes and does not find either a vazaha or a Malagasy with whom to build a stable attachment. Though she is young in years, just twenty-one, her lack of family resources and networks, along with her having a child, puts her in a precarious, humiliating position. Unlike many jeunes, Flavienne defined herself as "someone who went out at night"—that is, she worked as a prostitute. She avowed the position; she also lamented it.

Flavienne's parents came from the midsized towns to the north of Tamatave, but she had grown up in the city. By the time I met her, her parents had long divorced. Her mother had recently remarried and "no longer cared for her because she loved her new husband so much." She recounted how she first started to prostitute herself:

> I had a boyfriend, and I was pregnant. The child had been in my stomach for four months when he left. The child was born and he came back, but after a while he left again. I was alone raising the baby. I live in my mother's house, and I do not rent, but I look for enough food to eat. My other siblings are all married [with houses of their own], and I alone remain at home. My friend suggested that I not just sit around but go out at night, seeking money, something to buy food with, and I started doing that. It wasn't my heart's will. Rather, it was because I had suffered so much that I did that. Later my

child fell ill because his bone was out of joint. And we stayed in the hospital for a month, but then we had to leave because we didn't have money to pay. There was no one to care for us, for my mother abandoned us when the child fell sick. I still haven't paid the hospital. I finally brought him to a masseuse, and he was cured, though he still can't walk. His father doesn't do anything for him. Only I care for him, and I go out at night [work as a prostitute] to feed him.

Flavienne sometimes talked of trying to find a vazaha. She often ventured over to the Queens, or even the higher-end Neptune Hotel, which she jokingly referred to as her factory. Her one experience with a vazaha ended when he refused to go with her because he didn't believe she was more than seventeen and she didn't have her identity papers, yet more proof of her bad luck. Her life had an almost Dickensian quality of misfortune. She worked just to feed herself day to day, claiming that even her own mother didn't love her. For Flavienne, there sometimes seemed to be no imagined future.

Sylvie

Sylvie's story is similar to Flavienne's, further proof of the unhappy circumstances that await young women who fail in the sexual economy. Like Flavienne, Sylvie had started out with a Malagasy man and ended up on her own, with few options:

I was married for six years, and my husband drove a truck. Last year he was in an accident and died. In my husband's family, if your spouse dies, you are supposed to go to live with your in-laws for a year. So I went to live with them in Diego [the large port town in the north of Madagascar]. My sister-in-law is married to a vazaha, and she came back to visit from France and told me, "You'd better go get some work, because people here are really difficult" [they will not appreciate your not contributing to the household]. I went and got work in a restaurant, but my sisters-in-law would ask me for money all the time. Finally they drove me out, and I returned home to Tamatave.

Sylvie was still better off than Flavienne, in part because she did not have a child to take care of. She also was able to move among her kin to take advantage of free meals. She had a boyfriend who knew she worked as a prostitute when he was not there. Since he could not support her fully, he had little choice but to accept it. Nonetheless he seemed more interested in preventing her success than promoting it. At one point, he even sabotaged her efforts to find a vazaha:

> When I worked at Chanville [a knitting factory], a vazaha came by who asked the girls who were working if they wanted to have a correspondent [*koresy*] in Europe. And he took our pictures. A man wrote to me, and I sent him my photo. I wrote back, but then my boyfriend caught me. He followed me down to the post office to spy on me. I do not know what he did. Maybe he called that man in France so I never heard from him. Later I wrote to him again, and he wrote back saying he had a girlfriend, but she was too vulgar for his tastes. He preferred me. He asked me to send him a topless photo of myself. I sent him my photo, but he still hasn't answered me. I was so ashamed taking that photo. I went to the beach to do it, and I asked the photographer not to tell anyone.

Despite the forlorn tenor of this story, Sylvie never appeared as down-trodden as Flavienne. Still, her narrative suggests she remains in social limbo. She appears to have become a perpetual social dependent. Even her efforts to improve her social status ended in the humiliation of posing top-less on a beach, then sending the photo and never getting a response. Less successful women like Flavienne and Sylvie who slide into a stigmatized sand path prostitution, in which they have sex with poor Malagasy men just to earn money to buy the next meal, are cruelly mocked. In fact, all the neighborhood boys called them "the deformed Marimars," an allusion to a popular soap opera in which a poor girl marries a rich man. Flavienne and Sylvie were deformed because they had failed.

Although both Flavienne and Sylvie had relationships with local men, their circumstances make it somewhat less likely, though not impossible, that boys from their own neighborhood will want to set up a household. Dezy, a young man who wanted to start a business but had no capital re-marked, "If people didn't know that a woman had been a prostitute they might marry her, but for me, I would never want to marry a girl I knew had been a prostitute because I would fear the diseases I might catch from her." Dezy's remark about disease was unusual; many others talked about loss of honor from marrying a former prostitute.[14] Several other young men commented that women who were prostitutes married people from "elsewhere"—not boys from their neighborhood—an interpretation that fit well with the idea that these women seek out vazaha. Those who fail in the sexual economy also contribute to new patterns. Their experience normal-izes unreciprocated dependence as a condition of adult life. It contributes to the disintegration of the networks of exchange that knit families together. Not all young women achieve the valued adulthood they so desire.

Between What We Imagine and What We Create

In his essay on the "mirror stage," Jacques Lacan (1968 [1949]) depicts how the unformed infant assumes a more coherent "I" through seeing his image in the mirror provided by those who populate his social world and enable his development. Forming an acting subject requires interacting with an image that creates an illusory wholeness, though the one can never be reduced to the other. Similarly, in Tamatave young women searching for vazaha, and the many other Tamatavians who eagerly watch for their success or failure, conjure an image of the future. These actors create their image out of their everyday conceptions of jeunes and the nature of the life course, which are central to the mundane ways they imagine their future lives unfolding.

The transformations in intimate relations that these women contribute to as they move toward that future cannot appropriately be characterized by a language of radical rupture as some approaches to the role of youth in social change imply. Nor can they be reduced entirely to the transformation of existing symbolic structures as some accounts of structure and history might imply. Rather, women's participation in the sexual economy underscores the importance of the uneven dialectic between image and action for understanding generational change. The representations of change and the future contained in the many stories that circulate about young women who marry vazaha provide a seemingly coherent image that organizes and guides people's actions. Young women search for Europeans in the sexual economy as they try to build a future as valued and respected adults who can care for others under the new conditions created by neoliberal economic reform. The (re)opening of Madagascar, the recent influx of Europeans, and the difficulty of obtaining respectable steady employment have converged with the knowledge and practices associated with jeunes to increase the number of young women who pursue Europeans. Even though they are a minority of all young women, jeunes' participation in the sexual economy, and the discourse about them, teaches others new ways of engaging in these practices. Jeunes carve new paths across old terrain, circulating knowledge and social connections that not only encourage others to follow their lead but popularize some of the skills and knowledge they need. Perceptions of social change focused on this particular group create a representational feedback loop influencing others' ideas about what is possible and how to achieve it.

But there is no simple relation between the discourse of radical transformation that promotes the practice and the much more subtle effects created when others—many of whom are not perceived as jeunes—actually take it up. In fact, when one probes how young women's relationships with vazaha contribute to patterns of social change, it turns out that new practices arise in incremental ways, always in unpredictable tension with older patterns. Existing lines of attachment or cleavage within Tamatavian intimate life all are sharpened and reworked in these relationships: the kinship between mothers and daughters; the tension between the ideal of gender as a stable difference and its constant negotiation through the exchange of resources; and the tension between fitiavana as reciprocal exchange versus fitiavana as self-sacrifice. No single case encapsulates all these processes. Rather, some relationships have gained more salience than in the past, just as some aspects of relationships appear more important or open to contest. New possibilities emerge in this context, but the threads of older patterns nevertheless remain relevant.

SEVEN

Other Futures: Women, Suffering, and Pentecostalism

The love of Jesus never disappoints.

—Claudine

If someone hits you on the cheek, then turn the other cheek. That suffering that you get when you pray and others chase and hound you is not heavy but light. Christians must all have their private, special sufferings. Their sufferings are not the same as the sufferings of those who are not Christian.

—Pastor at the Power of Faith church

In the church, there are many more women than men. Perhaps it is easier to preach to women than men, but for men, it's hard to convince them unless they have a revelation. It is the mothers of families [*renim-pianakaviana*] that carry the burden in most households, for example, if their husbands or children misbehave. Women have soft hearts.

—Maman'i Olivina

We saw in chapter 6 how jeunes' efforts to attain the futures they desire popularize seeking European men, even though the futures they imagine and the ones they create are often in tension with each other, and the desired outcome uncertain. My analysis focused on young women's quest for European spouses because these are the women Tamatavians emphasize in their own understanding of the forces underpinning contemporary change. In foregrounding the role of jeunes, however, I deliberately backgrounded certain aspects of Tamatavian social and cultural life that have their own role in generational and cultural-historical change. After all, over the course of this book we have caught many glimpses of other life paths embodying other ways of interpreting, or deploying, shared ideas or images, especially those offered by the church.

The church is not a homogeneous institution. Both the Catholic and the Protestant mission churches have long played an important role in disembedding urbanites from the world of their ancestors, providing some a route to upward social mobility other than that offered by the colonial and later the national administration. Here, however, I focus on the role of the Pentecostal churches because participation in these churches provides the clearest contrast with the life strategy associated with jeunes, who seek salvation through foreign alliances in the sexual economy. Not only does Pentecostalism offer different ideas about métissage and clothing, as we saw briefly in earlier chapters, but Tamatavians tend to see the pursuit of vazaha and joining Pentecostal churches as contrasting ways to achieve prosperity that have accompanied economic liberalization. While some women build long-term alliances with vazaha, and more fashion a life by moving from man to man, continuing to work the sexual economy, many others become wives and mothers, building families with local men. When these relationships fail to provide them with the lives they had hoped for, they often turn to Pentecostal churches. Pentecostal beliefs and practices offer significant alternatives to contemporary political and sexual economies in creating a future. It is to this alternative path that I now turn.

Although adult women predominate in most Pentecostal churches in Tamatave, there are always other people who belong to these congregations. Male pastors led many (though not all) of the evangelical churches in the city, and there were always men among the fervent adherents of any congregation. Women usually bring their children, and sometimes young people come who have no immediate family connection to the church. I also encountered former jeunes, who had clearly failed on the nightclub circuit and found their way to the church—sometimes with parental prompting. Viviane, who was only twenty-one and already had a baby, told me, "I used to be very naughty and go to nightclubs, but once I started praying I changed." Her time as a jeune, it seems, had ended before it could really begin.

In addition to the comparative lack of men, I quickly found that, for the most part, youth were only temporarily or partially committed to Pentecostalism. They came and went in church youth groups, and bore babies out of wedlock despite the pastors' preaching, but in several cases they also showed up in the meetings of a prostitutes' association, much to my assistant's amusement. By contrast, over the course of my fieldwork in Tamatave it became clear that adult women were the most committed members of the new churches. They made up about two-thirds of every congregation.

Again and again, regardless of their own religious affiliation, Tamatavians explained that adult women participated more because mothers of children (*reninzaza*) suffered the most, making them more open to the church's redemptive message.

When Tamatavians say women suffer the most, they refer implicitly to the problems created by Tamatave's ferociously competitive social world, where those who have less to give are less firmly embedded in networks of fitiavana, where those who are poor are mocked, and where everyone wants to be "considered." In contemporary Madagascar, economic conditions sometimes articulate with the gendered life course to prevent older women from attaining valued forms of personhood. As she ages, any given woman has access to only a few pathways to success, and many are excluded from the more respectable routes to status and comfort. This exclusion is particularly likely when women depend on husbands who either do not have money or spend it elsewhere. *Mijaly* refers to the very concrete bodily and emotional suffering women experience when they do not have enough money to care for themselves or their children, or when men either withhold resources or are violent.[1] Local ideas that see women as more emotional, and that construe emotion as potentially dangerous and disabling, making women more fragile than men, further inform these views on women's religious lives.

At least at first, Pentecostalism attracts these women because it offers a prosperity gospel according to which Jesus Christ bestows material goods and physical well-being on those who embrace his teachings. Pentecostalism's offering a solution to economic problems is a central part of its appeal, as many scholars who have examined the relation between economic development, globalization, and Pentecostal practice point out (Bornstein 2003; Comaroff and Comaroff 2003; Csordas 1992; Gifford 2004; Hackett 1995). Women come to be cured of afflictions, to gain money, and to build the networks of fitiavana that define valued personhood. With the exception of curing physical ailments, these goals resemble those of young women who work the sexual economy and seek vazaha. The same powerful sense of humiliation, hurt pride, and anger that drives some women to pursue vazaha motivates other women's turn to Pentecostal churches. New converts continue to share many of the same notions of self, social value, and material progress as their non-Pentecostal counterparts.

This desire to obtain resources through prayer, however, is only one moment—and perhaps not the most important—in what may turn out to be a much longer process of engagement with a religious community. Eschewing the secular economic striving that is so important to life in Tamatave, Pentecostalism offers believers alternative ways to experience their interactions with others. Ultimately, it offers a different conception of what it means to be a person and of how the person relates to her social world than the common wisdom that predominates in the aspiring, yet struggling, households of Tamatave. Pentecostalism promotes an intense and, these women say, deeply satisfying relationship with Jesus. It gives them a new way to interpret the suffering associated with being poor. When women become truly involved, they remove themselves from the competitive interpersonal interactions that underpin local theories and practices of social change associated with secular aspiration. Their involvement leads them to build the future in new ways.

Yet Pentecostalism also draws on some of these same entrenched social interactions and practices, recontextualizing them to suit a new logic. As I will explore in the following pages, the social competition, anger, teasing, and exclusion of others that are such an important part of turning away from existing life worlds and forming new communities continue to operate, as does these women's desire to form households from which they can generate new life. Love, jealousy, anger, sharing, and withholding are all crucial, but these emotions and their accompanying actions are rearranged through Pentecostal churches. While the mere fact of living in Tamatave disembeds urbanites from the rural contexts they were once rooted in, membership in these churches produces an additional disembedding: it separates members from their urban communities and commitments, substituting new social networks and new pathways to the future.

By examining how change happens among women who join Pentecostal churches, we can see that the emergence of a new generation of adult actors is only one of many possible moments when personal change articulates with, and may transform, wider cultural and historical structures. Not only does the discourse about jeunes operate as a synoptic illusion in relation to a social field that includes people who do not fit neatly into this dominant generational representation. It also obscures how people continue to change over the life course in ways that often draw from many of the same social logics and experiences that characterize generational change. We can also begin to see how different groups imagine their paths in relation to each other. Those who join Pentecostal churches and those who pursue well-being in the sexual economy may see themselves as fundamentally different, but their practices are deeply entangled with one another. Pentecostal preachers constantly use jeunes as negative examples to teach their followers how not to behave: recall Pastor Aimé's sermon on métis Christians who washed the clothes, made the bed, and then went searching for other men besides their husbands. Meanwhile, jeunes mock the styles and assumptions of Pentecostals. Jeunes imagine their own futures in relation to the rural world from which they wish to distance themselves, to be sure. But they also imagine their own paths in contrast to the women who most visibly disapprove of them but who may also succor them and offer a practical alternative when their lives as jeunes fail. Women who enter Pentecostal churches in turn respond in part to the possibilities and constraints made visible in the lives of jeunes. The people who engage in the contrasting practices of sex and salvation imagine their paths in relation to each other all the time. In Tamatave the futures enabled by sex always take place in relation to the alternative routes provided by salvation.

Another Disembedding: Turning toward Pentecostalism

The rise of Pentecostalism in Tamatave has paralleled its rise in many parts of the world.[2] Like Pentecostal churches elsewhere, those who have come to Tamatave in the past ten years emphasize the importance of receiving grace from Jesus through close adherence to the Bible and thereby being born anew, a radical transformation that supposedly creates an entirely new person. Regardless of which aspect of Pentecostal doctrine a particular church emphasizes, entry into the church is premised on conversion. According to Pentecostal doctrine, people convert because they receive a sudden revelation from God. Listen to Pastor Fanja, the female pastor at the Power of Faith Church, as she explains what it's like to have a revelation by comparing God's wisdom with that provided by ancestral custom.

> There are two kinds of wisdom. There is that wisdom that comes from God and that God gives you, and there is that wisdom that comes from the land, which is the inheritance of your ancestors. But with ancestral wisdom, you see that it is only within your house that you show your good behavior. For example, maybe someone respects his parents at home, but when he leaves he behaves in a completely opposite manner! But if it is wisdom that comes from God, it isn't just in the house that you enact it. *You carry it everywhere within you. No matter where I am, I can't do things that go against the word of God, because God has already put wisdom that comes from him inside me.*

Conversion implies a powerful internal transformation that makes God one's most important interlocutor. Likewise, women sometimes spoke to me about the differences between their past and present selves by emphasizing how, in the past, they would carry the Bible to pray on Sunday but

Figure 7.1. Pentecostal prayer meetings gather the faithful to pray and be healed. Courtesy of Pastor Aimé, Power of Faith Church, Tamatave.

continue their evil ways on Monday. In these stories, redolent with Pentecostal doctrine, their good behavior figures as mere facade. It is not internal to them but contextually based. They said that when they converted to Pentecostalism, by contrast, God touched their hearts, transforming them internally. Another woman explained, "Wherever I go, I think of Jesus. Even if my eyes don't see Jesus, I believe he dwells within me. He is in my heart, he is always with me."[3] All conversion narratives emphasize a period of suffering or danger (typically sickness) that God transforms into a life of peace and prosperity. This transformation then leads the person to recognize the power of Jesus. Claire's conversion narrative illustrates this dynamic.

Claire was the daughter of a night watchman who lived with his family in a small house on the school grounds. When the Power of Faith church first arrived in Tamatave, it held services in the school building. As part of his evangelizing effort, Pastor Aimé offered to pray over people to cure them. Claire was having stomachaches at the time, so she allowed the pastor to lay hands on her. But Claire didn't believe, and she grew sicker still. After a month God appeared to her in a dream, saying, "My child, follow me and your illness will be cured." Claire started to pray again, sincerely this time, and was cured. She converted to Pentecostalism. According to Pentecostal belief, Claire's revelation meant she was born anew as someone who believed in the power of Jesus Christ to save humans from sin and suffering. In becoming a new person, she was thought to develop new tastes and proclivities. To all appearances, she did. She no longer wanted to wear clothing the church deemed immodest, and she took enormous pleasure in studying the Bible and singing at church.

For most Tamatavians, regardless of whether they are Pentecostal, what these churches prohibit is as important as what they encourage. Pentecostal doctrine insists that believers should *not* engage in competing religious practices—they should not be "métis Christians" (see chapter 5). In addition to ceasing to observe basic ancestral rites, new converts should explicitly reject the temptation of worldly things. They are supposed to forgo sexual relations outside marriage and renounce the sexy, immodest clothes of Tamatavian jeunes. They are also exhorted to give up the alcohol so integral to sociality in much of Tamatave. This turning away from "worldly things," however, does not imply the rejection of all consumption. Rather, those who convert should consume in ways that build and reproduce Christian families and homes living according to biblical precepts (Austin-Broos 1997; Brodwin 2003).

These choices mean new converts no longer take part in some of the activities that are central to other Tamatavian households. They refuse to participate in many ways: by abstaining from drinking or smoking, by denying any interest in the fashions that preoccupy so many others, and by not eating the meat that other family members bring home from a sacrifice.[4] Usually, new converts also reject the Catholic or Protestant churches that their families previously belonged to.

The refusal of certain shared practices embodies a politics of participation and exclusion with widespread implications. As we have seen, in everyday life the best way to express love, affection, and loyalty is to share money, things, labor, and food. Often east coasters express such attachments and commitments in rituals, which until fairly recently were one of the most important ways to publicly display wealth. In Tamatave, and along the east coast more generally, taking part in such a ritual requires much more than just watching events unfold. It indexes a whole set of political, social, and emotional loyalties. Recall the words of Josef and Ramarie, the older villagers in chapter 3 who emphasized that you couldn't go to a bone turning and not participate—to *really* understand, you had to get down on your knees and sort through the bones. In rural areas, one common way to signal political loyalty is to attend another family's ritual. Conversely, not showing up for a ritual you've been invited to implies a break in social relations. Failing to attend a ritual, or to eat food that is offered, implies rejection of a social and political relationship. No one needs to say much; it is only necessary to see who joins in and who stays away. A great deal can be inferred from such observations.

Within the "ancestral" Catholic and Protestant churches, most people inherit their faith from their parents. Like farming a family field or living in a certain house, belonging to a particular church is an "inheritance from the ancestors." There are, of course, some circumstances where family members expect others to change their faith—for example, it is normal for a woman to adopt her husband's form of Christianity when she marries, just as she ideally goes to live in his house. In contrast, most people join Pentecostal churches not because they have to, and not because their parents belonged, but because they themselves choose to. In this sense an older woman's decision to join a Pentecostal church is not unlike the choices faced by jeunes who find themselves forced by circumstances to carve out partially new paths. But unlike jeunes, whom everyone expects to transform themselves as part of a normative process of "seeking," the choice to join a new church includes a willful, personal rejection of one's old community and family. Such a break implies that the old paths to success have failed.

Consequently, in most cases converts' families become very upset when their kin join Pentecostal churches. Claire's narrative exemplifies the kinds of tensions that can arise when one family member decides to convert:

> My father is the school's watchman and my mom sells things. They don't pray, and they remain caught up in worldly matters. In my family there are many who aren't saved, for I alone have been called by God. My father is possessed by a *tromba* [spirit], and every night that spirit comes, and my parents serve it [hold the rituals the spirit demands]. But in terms of what makes me a child of God, I cannot do that. God wants them to stop serving the devil. My mother doesn't give me a hard time about my praying, but my father doesn't like me to pray. The spirit who possesses my father says I do things I haven't done. He [the spirit, speaking through the father] says that I go with men. And my father says that the spirit speaks to him and tells him what I do. My father says, "If I catch you with men I'll cut you with a knife, for you must be twenty years old before you [sleep with men]." He does that when he is drunk. And I am sad for him and I pray.

Claire uses specifically Christian language. Though her father, while possessed by the spirit, threatens to cut her with a knife if she goes with men, she says only that she is "sad for him and prays." Hers is a language of Christian suffering and forgiveness that answers anger with a prayer for salvation rather than with retaliation. Claire feels that she models Christlike behavior by sadly, resignedly, hoping for her father's conversion.

Similarly, Maman'i Lala, an older woman whose husband worked as a mechanic, lamented that her family still harassed her for abandoning Catholicism to join the Power of Faith church. Like Claire, she emphasized that she tried to "teach them" or enlighten them rather than responding in kind. Both Claire and Maman'i Lala use a Christian language of forgiveness to manage a situation that might otherwise lead to a confrontation. But note, too, how they use this language to justify their turning away from, and excluding, others. This time, however, the "others" are not those who are poor or those who don't give recognition, but unbelievers in general.

Pentecostals' refusal to engage in the practices central to much of Tamatavian daily life also makes them vulnerable to criticism in the wider public sphere. They become a foil against which jeunes sometimes define themselves. Mamitiana, the young women I cited in chapter 3, confirmed this when she remarked, "There are those who don't follow the fashions, and they really suffer! One kid who lives near me, her parents pray at the Pentecostal church, and she can't follow the fashions and wears long skirts all the time. And when she comes to school everyone teases her and calls her ma soeur [my sister]. She really has an inferiority complex." The Pentecostal schoolgirl's failure to wear fashionable clothing sets her apart. Her choice of clothing implies that she shares neither her peers' aspirations nor their understanding of how the world works. This young woman is simply obeying her parents. Nevertheless, her peers see her as having chosen an alternative path. They accuse her of differentiating herself, implying that she is superior to them.

When their kin blame them for converting, saying it is bad to change faith, Pentecostals often respond by arguing that all forms of Christianity are related. They claim that the shift from one kind of Christianity to another is a less radical break than critical family members perceive it to be. Fanja, the female pastor at the Power of Faith church, argued, "Many people say it is bad to change faith. Like me, I was a Catholic, and I worked in the church. But when I moved to the new church many people chased me for having betrayed my faith. But to me, it isn't the church that is faith—that is just a label or a name. Like flowers, they each have their name—dahlia, or *belle du jour*. So too, the name of the church doesn't mean a lot to me. At the Catholic Church or at the Power of Faith church, I am still serving Jesus Christ."

Since on another occasion Pastor Fanja had told me how unsatisfactory Catholicism was, her claim that all churches are the same and that it does not matter how she worships Jesus Christ is somewhat disingenuous. Clearly, she thinks belonging to a Pentecostal church is more compelling from an experiential point of view, and more righteous from a religious one, than belonging to the Catholic Church. Setting aside the logic of her justifications, however, these narratives indicate that while joining Pentecostal churches offers congregants the benefits of salvation, it comes at a cost. But given the social tensions and criticism that conversion creates among one's kin and neighbors, why are these churches are so popular? To be sure, the practical benefits provided by Pentecostal communities are part of the answer. But the appeal runs deeper.

Continuities and the Allure of Pentecostalism

When women first start to attend these churches, they often assimilate Pentecostalism to their urbanized perception of the demands and habits of ancestors. According to traditional Tamatavian common sense, people honor ancestors, and ancestors reward them with health, wealth, fertility, and prosperity. People also make deals with their ancestors. It is common, as we have seen, for people to make vows such as, "If you help me find a vazaha to marry, I will return here and sacrifice a bull to you." Ancestors are entities to be appeased and bargained with.[5] Both Claire and Maman'i Lala remarked to me on different occasions, "I will just not leave Jesus alone until he hears my prayers and gives me what I want." Their statements imply that the two parties are hierarchically related, but that they can negotiate nevertheless.

Although church doctrine holds that people must not pray to ancestors, many practitioners continue to believe that material success is the surest proof of ancestral blessing. Both those who have converted to Pentecostal-ism and those who have not sometimes fight over the right way to be religious, by comparing who is more efficacious: Jesus Christ or the ancestors. Maman'i Lala explained,

> My family chases me, because I won't participate in a *famadihana* [bone turn-ing]. They say, "Why won't you do a bone turning? Our ancestors, they are powerful! And when people have finished a bone turning ceremony they have wealth." But I always say, "The dead don't bless the living. If they could bless, then they'd still be alive." And they retort, "If this Jesus of yours is so great, why is it that people who pray are still poor?"

Maman'i Lala used the same logic to justify abandoning Catholicism and ancestor worship, which she saw as intertwined. She acerbically remarked,

> When I was a Catholic, I also did ancestral ways, and I didn't see what good it did me. I went with my mother's family to my grandfather's tomb. Everyone was making vows to the tomb, so I did too. I vowed, "If I complete a house in Tamatave, then I'll bring you money." But I waited and waited and I never got that house. I was already deeply into the [Pentecostal] church before I obtained a courtyard, and now I have a house that I rent out.

Similarly, the pastor's wife at the Assembly of God church used to com-plain that if ancestors were so great, then Malagasy should all be richer than they are: Madagascar's poverty was proof of ancestral failure. She also com-plained that ancestors were too demanding, always making their descen-dants sick so that they would sacrifice cattle or refurbish their tombs. By contrast, she said, Jesus only asked that you pray to him. For these women, poverty signals ancestral impotence.[6] New converts hope that Jesus will be-have like a more powerful ancestor.

The Promise of Prosperity

At least at first, it is usually the promise of prosperity that attracts women to Pentecostal churches. Take the beginning of a sermon at the Rhema church, in which the pastor went on at length about the luxurious homes she'd seen on a recent trip to the neighboring island of Réunion: "When I went to that meeting in Réunion, I was very surprised because the house I lived in there was truly beautiful. The shower was much nicer than the living room in my own house! The car that picked me up [at the airport] if it wasn't a 4×4, it was one of those new kinds of cars, really luxurious!" Though in this case the pastor used the example to prove that people should be generous to their guests in keeping with Christian teaching, she also implied that God will grant you riches like those of her Réunion hosts if you follow his ways. The audience may have appreciated her talk of travel and her glamorous experience in Réunion and gained a sense of vicarious pleasure. But they also hoped to attain such pleasure more directly for themselves.

Maman'i Lala, for example, clearly joined the Power of Faith church because she believed it would enrich her. One day she remarked to me in exasperation, "Before, the end of the month [payday] would come, and my husband would only hand over a few pennies." She went on to describe how he had even tried to stop her from going to church, complaining, "You are always going away [to church], but we have nothing here at home." She kept attending services nevertheless and planned to give her land to the congregation so they could build a new church on it. She was sure her gift would bring wealth in return. Noting the various needs she hoped would be met as a result of her generosity, she remarked: "We need to repair our house, and also to get electricity. I wish I wasn't poorer than the rest of my family—my heart will be sad if God doesn't grant me parity with my siblings." Maman'i Lala then described a vision the pastor had had of what would come to her if she gave her land to the church:

> The pastor has already had a vision of my house. Our house was very huge, and there was someone who was very old and ugly who came to the door. She asked me to invite her in, for there was nowhere for her to go. And I said, "I don't have enough for myself, so how am I supposed to help you too?" But then the words of God came to me, "Be keen to invite guests into your house." And I brought her in. She was very dirty, but I made her coffee and gave her bread and a bath and clean clothes. I went to buy coffee. Well, there is a Bible where I keep my money, and I went to get my Bible, and I looked, and my Bible wouldn't shut, it was so full of money. I was amazed. And then I went

to look and the coffee box was full, and so was the sugar jar. I turned back toward the old woman, and I said, "You are my Lord and my God." She had disappeared. But my house had turned into a many-storied abode.

Maman'i Lala's narrative of her pastor's vision encapsulates both the competitive social dynamics and the desire to be generous and give to others that structure many women's intimate lives. It is no accident that she wants a house, the symbol of married respectability for east coast women, though she wants a bigger and grander one than she has now. As she remarked on another occasion, "Women's jo [honor, respect] comes from love within their household." The house is the concrete embodiment of that love. Her dependence on her husband's wages, her anger at not having adequate resources, her malahelo-inducing interactions with her siblings, and her intense desire to outdo them, or at the very least keep up, sharpen her sense of frustration. All these elements combine to make the church's promise of wealth for the faithful particularly appealing.

Reforming Men

In many contexts, Pentecostal converts find that through their participation in the church, their husbands' interests become more aligned with their own (see also Brusco 1995; Gill 1990). Where before men may have spent their money drinking or supporting other women, men who convert to Pentecostalism sometimes become more committed to their wives and families, in keeping with church doctrine. So too, women like Maman'i Lala also hope that by participating in the church, and by praying to God, they will be able to reform their husbands. Madame Josephine's story epitomizes the combined promise of instant wealth on the one hand and the hope of reforming men's behavior on the other that often constitutes Pentecostalism's initial attraction. Pastor Aimé recounted,

Madame Josephine, her husband used to drink rum all the time. And she had an aunt who already prayed. The aunt spoke to me, saying that her brother's daughter had problems and that we should go and help her. That Sunday Madame Josephine came to church. We gave her our opinions, teaching her that when he was drunk and had come home, not to put him outside on the ground but to help him into bed and to show him that you love him as a wife should. That way he will realize what he's doing and stop his bad behavior. Well, Madame Josephine, she listened to our advice, but later God tested her again. They had lots of debts. The debt collectors came to take away their money. They brought the police with them. They said that if the debts weren't paid, they would put her husband in prison. Madame, she came to tell me what had happened, and I said, "We shall pray, for God is trying to change your husband." And she believed me, and so we both prayed. The next day when her husband went to work, he found money on the ground, and they paid the debt off. Her husband saw that miracle, and he came to his senses. Now he has quit those habits. And they both continue to pray here.

Madame Josephine did indeed become a fervent believer, but this is not always the case. Pastors often complained to me that converts valued only the material goods they hoped to gain, as opposed to eternal salvation. Pastor Fanja remarked, "There are some [converts] who have many problems. They become very grouchy and blame me, saying that it is my fault when they do not get what they want and that I don't know how to care for them. There are even those who quit the church. Because those people, they pray to get rich, not to go to heaven. It is of the flesh, not the spirit. But Andriamanitra [God], he looks at your character." Similarly, her husband, Pastor Aimé, explained how sometimes, when a man's behavior starts to change, the woman feels she has achieved her primary goal and abandons the church. "There are those who just want to make their spouses behave. That is why they pray. Often we go to visit at the house, and we'll meet the man. And we'll preach to him, and when he's heard God's word he'll start to change. When the woman sees her husband changing, we stop seeing her at church! And then she is lost to the path. But she doesn't know that when she is lost to the path her husband too will return to his bad ways." For many women, the practical promise of Pentecostalism constitutes its spiritual efficacy, much to the pastor's dismay.

Creating a New Social World

Although Pentecostal discourse emphasizes that conversion and involvement in these churches are personal, enabled by divine revelation, conversion is also deeply social. Much as young women's entry into the sexual economy is a personal reaction to a social provocation, and new entrants are taught the ropes by women who have been there longer, so joining Pentecostal churches involves learning to be fluent in a new idiom for understanding, explaining, and acting in the world, a new idiom that fellow churchgoers reinforce. The adoption of certain narrative conventions plays an important role in this transformation, as Susan Harding (1987, 2000) has argued. But narratives are only one small piece of this process, which also includes an imaginative reorientation as new converts come to adopt new forms of worship and new ways of seeing (Luhrmann 2004).

Evangelizing: Tales of Suffering and Redemption

Evangelizing, many scholars of Pentecostalism have pointed out, is a crucial part of this religious movement (Chestnut 1997; Stoll 1990). Of course, church members in Tamatave regularly go out on "crusades" to spread God's word. But perhaps the most effective method of evangelizing is sharing stories of suffering and exchanging information—much as neighbors would share which doctor is most effective or where to buy the best meat. Getting water at the pump and chatting outside the local store in the evening not only are occasions for people to compete, as I described in chapter 3. They are also moments when neighbors helpfully share their experiences. Often women will hear a neighbor's tale of suffering and invite her to church, reassuring her that, if she shares her pain with Jesus, her load will be lighter. As a banner at the Assembly of God church reads, "Jesus is your best friend. He forgives your sins, releases you, cures you, and solves your problems."[7] Though the exact phrasing varied, this was a promise adherents often offered to attract others to the church. At other times, a pastor's preaching or a neighbor's gossip may arouse curiosity and draw them to the church.

Jeanette was Maman'i Olivina's neighbor, and Maman'i Olivina used to preach to her regularly when she saw her on the sand paths. At first Jeanette resisted her overtures, but eventually she conceded and tried the Pentecostal church. What she found there moved her.

> I went to pray that very Sunday, and I was amazed to see everyone bringing out what was in their hearts. It wasn't like the church that I was used to. . . . I looked, and I could see that they were all really speaking to someone [Jesus], and I was amazed. "Who are they talking to?" I asked myself. There were no crosses, but the word of God was hung on a banner. I didn't know very much about the Bible; I had hardly studied it. The pastor went up into the pulpit and began to pray. And I said to myself, "He looks very different from what I am used to." In the Catholic Church they wear a long white robe, but this man was dressed very simply. He started to speak, and it was *as if he'd seen right through me and knew my life.*

The comment that "it was as if the pastor had seen right through me" or "the pastor somehow knew my life" is a common refrain. Jeanette found this sense of someone watching with sympathy deeply compelling. It offered her a novel kind of recognition that felt very different from what she experienced in the sandpaths of Tamatave, prompting her to return to the church. Her comment underscores the important role of the pastor and church services in reorienting women's commitments.

Sermons

Drawing from a mix of personal experiences and stories about people they know, interspersed with biblical allusions and explication, sermons often contain a running critique of daily life in Tamatave. By simultaneously alluding to their congregants' experience, evoking their suffering, and associating it with biblical themes, pastors work to reframe the way their flocks look at the world. They teach congregants to see the work of the devil and the hand of God in the mundane details of their daily lives.

In one Sunday sermon at the Power of Faith church, Pastor Aimé explicitly addressed the problem of "not having" and the kind of "complex" that urbanites are said to acquire when they feel inferior because of poverty. He announced, "Sadness and tears are for the devil. We are stronger than our enemies. Get rid of all your complexes, for God does not want that. My sisters and my brothers, the lack and sickness that are your problems, we will solve those problems today." On another occasion, Pastor Aimé began his sermon by reading from Genesis about Jacob's dream, in which God appeared to him. He then went on to address how Abraham had feared God and how his grandson, Jacob, should have followed his grandfather's path, using this story to talk about the importance of God's work. Yelling at the assembled crowd through his microphone, Pastor Aimé asked, "Do you want to see God's work?" The congregation, already sweaty from dancing, yelled back, "Yes, we do." At which point Pastor Aimé started to lecture, talking about how fervently Jacob had loved God. He then asked the assembled group, "Do you love God?" and they cheered back, "Yes, we do." He again began to lecture:

> Angels bring orders from God every day. There is an angel with you. A bodyguard. Jehovah's angel is the strongest bodyguard of all. He protects you. Do not be afraid, for an angel protects you. But the thing that blocks you, that makes you unable to fly to heaven, is your sins. Are you afraid? Is something troubling you? Today we are cutting off the devil's head. Your illness will leave you. Your problems will leave you.

Figure 7.2. Pastor Aimé, Pastor Fanja, and their baby.

In this sermon, as in many others, the pastor likens the things that harm women and cause suffering to the devil in his many incarnations. But Jehovah's angels protect the faithful. For many women who don't have enough money, who feel frustrated trying to forge rewarding relationships with their husbands, and who are beset by jealous neighbors and consumed by their desire to succeed, the promise of such protection is compelling indeed.

Many of the pastors who live in Tamatave make a living through tithing by their congregations. Through their pastoral work they become well acquainted with the intimate problems that beset Tamatavians. At times they explicitly speak to the problems women experience within their households, and they advise women and men how to behave. One sermon at the Rhema (Revelation) church was devoted entirely to marriage, and the pastor began with the tensions created when in-laws exert too much power within the household. But her focus quickly shifted, and she began to lecture men not to wander and women to work harder at keeping their husbands' attentions:

> The household is about bending to each other, and honoring each other. No
> matter what problems you face, do not give up your spouse. My brothers, no
> matter how sweet a woman's perfume is outside your house, even if those girls

outside your house are really lovely, let them not seduce you, because your wife is much better than that. Love your spouse with your whole heart. For those women who raise children, may you keep your children clean. Because if your *lamba* [wrap] is soaked with kid's piss and you do not change it, your husband will grow tired of you.

Although this pastor lectured the women as much as the men, in many other cases pastors offered direct encouragement to women in difficult situations. Pastor Aimé remarked one Sunday, "We are Christians who will always walk forward. We cannot but do battle. Even if your front teeth are all broken by the punches your husband gives you because he doesn't want you to pray, that doesn't matter, because you'll get new [false] teeth once you get money. The wisdom of God and the love of God are not bought with money." Here too the pastor likens the woman fighting with her husband, or struggling within her community, to a Christian soldier doing battle with the devil. He reminds his flock that no matter what obstacles they face, they must persevere in their faith. But he subtly implies that faith can produce money. The love of God may not be purchased, but he also implies the opposite, that faith can, in fact, bring wealth as a form of blessing.

The Appeal of Emotional Practice:
Singing, Dancing, and Speaking in Tongues

"Pentecostalism is a religion of emotion" (Hurbon 2001, 134). Whereas the pastors' sermons teach women to encounter the world around them by pursuing righteousness and overcoming the many obstacles in their paths, practices like communicating directly with Jesus, speaking in tongues, or performing exorcisms articulate with and enhance local conceptions of women as more emotional beings. It also gives this otherwise denigrated capacity—which in traditional contexts makes them spiritually more dependent on men—a positive valence. There is an ecstatic, emotional quality to Pentecostal services that makes them seem especially appropriate for women as they are locally perceived.

Religious services include extensive singing, dancing, testifying, and being filled by the Holy Spirit.[8] The Power of Faith church, for example, was a large temporary structure, palm-roofed and traditional, that the pastor and his wife had managed to erect on borrowed land. The young women's dance troupe, led by the pastor's wife, occupied the first half of services. The girls all wore skirts below the knee, with white blouses, and wore plastic bags cut into ruffles around their wrists to accentuate their hand movements. The song was a praise song that repeated the words, "It is pleasing to go with Jesus because he gives you miracles."

At other churches, like the Rhema or Pentekotista Afaka (Pentecostals Saved), services focus more on the blessings of the Holy Spirit and on speaking in tongues. Mamy, a middle-aged woman, explained,

> We in the Rhema, we believe in the blessings of the Holy Spirit. There are some revival churches that don't use that too much, but we do. If you pray on your own, then you may receive your own strength from God. That is a rhema (revelation). When you really pray well, you may start speaking in another language—maybe in English or French—but I don't know English or French! Maybe I'll speak in Hindi or Japanese or Chinese! That can really happen. When you are very close to God and then you pray, then the power of God comes down to you. Then people start to speak in tongues. It isn't everyone who does that, but only some. When the power comes down, you feel him coming into your body. When his strength works in you, then you speak prophecies.[9]

These practices foster an emotionalism found in many other Pentecostal contexts.

Tamatavian Pentecostals' emphasis on teaching women to manage anger appears to be a local elaboration of this more general tendency. As I have suggested, women not only are perceived to be more emotional beings. They are specifically said to be less capable of controlling their anger. And anger, combined with humiliation and hurt pride, is part of what motivates people to turn away from old social connections and seek new ones. Pentecostalism articulates with this dynamic by teaching women to cast out anger and cultivate the Christian virtue of turning the other cheek. Pastor Aimé exhorted his flock one Sunday, "Do not let the setting sun see your anger tonight." At the same time, rather than seeing anger as a sign of weakness that makes women unfit for the religious domain, Pentecostalism associates anger with the devil. Pentecostal rites and beliefs encourage this association by portraying anger and other negative feelings as the devil's ruse to provoke Christians to bad behavior. Many services also include exorcisms, in which women lay hands on the sick and forcibly "drive out the devil." In these rituals, women mobilize negative emotions they may well feel toward some people around them and channel them in a holy battle with Lucifer.

Connecting Church Lessons to Daily Life

As they are drawn into the pastor's sermons and spend time at church, women learn to see both the miracles wrought by God and the temptations of the devil in the minutiae of their daily lives. It is difficult to overemphasize how much time members of the same congregation spend together and helping each other. Over the course of my fieldwork, I quickly discovered that the best place to find my informants was not at their homes but at church or at each other's houses. They visit one another constantly. They also go on evangelizing trips together. Over time, congregants take what they learn in church and bring it into their homes in many informal domains—for example, prayer groups at friends' houses or reading the Bible at home. Two practices in particular connect people's everyday experience to the narratives they learn in church: being tested by God (*fitsapana*) and bearing witness (*manao vavolombelona*).

In the first case, a woman experiences things in her life that she interprets as God's testing her faith. Voanghy, a young woman who was a fervent member of the Assembly of God church, recounted a recent test:

A fitsapana that happened to me was this. I went to our kin's house, and I hadn't seen them in a very long time. My uncle was very happy to see me, and he gave me food to eat and drink. But there was blood in that food, and at the church we don't eat blood. But my uncle, he'd gone to so much trouble, and it was really difficult not to eat. But if I ate that blood, it was a kind of test that God was giving me. "You say you serve me, but I'll give you this [forbidden food], so will you eat it or not?" But I didn't think about God. I just kept thinking about how my uncle was trying to care for me, so I decided to taste a little bit. When I got home, I was terribly weak. And they called the pastor and almost called a doctor, but I wouldn't let them. And the pastor said, "What has happened?" And I said, "I don't know." And the pastor said, "Is there something that you have done that does not accord with the will of God? Reflect on what you have done, because sickness does not come without reason." Though I could barely stand, I bent down and prayed. And a spirit came to me that said, "There is something that you ate that goes against the will of God. You promised not to eat it, yet you ate it. Why did you do that? Don't you know that I am God and that I am watching your character?" When I apologized, the sickness started to abate.

It is fitting that Voanghy's test had to do with her kin and tabooed food. After all, taboos—things the ancestors have forbidden their descendants to eat or do—are the way ancestors demand loyalty. Enacting them is a clear statement of family allegiance. Voanghy felt torn between the kindness shown by her unconverted kin and her desire to follow her faith. That she fell sick and was cured when she repented merely reinforced her faith and reminded her to whom she really belonged. It also enabled her to draw further connections between mundane things like eating food with blood in it and God's power.

Not only do pastors' sermons interweave biblical stories with allusions to people's concrete difficulties, but people bring their tribulations and triumphs back to church, where they publicly narrate them as proof of God's power. Bearing witness (*manao vavolombelona*) to the miracle of God's power is another practice that explicitly reinterprets daily happenings in light of the church's religious message. The classic testimony recounts a sick person's miraculous cure through prayer and God's blessing. But there are many ways that congregants see God working in the tiny details of their lives, such as finding money just when they have nothing to eat or getting a job when they are most desperate. Often, at the end of church services the pastor will call people to the front to tell their stories. One day at the end of services at the Power of Faith church, Fanja, a young woman in her twenties, walked up to the front when the pastor asked if anyone wanted to bear witness. Her narrative conveys a sense of what "bearing witness" is often like:

> When I didn't pray, nothing I did worked out. Often there was something I needed to buy, but when I'd get the money for it, I would just waste it on something with no meaning. I'd go to balls all the time and go with men. Often the kids at the balls were very badly behaved. I'd be angry all the time. But now God watches over my life. When I have a problem, I bend down to pray. Before, when I did not pray, I was always having accidents. On the twenty-third of June, I was hospitalized for six months. But since I've started to pray, cars come close, but they always miss me. I walk on the street, and there are often car accidents, but instead of hurting me they hurt other people.

When Fanja told the congregation how God protected her, everyone clapped in delight, confirming her experience.

Performing a New Self: Clothing, Social Relations and Suffering

Women's time in the church, and their growing social world focused on fellow congregants, brings them to a different conception of the relationship between God and humans, and of material wealth and personal value, than the one that pervades secular Tamatavian daily life. Although the prosperity gospel is important, especially at first, another prominent strand of Pentecostalism holding "blessed are the meek, for they shall inherit the earth" mitigates these ideas. Women may start by treating Jesus like an ancestor, but over time they learn that God's greatness suffuses all experiences. They learn to apply the lessons they learn in church to their own lives. The Pentecostal social and religious world they participate in is slowly internalized and becomes part of their sense of self.

Not surprisingly given the importance of clothing in both the creation and expression of social relations in Tamatave, clothing also plays a prominent role in how Pentecostals express the new self they say they have acquired.[10] Jeanette said one of her first observations about the new church had to do with the different role of clothing. Recounting her first visit to Pentekotista Afaka, she remarked, "It wasn't like the church I was used to [the Catholic Church], where everyone was just looking at your clothes and shoes and checking out whether you had blown your hair dry. Rather, I could see they were all speaking to Jesus privately." Jeanette said her conversion and commitment to Pentecostal ideals led to a different relationship with clothes. "My mind was calm, and I no longer liked profane things. When I got dressed in front of the mirror, and put on worldly clothes, I would hear a voice speaking to me, 'Take those off, they are terrible!'—the profane clothes I liked, they were shorts, because I was a real tomboy!" Mamy made a similar observation when she recounted how she had come to realize that wearing her beloved pants was wrong:

> When I first started praying, I wore velvet pants to go out. Because I really loved those pants! One day I went out and the pastor caught me wearing them. I thought he was going to scold me. But it wasn't for that reason he called me over, but to encourage me to pray more frequently. Eventually it was my own thoughts that made me realize I shouldn't wear those pants. When I put them on, a voice came into my head saying, "Take off those pants." I said to myself, I shall sell these pants, for they are bringing shame on me."

For Mamy and Jeanette, the new relationship with fashionable clothing, the commodity that most clearly embodies the entanglements of everyday sociality in Tamatave, becomes iconic of their rejection of old ways and old relationships and the creation of a new self.

By ennobling sacrifice and promoting the practice of endurance, women's experience in the church also transforms their experience of suffering. It gives them new scripts for interpreting otherwise painful interactions with their husbands.[11] Take, for example, Jeanette, who constantly fought with her husband, who did not approve of her participation in church. He saw it as insubordination to his authority and constantly chastised her for it. Rather than concede to her husband's demands, Jeanette interpreted everything that happened to her as part of her private conversation with Jesus. When her husband threatened to burn her clothes if she kept going to church, he accidentally burned his own clothes—a mistake she read as a miraculous sign of Jesus's loyalty to her. When they fought and she was able to master her anger and turn the other cheek, she thanked Jesus for giving her inner peace. When he used Malagasy medicine to drive her back to the Catholic Church, she dreamed that the devil spoke to her and said, "Stop talking to Jesus all the time." But she soon learned how to drive out the devil in the name of Jesus. At one point she told me she even started sleeping in the living room, a subtle way to say she refused to have sex with her husband. When I asked whether she ever thought of leaving her husband, she replied, "No, it isn't in my thoughts to leave him, because God doesn't appreciate when you abandon your spouse except for death. But I beg Jesus to help show him that I am his alone."

Pirette, who was fifty and the mother of four children, offers a related example. Her husband was a policeman who treated her violently and took many lovers, cutting her off from the networks of exchange and fitiavana in which she wanted to be embedded. His actions eventually drove her to seek solace in the church. Over time she became increasingly engaged. At first she hid her religious commitment from her husband. Rather than preaching the gospel to him, she showed her proper wifeliness by caring for him despite his drunken rage, as pastors frequently advise. Eventually she revealed her conversion. He took the news well, asking only that she limit her time at church, since she had a household to attend to, and not preach in public, which offended his masculine pride, since it implied he could not keep his wife "in the house." Eventually Pirette found she could not curtail her religious activities: her love of Jesus and her desire to accompany her fellow churchgoers on evangelizing missions overrode her desire to obey her husband. She concluded by remarking that in any case he was not totally reformed: "Sometimes he's well behaved, sometimes he's naughty." Both Jeanette and Pirette's involvement in the church meant that their husbands' behavior no longer affected them in the same way. Jeanette interpreted her suffering as a part of a private conversation with Jesus, while Pirette blamed her husband's behavior on the devil and saw it as a way to test her faith. Revaluing suffering, promoting the practice of endurance, confirming their belief in the righteousness of their actions, and providing a sympathetic audience for their continued faith are all Pentecostal contributions to Pirette's and Jeanette's new experience of their husbands.

Yet despite these women's expressions of transformation, it is also true that from the observer's point of view, they need to prove that they really have transformed. After all, since Jesus died for people's sins, Pentecostals must consistently repent and live in a godly way; there is no formal proof of absolution. Consequently, women's personal relationship with Jesus is never as completely free of the surrounding context as Pentecostal doctrine implies. Rather, congregants rely on the image of sin—and here jeunes with their sinful, métis practices figure prominently—to build their Christian self. Given how central the exchange of resources and the competitive dynamics of humiliation are to social life in Tamatave, and that these relations always carry an ambivalent valence, it is fitting that relations with non-Christian kin, neighbors, and commodities are important for constructing a Christian identity. Some of the same interactions and modes of creating value that propel women into these churches in the first place are now drawn into producing a new Pentecostal person.

In their daily lives women often use their negotiation of relationships with unconverted kin to simultaneously produce and express this sense of inner transformation. Women in Tamatave did not convert to Pentecostalism to repudiate their kin's demands for financial support (Meyer 1999) or to avoid witchcraft accusations, so that they could accumulate more wealth (Bornstein 2003). To the contrary, most converts explicitly tried to maintain their relationships with their kin while honoring their religious commitments, a tension made explicit in Voanghy's narrative, where she recounts how God punishes her for eating her uncle's food.[12] Pentecostals' efforts to maintain relationships with kin are due partly to their precarious economic circumstances: someday they may have to turn to them for support. But it is not only a practical matter. While Pentecostalism is often thought to be different from other forms of Protestantism because of an increased emphasis on the supernatural (Meyer 1999), what is striking in Tamatave is the emphasis on moral uprightness and visibility (see also Austin-Broos 1997; Robbins 2004b). Women converts use their relations with kin and neighbors to demonstrate what it means to be a good Christian.

By self-consciously discussing their actions as Christians, in contrast to their "worldly" kin, Pentecostals produce the very experience of themselves as different that they claim to already have. When I asked about her relations with her kin, Maman'i Lala explained,

We cannot separate from them, but we must convince them that what we have done [in giving up ancestors and rejecting Catholicism] is right. And so we pray that God may change their hearts of stone, and that their hearts, which depend on the worship of idols, may change. We model good behavior for them. And when there is a meeting of the family we try to convince them to pray. If there is a disagreement we say, "We need to love each other for that is what God asks of us." That is what we teach our family little by little.

Despite her family's anger at her conversion and her abandonment of ancestral practice, Maman'i Lala never broke relations with her kin. Nor did she snub them. Rather, she kept trying to convince them she was right by modeling Christian behavior. Their intransigence enabled her to occupy the moral high ground. She established her Christian selfhood by continuing to be kind despite their anger.

By interpreting certain interactions with kin or neighbors as the devil's temptations, women further avoid the competitive dynamics of Tamtavian social life. Mamy told me, "Before, I didn't get along with people, and I loved to fight! I didn't know how to bend or give in, for I didn't have a joyful heart near to God." Mamy went on to explain that she had succeeded in calming herself the day before: "Yesterday there was someone we sold clothing to. They were mad at me for something that had no meaning. They wanted to fight me. But I said, 'I will not fight you.' And I went away. The devil knows well that I really loved to fight before, and he often tempts me, but because of the prayers I have done, the devil will not get me." For women who are not involved in Pentecostal practice, such altercations are likely to lead to the competitive interactions that drive younger women to seek vazaha or other options. For Mamy, however, the interaction became an occasion when she could reestablish her new Christian sense of self by turning the other cheek. As long as they remain committed to Pentecostalism, Jeanette, Mamy, Pirette and others like them have opted out of the competitive dynamics that help make history in Tamatave.

New Opportunities

Jeanette, Mamy, and Pirette not only disembedded themselves from old relationships but also embraced new ones. When women spend more time with their fellow congregants, church membership reorganizes kinship to create a new family of believers. Although sometimes people drop out of the church because of family or other kinds of pressures, when they do remain committed, they are slowly pulled away from their communities. Over time they form a community of religious adherents that stands apart. They are welcomed into a network of believers who help and support them.

Women often find that the church offers new activities that they enjoy and that make them feel valued. When women speak prophecies, they sometimes become informal healers. And I have already described Pastor Fanja, the female pastor at the Power of Faith church, who had a central role in leading church functions. Many younger women in the church told me they wanted to become pastors. Some excelled at preaching. Olivina, Maman'i Olivina's daughter, said, "I want to be an evangelist so I can go out and move about. As the Bible says, 'A prophet is never listened to in his own land.' But when I go far way sometimes with the church, I feel very powerful because I preach to people I don't know." Olivina's desire to "move about" is particularly striking given the middle-class expectation that women should stay close to home (and that those who move about are morally suspect). For these women, the church offers both an alternative model and an alternative set of ways to build a positive sense of self. Their sense of valued personhood no longer comes from dispensing resources within a network of kin or showing off to neighbors. Rather, they reorient such motives toward a group of believers and arguably a new kin group.

Inversions: The Dialectics of Social Goals and New Meanings

All too often, anthropology resists taking religious matters seriously. Nowhere is this tendency more visible than in the study of Christianity. As Fenella Cannell notes in a volume on that topic, "Religious phenomena . . . may be described in detail, but must be explained on the basis that they have no foundation in reality, but are epiphenomena of 'real' underlying sociological, political, economic or other material causes" (Cannell 2006, 3). The alternative is to examine the adoption of Christian practice as a compelling and coherent cultural system in its own right. By examining how people draw on new religious frameworks to fulfill existing social needs, the first approach tends to emphasize continuity with existing cultural and material concerns (Sundkler 1961 [1948]). The second foregrounds rupture, analyzing the worldview that emerges as people are drawn into a new discursive system (Robbins 2004b; Marshall 2009; Keller 2005).

The way that Pentecostalism provides Tamatavian women a different path to the future from that offered by the secular economic striving that pervades so much of life in Tamatave complicates these oppositions. Women enter the church with practical goals and aspirations, aspirations that are largely continuous with those of the jeunes and their other non-Pentecostal peers.

Pentecostalism appeals to them because it appears to offer them money, revenge, social respect, and control over their own lives when their more traditional involvement in local kinship and sexual economies, and their participation in the older Catholic and Protestant churches, has failed.

Conversion, however, is not the same as commitment (Keller 2005). Women may enter the church with instrumental goals, but not all women find what they want, and many drop out. When women do stay in the church, it is because they have been drawn into new ways of interpreting their place in the social world that reconfigure the competitive dynamics of Tamatavian daily life and retool the instruments they use to achieve satisfactory personhood. Women's participation starts as a serendipitous convergence between certain aspects of Pentecostal ideology, local conceptions of women, and women's desire to pursue traditional goals. This convergence, however, does not result in syncretic forms of religious practice. Rather, as Pentecostalism inserts itself into Tamatavian social life, it intervenes in the competitive interactions that create historical change from below, producing new conceptions of personhood and new religious communities.

Women do not gain new paths to the future simply because they suddenly obtain wealth or find social support in new communities. Nor do they transform themselves through the wholesale adoption of a new perspective, as if old glasses were pulled off and new ones put on. Rather, there is a dialectical interplay between the problems that these women face and their use of Pentecostalism as a way to solve them. As a result, the problems that women encounter and the solutions Pentecostal practice offers become incorporated into a new worldview. This new perspective on social life is created in part because participation in Pentecostalism changes the valence and meaning of key elements of their prior ways of interpreting both themselves and their social worlds. It produces another form of disembedding, one that amplifies that which occurs when people leave the countryside and settle permanently in Tamatave.

Many transformations occur that attest to this complex dialectic between social goals and new meanings when people convert and become committed to the church. A woman may solve the problem of attaining money to buy fashionable clothes by reinterpreting the significance of clothing and the ethical burdens that attend seeking it through transactional sex. Sexy or fashionable clothes now indicate moral weakness, while modest clothes signal not poverty and lack of connection, but moral strength. The meaning of fashionable, expensive clothes trades places with that of simple, modest ones; they are inverted.

The same process of inversion takes place with respect to a complex of related cultural practices. Instead of interpreting their emotionality as a sign of weakness that can harm others, women can value it as a quality that enables them to achieve a special connection to God. Instead of asserting her power and self-worth by starting a public fight with the husband who returns home drunk, a woman can demonstrate her virtue by caring for him. (In so doing, she may even create new opportunities to change his behavior.) Instead of being consumed by the sentiment of malahelo when their kin reject them for being poor or for having converted, women can demonstrate moral superiority and find affirmation from a community of like-minded peers by continuing to be kindly to the very kin who turned them away.

It is not enough, then, to look only at how emergent generations like those epitomized by jeunes create change. By examining the dialectics of inversion that take place in Pentecostal churches we can see how the futures offered by salvation and those conjured up by jeunes become important conditions of each other's possibility. Together they bring new life paths and new futures into being.

EIGHT

How the Future Comes into the Present

Events often crystallize and make visible processes that have long been under way. I started working in Madagascar in the early 1990s, just as the country was adjusting after the fall of the Soviet Union. The failure of the socialist government to deliver on its promise of economic prosperity had produced massive unemployment and strikes in the cities, forcing President Didier Ratsiraka to accept elections. By 1993, and increasingly over the ensuing decade, Madagascar's government embraced free-market economic liberalization and reform.

When I returned for a second round of fieldwork in 2000, I quickly found myself fascinated by the emergence of a new, widely recognized kind of young people—jeunes—who had emerged on the urban scene. Little did I imagine, even a few months before writing this culminating chapter, that by 2009 a strikingly typical member of this popularly recognized category would claim political leadership of Madagascar and, with the backing of the army, reject the political and moral authority of the generation that preceded him.

The facts are these: Andry Rajoelina, the former mayor of Antananarivo and the leader of the political opposition to President Marc Ravalomanana, declared himself president of Madagascar on March 13, 2009. His announcement followed two months of street protests in which some one hundred people died. Though tensions had emerged between Rajoelina and his rival some months earlier, the climax came when his supporters marched on the presidential palace demanding that Ravalomanana relinquish power. At President Ravalomanana's orders the army fired on the crowd. Some thirty protesters were killed, and many others were injured. The army then mutinied, throwing its support behind Rajoelina. In a subsequent civilian march, the opposition seized the presidential palace and the

Figure 8.1. Before his bid for the presidency, Andry Rajoelina owned radio station VIVA.

central bank. Ravalomanana stepped down, ceding power to the military. Andry Rajoelina declared himself president; the high court ratified his status as the "president of the transition process," even though he was six years too young to become president according to the Malagasy constitution.

Protests from the international community and Ravalomanana's supporters notwithstanding, Rajoelina continued to act as president. In August of 2009, leaders from the different political parties—not only Rajoelina and Ravalomanana, but also former presidents Ratsiraka and Zafy Albert—met to work out a power-sharing agreement between the different factions. Rajoelina refused to honor the agreement. Under continued pressure from the international community, however, Rajoelina has, at least as of January 2010, agreed to organize new elections and begin a transition process. Still, it remains to be seen what the future will bring.

Although Rajoelina's youth is notable, most relevant to my story is the way he exemplifies many aspects of the social category of jeunes, though he can claim more economic and social capital than many would-be jeunes in Tamatave. Rajoelina comes from a middle-class family; his father fought for the French army in Algeria. Though his family had the means to pay for college, Rajoelina nevertheless quit school after receiving his baccalaureate (the diploma awarded at the end of high school in the French system). Like those jeunes I described in chapter 5 as cynical about the ability of schooling to guarantee a future, Rajoelina was intent on social ascent through business, not schooling. Throughout the 1990s, he had worked as a disc jockey in the bars and clubs of Antananarivo, "animating," as one says in French, gatherings for other jeunes in the capital. He built up a printing and poster company, then diversified, opening his own radio station, VIVA. He was clearly a master of the hip new media that exploded in Madagascar with the growth of computers and telecommunications in the 1990s.

It is also notable that Rajoelina's desire to copy and then usurp Marc

Ravalomanana long predated the events of 2009. In 1999 a prominent business magazine named Ravalomanana "manager of the year." Then in 2000 it chose Rajoelina. Two years later, when Ravalomanana won the presidential elections, Rajoelina took note. He started keeping company with Ravalomanana's daughter. He said in an interview with *Le Monde* that he "made Marc Ravalomanana his model" (lasa maodely) (Rémy 2009).

Though he may not have been born into the political establishment, Rajoelina cleverly used the connections he made in business to forge relationships with the capital's political elite (Galibert 2009). He also founded his own opposition party called the Tanora Malagasy Vonona—"Determined Malagasy Youth"—which was widely dubbed the TGV (Train à Grande Vitesse), echoing the name of the French high-speed train (his nickname is Andry TGV, and political jokes about the "train pulling into the station" or "trains going off rails" abound). For a diverse array of actors, not all of whom are ideologically aligned with him, this jeune offered a "fast train" to the future.

Andry Rajoelina's story exemplifies how attainment of adulthood in new socioeconomic conditions, and the emergence of groups like jeunes, can change the course of history, extending beyond private lives and contributing to shifts in public culture. Indeed, his story can be understood as a more widespread "jeunification" in which many of the skills, practices, and assumptions about everyday interactions that jeunes helped popularize quickly enabled a jeune to intervene in national politics. But it also shows how even when a new generation accedes to political power, it never achieves total rupture with the past. The fact that all of the former presidents of Madagascar participated in the Maputo accords, and that Rajoelina has incorporated people from earlier opposition movements into his government, reveals just how partial this process really is.

Not just a jeune, but also evangelical groups, played a role. Although one might expect the women who belong to these churches to oppose someone like Rajoelina, given the opposition between jeunes and Pentecostals depicted here, it is also clear that the strategic political alliances formed in moments of political upheaval transcend these quotidian oppositions. During his seizure of the presidential palace a group of *mpiandry*—evangelical Christians healers who specialize in driving out the devil and laying on of hands—publicly searched for evidence that Ravalomanana had been using secret "medicines," the very kind of magicoreligious practice that Pentecostals associate with the devil.[1] That exorcists went to seek out medicines in the first place, and that their findings were so widely publicized, is a practice that likely began under Ravalomanana, whose own ascension to power, only a few years earlier, had also featured his Christian supporters. Nevertheless, it suggests how profoundly some aspects of evangelical Christianity, which came to prominence as part of the same sociocultural processes that produced jeunes, have penetrated national political culture over the past decade. Not only a jeune but also many who participate in the new evangelical churches have become visible on the national stage.[2]

Reexamining the Role of Generations in Historical Change

If Andry Rajoelina's rise to power illustrates the role of jeunes, lasa maodely, and the complementary rise of evangelicalism, it is also true that particular cases foreground some aspects of the way generational change enters into broader social and cultural transformation while backgrounding others. To highlight the more general lessons to be learned from this ethnography, I pause to consider how my analysis of women's efforts to achieve the future in eastern Madagascar contributes to these broader concerns. One of my goals throughout this book has been to theorize generational change in a way that does not rely on the language of crisis, rupture, and lost generations so common in academic and popular accounts. As I argued earlier, the language of crisis tends to homogenize an otherwise heterogeneous social landscape, as if all social groups experienced social, economic, and political change in the same way. Such an overgeneral rhetoric obscures more than it reveals about the processes by which new patterns emerge.

When we try to examine these processes in people's daily lives in an old port town on the shores of the Indian Ocean, where people have centuries of experience integrating themselves into far-flung global networks, we can begin to see change less in terms of loss and replacement, the images that dominate so much writing about young people on the global periphery, and more in terms of historically contingent moments of synergy as new practices meet, merge with, and are transformed by older ones. This sequence is partly captured by studies of culture and history. Sahlins's examination of what happened when the Hawaiian women paddled out to meet Captain Cook and his crew, with its emphasis on how people apply their old beliefs to novel situations, thus transforming their ideas, helps illuminate young Malagasy women's rush to find vazaha and shows some of the likely consequences. Sewell's insistence that any cultural context includes multiple structures that are only loosely articulated so that cultural schemas can never fully explain how and why something becomes a resource at a given moment, direct our attention to the global economic and political factors that make vazaha figure as a resource at this particular time. And Mannheim's insight that generational emergence is loosely analogous to what happens when people from different cultures come into contact allowed me to see the often ahistorical field of youth studies in more historical and processual terms. His concept of fresh contact revealed parallels between young people's achieving adulthood and cultural encounters where I might not have seen them.

Yet when we move away from Mannheim's speculative essay and from the historical material used by Sahlins and Sewell to focus on how living young people seeking to create their futures draw from the past to confront constraints in the present, we gain an added perspective on these matters. Above all, what we get in addition is Tamatavians' ideas, *their* representations of change as well as an experience-near view of their agency in making change happen. My argument for a representation-mediated approach to generational change, one that attends to the work of the imagination in shaping how the future comes into the present, flows from the observation that Tamatavians' ideas about change shape change, if not always in the ways they anticipate. East coast Madagascar is not the only place where people "see," "desire," and "copy" one another as a means of forging their futures, though local Malagasy ideas make this aspect of social change particularly apparent. But an experience-near view of these forces at work provides insight into how jeunes' and Pentecostals' motives, conflicts, and desires for the future converge with contemporary social and economic circumstances as well as with new practices coming from beyond Madagascar to propel change. What I refer to as disembedding, the interconnected processes entailed by lasa maodely, and the intensification of change that occurs at moments of historical convergence all make important contributions to understanding the complex dynamics at work.

Disembedding

Following my informants through the sand paths, bars, and Internet cafés of Tamatave and watching young women try to build viable lives in the sexual economy, or accompanying women when they join Pentecostal churches, reveals the importance of disembedding—the way actors are drawn out of older practices and become amenable to new ones. By offering some possibilities and prohibiting others, a particular practice shapes those who engage in it. I use the term disembedding to examine how, over time, people become alienated from particular social contexts or life worlds, coming to feel that those old ways of organizing social life are less compelling or promising, a development akin to deterritorializing. When anthropologists or sociologists write about "acculturation" they show that people move across cultural boundaries, but they do not reveal much about how people let go of discrete skills, orientations, and dispositions and adopt new ones. As we have seen, people must cut their sense of obligation to some people if they are to make themselves available to others—by returning home to an ancestral village less frequently, by sending cash instead of attending a ceremony, and perhaps by coming to believe that a particular ceremony is a waste of money.

My aim here has been to draw attention to the social processes that propel people in and out of the contexts that shape, subject, and produce in them particular kinds of commitments.[3] Malagasy life makes disembedding particularly apparent because of the enormous importance given to ancestors rooted in particular parcels of land. In such circumstances, disembedding is a particularly evocative image. Making people movable—propelling them outside local, geographically constrained networks and making them available to new practices—is a necessary precursor to the emergence of any social formation.

Disembedding has long been a feature of the practices and assumptions that have shaped the life course along the east coast, and it takes place in other parts of Madagascar and Africa as well (see Austen 1999; Bloch 1999; Feeley-Harnik 1991; Graeber 1995). Recall that along the east coast, young people are supposed to leave their rural ancestral villages and "seek" their fortunes. Sometimes people find their fortunes just a few kilometers from where they grew up, as when a young man goes out to cultivate a piece of fallow land or a young woman marries a man from the next village. In these examples, young people take on new practices or make new connections, but they do so relatively locally, so that appropriating and adapting existing cultural practices entailed in becoming adult involves only tiny oscillations within an existing pattern. However, some east coasters long have moved to other parts of Madagascar to pursue a future far from home. The centrifugal tendency—the need to find the resources to "make oneself living" that propels young people out into the world—has long been matched by centripetal forces that pull people back to their homelands. Seeking blessing from one's ancestors, which traditionally could be done only by returning to an ancestral great house, is one example of how people are often forced to return to older circuits of relationships even when they move away. Yet as I have suggested, over time, sending money home rather than participating directly in a bone turning can make them less committed to kin relationships. Such abstracting can contribute to more radical disembedding, further exposing young people to new practices.

Lasa Maodely: Synoptic Illusions, Looping Effects

When people search for new options, they almost always have to take their tools from the cultural materials at hand. At the same time, the young women who search for vazaha infuse older categories for interpreting women's relationships with men with new associations and meanings. When women use Web sites to find vazaha or seek them out in the new clubs, when they rely on the Internet or television to learn new styles that will attract European men, they change the nature of courting and romantic relationships, infusing the traditional courting practices with the style and know-how associated with being jeunes. They recombine existing categories and practices in new ways or enact them in new contexts, creating new associations and producing new models.

The jeunes who embody a new way of being young that is explicitly associated with new media and technologies brought by recent globalization, as well as the women who build enduring relationships with vazaha, become what Tamatavians call "maodely"—achieving ways of succeeding in the world that others aspire to and copy. Though the experiences recounted in earlier chapters have relied for the most part on women's perspectives, and though contemporary Tamatavians emphasize the role of young women in their imaginings of cultural change, the basic principles also apply to men: recall that Andry Rajoelina saw how Marc Ravalomanana had used his business as a stepping-stone to political power, and "he became my model."

The people who produce these models, however, are but a minority of all the young people who live in Tamatave or Antananarivo. Much as those who become iconic of jeunes simplify and condense a wide range of positions and interests among young people in Tamatave, so too the young women who are recognized as seeking vazaha represent a simplification of a complex social field. Neither stereotype of "youth" is representative of all young people. These social categories always stand as part to whole, while somehow seeming to exemplify the whole. Consequently, like all recognized categories of people, they simplify and distort lived experience.

But both by helping people to interpret changes in the world around them and by guiding their actions, this kind of representation, with its simplifying qualities, contributes to the spread of new information, fashions, and social networks. It is a crucial part of how the imagination of change shapes change in social life, contributing to a reflexive feedback loop between action and the image certain actors want to attain.[4] Though only a tiny fraction of women ever succeed in respectably marrying foreigners (although there are certainly more such marriages than in the recent past), this group of successful young women popularize the attempt, since others copy their model. There is nothing random about the growth and spread of these new models or practices, though to an outsider it might look that way. Rather, they spread through the thick sociality of life in the sand paths, where almost everyone lives in close quarters, everyone watches everyone else, and everyone wants to succeed. They spread when a young woman achieves a liaison with a vazaha, then brings her little sister to live with her and help out around the house. The sister then both learns how to behave and sees the advantages (or disadvantages) of such a relationship.

The strategies enacted by jeunes and taken up by the young women who pursue vazaha can be understood only in relation to the Pentecostal women who most vividly embody an alternative set of choices. In part this is because the process through which women come to adopt Pentecostalism shares many similarities with the changes embodied by jeunes. After all, when women who belong to Pentecostal churches evangelize and share their stories of suffering and salvation, they too become disembedded from older networks of social relations. When they succeed and find happiness, they too become models for others. And like the jeunes who pursue vazaha, by joining the church these women too draw on some very long-term strategies for achieving a modern identity in Tamatave. At the same time, by taking these other women into account, we can begin to see how the dialectical movement between image and action always takes place in a multitemporal field among actors of different generations: the popular representations of young people, and of young women in particular, are not simply a part of how jeunes think about themselves. They are also part of how some members of older cohorts try to differentiate themselves from their successors, further changing the social landscape in Tamatave.

Pentecostals use of jeunes as negative examples suggests that young people's back-and-forth behavior, in which they sometimes enter the church for a short time but do not ultimately commit, is not just about demographics. From the perspective of nonconverts, of course, the fluctuating commitment of youth who do join Pentecostal churches has more to do with their changing needs and desires than with their salvation. From a Christian perspective, however, this behavior reinforces the basic dynamic by which people get tempted away from God and return again and again. Jeunes are (unwittingly) part of the cultural logic of Pentecostal Christianity, which requires that there be sinners so they can be saved. However to partake of this logic, people have to see themselves as sinners in the first place. They require constant reminders of what sin is. Only by first recognizing themselves as sinners can they later constitute themselves as saved. Consequently, Christian discourse about sinners and the saved shapes and reinforces a constant movement from the sexual economy into the church and back. The representations of practices, and people's perceptions of change and how they talk about it, are always also part of how those practices work.

If we are to take seriously the idea that generational change requires imagination, we need to attend to how people's choices are always worked out in relation to others they see around them. Any group needs a foil against which to imagine its own choices and make them real. Jeunes and Pentecostals fulfill this mirroring function for each other. Even as we seek to illuminate the emergence of a new generation, and the way change becomes mediated in the lives of the young, we can understand the meanings of sex only in relation to salvation.

Convergence and Intensification

Disembedding and the emergence of new models occur constantly in daily life, but whether they gain enough momentum to create a broader shift in cultural practices depends on their convergence with wider social and economic circumstances. This convergence can in turn lead to intensification, a term I use here to refer primarily to an increase in concentration or force.

Though disembedding is partly enabled by long-standing east coast ways of orchestrating the life course, the encompassing relationships of the state and political economy always shape the degree to which "searching" makes available genuinely novel ways to "make oneself living" and entices young people to adopt them. Disembedding may lead people out of local settings, but it does not impose the new practices they adopt: there is no teleology built in. During certain moments of the colonial period, for example, at least some peasants managed to go to school and find jobs in the colonial administration that pulled them away from rural areas. Although this pattern might have led to a more radical disembedding, during the late socialist period, as the impoverished state retracted, some civil servants went back to farming to earn their livelihoods. Disembedding was still at work, but the lack of opportunities to propel people out of existing patterns made the change less striking.

Global political-economic relations and technology also powerfully combine to provide new models and to shape whether they are adopted and what their effects are. Jeunes popularize new styles of courting and romantic relationships, but the maodely of marrying a vazaha could not have spread as it has without significant changes in the global political economy. Especially important among these are the new modes of communication and transportation bringing more foreigners to Madagascar, at least for a time. The growth of the Internet and the spread of cell phones have also played an important role; in earlier times, young women would have had to rely on the cumbersome task of getting kin in France to help arrange such relationships. Now, if they have the stylistic and practical knowledge associated with jeunes, they can walk into an Internet café and seek such connections on their own. Likewise, when they do achieve such alliances, their boyfriends can call their cell phones directly, bypassing the watchful eyes of worried parents and jealous neighbors.

In this respect, the category of jeunes exemplifies the radical disembedding that can occur when the right circumstances converge. As a mobile, performative category that some roughly middle-class young urbanites adopt, jeunes emerged out of the confluence of a new cohort of young people "seeking" at the precise moment when older structures like schooling and access to government jobs failed, and images, commodities, technologies, and Europeans flooded into Tamatave. Even with such a convergence, jeunes' pursuit of vazaha does not create one sudden cultural transformation, as if a kaleidoscope was turned and the crystals suddenly fell into a new shape. Rather, there are a small series of oscillations in each person's gendered and generational relationships that can magnify and solidify or dwindle and disappear depending on wider circumstances.

The Affective Dimension

To consider how women move across the uneven terrain that leads from present to future is to take seriously local ideals of what it means to attain valued personhood and to recognize what a deeply passionate quest that is. By attending to quotidian concerns, I have sought to perceive, and give analytic weight to, the everyday hurts, slights, and exclusions that motivate people to carve out new paths as well as the exhilaration and hope inspired when others in difficult circumstances see them succeed. Other scholars have observed that affect—a term I use here to signal a network of emotions that is individual and yet central to public social life—provides a central dynamic force in constituting historical events.[5] My east coast ethnography makes it clear that emotions enter historical process long before they ever become visible in uprisings, revolutions, or elections. Neither love and anger nor the sharing and withholding of resources are topics to be analyzed after the real work of examining socioeconomic or political change is done. Rather, they are the mediums through which individuals participate in and contribute to these changes.

When a young woman is rejected by a man, or when she is mocked at the water pump because she does not have the latest shoes or a cell phone and then turns to the sexual economy for resources, it is never simply about wanting pretty things. Rather, "searching" is about what it means to be a particular kind of valued person. Exclusion, with the resulting anger and injured pride, on the one hand, and aspiration, desire, and pleasure on the other, produces the disembedding that has disconnected many Malagasy from particularistic networks and practices, making them available for integration into new networks or institutions. The sentiment of malahelo, the bitterness a young woman feels when she does not get the recognition she feels she deserves from those around her, motivates many to pursue new paths, seeking to be "considered." Hurt, anger, and the desire to exact revenge on Malagasy men who reject them, or who take more than one lover, are among the important proximate reasons young women pursue vazaha. Likewise, when older women decide they want to join the Pentecostal churches, it is more often than not because they feel hurt and rejected. They almost always enter the churches filled with a bitter sense of frustration that they have not gotten their due from social life. They may be at different points in their life courses, and they choose different paths, yet the complex of affective interactions that motivates their initial entry into new churches is much the same.

Affect is not just a part of disembedding; it is also crucial to why new models are adopted and how they spread. The simultaneous panic and excitement some Tamatavians feel as they see what they perceive to be new routes to the future, and assess their consequences, help create new possibilities. It is the intense desire to be "like others" or "to have what everybody has"—a phrase striving Tamatavians use to refer to "those who have," eliding the many who do not have—that makes them eager to adopt new models. These new models, and the people who use them to succeed, generate the excitement that makes talk about new practices—and knowledge about how to engage in them—spread, prompting people to hold a new vision of the future and reach out for it. Wounded pride, envy, and striving, as well as the desire to establish positive relationships characterized by reciprocal exchange, and the interpersonal dynamics of reaching out to—or turning away from—one's kin or neighbors, are a fundamental part of how changes happen.

The Work of Imagination and Generational Change

Precisely because so many people—Tamatavians and foreign scholars—privilege the moment when young people assume adult roles as a fulcrum between the reproduction of existing patterns and the adoption of new ones, new generations come to have a special force in social change. Like an actor filling up the stage, generations as an idea draws attention away from the many other types of change (personal, political, social, economic) that are always simultaneously at work and that in some ways enable it. Yet as I have sought to demonstrate, the emergence of a new generation of adult actors, with the kinds of change this makes possible, has much in common with the changes that occur when people move from the country to the city or adopt new practices later in life, like the women who convert to Pentecostalism. The way young people's steps toward adulthood transform social and cultural terrain is far more modest than it is usually considered. When the emergence of a new generation of adults does have a more lasting effect it is because it has contingently—serendipitously perhaps—converged with a number of social and economic factors in a particular time and place.

Despite how modest generational change usually is, scholars and local people themselves continue to give it enormous explanatory power. Perhaps for that very reason, generational change reveals with particular clarity how imagination features in social change more broadly. To be sure, my Tamatavian informants' concerns about sex and salvation are specific to their cultural and historical circumstances. My effort to analyze generational change while avoiding misleading models of crisis and rupture has led me to see it as fundamentally created by the ways people imagine the future and seek to attain it in their daily lives. It also sheds light on some common ways that actors, trying to bring the future into the present, create new patterns elsewhere. Any ethnographic analysis of change should use terms that give meaning to the actions of local actors. But it should also attend to the persistent tensions and interplay between the worlds we imagine and those we create.

NOTES

CHAPTER ONE

1. I borrow the term "experience-near" from Geertz 1983.

2. For an account of European conceptions of time in the context of modernity, see Koselleck 1985. For an account of time and the French Revolution, see Baker 1990. Donham (1999) examines time, narrative, and revolution in an African context. Finally, for classic psychological and sociological analyses of the role of youth in change in the American context, see Erikson 1968 and Parsons 1961.

3. Empirically, young people appear to be the most visible partakers in many symbols of globalization—whether as consumers of commodities or as users of the Internet (Cole and Durham 2008a, 2008b; Fass 2007). Journalistic or popular accounts tend to take this visible consumer youth culture in non-Western locations as evidence of globalization. Commenting on this tendency within popular accounts, anthropologist Ritty Lukose argues (2005, 915), "Youth is seen as a consuming group, the first to bend to what is understood to be the homogenizing pressures of globalization." Scholarly work on the topic has been more nuanced than implied by the popular narrative of global capitalism steamrollering the rest of the world (Lukose 2005, 2009; Mains 2007; Weiss 2009). Nevertheless, the reliance on the concept of youth culture in studies of youth and globalization suggests that the increased movement of new media, commodities, and images has created a global youth culture that strengthens certain cultural tendencies in the West while disrupting cultural processes in the rest (Maira and Soep 2005). It thereby reinforces ideas of rupture.

   Essentially, the idea of youth culture refers to a bounded subgroup within a society that has its own logic and rules (Hall and Jefferson 2000 [1975]; Hebdige 2000 [1975]). Analyses that use the concept of youth culture rarely attend to diachronic processes. But when scholars use the concept in non-Western contexts, they often inadvertently smuggle in assumptions about history. They especially tend to imply that the adoption of global youth culture creates change among the very group on whom social reproduction is thought to depend. For example, in his analysis of youth culture in Kathmandu, Mark Liechty (2003, 233) argues that stories derived from global youth culture "implicitly undermine local narratives of value and meaning kept in cultural circulation by members of earlier generations, rendering them less and less likely to maintain the narrative momentum needed to carry these Nepali cultural practices from the past into the everyday lives of young people in the present." Likewise, Alice Schlegel (2000, 86), though careful to point out that the global spread of adolescent youth culture does not *necessarily* lead to replacement of older forms by new ones, nevertheless emphasizes that it does tend to increase reliance on commercial products as opposed to homemade ones, potentially undermining local creative production. Such dislocation appears likely to occur in postcolonial contexts where a particular social group devalues its "own" way of life in comparison with that of the former metropole, making new, globally marked practices particularly appealing.

4. Another variation on this argument emphasizes the growing tension between generations. One volume suggests that owing to "rapid processes of change related to colonialism, modernization, social upheaval and disturbed demographic trends such as runaway population growth, this phenomenon [of generational tension] has assumed crisis proportions, fundamentally different from those in the past" (Abbink 2005, 11).

5. For counter examples, see Straker 2007 and Perry 2009. Both emphasize, in different ways, that despite economic hardship, many young people in Africa do in fact continue to be embedded in existing intergenerational relationships and have many of the same concerns as previous generations. While I generally agree with their perspective, here I want to draw attention to the way youth's discourse of crisis becomes entangled with scholarly analyses of the topic.

6. Whether referring to individual growth over time or social-historical change over time, stage theories share a number of assumptions. These assumptions include the idea that stages are ordered in a clear progression, that all societies and all individuals go through them, and that the stages are coherent in the sense that all people in a particular stage share key characteristics (for some classic accounts with respect to the life course, see Flavell 1971, cited in Cole and Cole 1989, 8; Fortes 1984; Grimes 2000; and LeVine and LeVine 1966). For a recent critique, see Johnson-Hanks 2002. For a classic account of how the life course intersects with historical events, see Elder 1999.

7. Take, for example, the emergence of particular cognitive capacities in children. In his analysis of children's cognitive development, the psychologist Jean Piaget (1977) argued that four-year-old-children are supposed to reason magically and egocentrically. Yet much subsequent research has shown that when it comes to matters that are familiar to them, or when the problem is presented as part of play, four-year-olds also reason in what appears to be a more adult way. The ability to reason in a particular way is not uniform across contexts, implying more variability than a stage theory of cognitive development would allow (LCHC 1983).

8. These arguments for heterogeneous and contextually sensitive patterns in the unfolding of the life course resonate with Deborah Durham's (2004) argument that the category of "youth" operates as a social shifter. "Shifter" is a term used by linguists to indicate the part of speech that simultaneously stands independent of usage and can be understood only in the particular context of an utterance (Gal and Kligman 2000). Thinking about youth as a social shifter avoids homogenizing the category by calling attention to the pragmatics of particular utterances and how the invocation of youth in a particular context contributes to the constitution of the category of youth itself.

9. See, for example, Cooper 2005; Rosenwein 2006; Sewell 2005; Walley 2004; Zemon-Davis 1983.

10. Where Sahlins emphasizes how individuals' pursuit of traditional goals under changed circumstances leads to a slow transformation in the way cultural categories

are positioned with respect to one another, Joel Robbins (2004a) offers an analysis of a group who appear to adopt a new set of values while not entirely discarding the old. He describes how the Urapim of Papua New Guinea find themselves caught between their traditional system of cultural values and that offered by Pentecostal Christianity. Before contact the Urapim were important participants in a regional system of trade, which gave them a sense of prestige and self-worth. Colonization, and later the arrival of missionaries, dismantled the trade system, sparking cultural change. Deeply humiliated by their loss of prestige, and already prone to moral self-questioning, the Urapim embraced the new cultural model of Christianity. But rather than reconfiguring the logic of their culture in a new pattern, as Sahlins suggests, they find themselves constantly living *between* the two systems. The pattern is not one of replacement or even renegotiation, but one of constant negotiation, played out—for the Urapim—primarily in the moral domain.

11. Sewell's (2005) empirical work offers exemplary analyses of the interplay between structures and events. For example, in his analysis of Marseille dockworkers' ability to retain their privileged position during the first four decades of the nineteenth century, Sewell starts from the premise that any temporal sequence is complex and will contain several levels of temporality, including trends (directional change in social relations), routines (patterned sequences of behavior), and events (temporally concentrated sequences of actions that transform structures, as with Captain Cook's arrival in Hawaii). He then goes on to show that the dockworkers were able to maintain high wages and ensure high levels of occupational inheritance for their children, even though occupational guilds had been legally abolished and there was, in fact, radical change taking place all around them.

12. See Durham 2008 for an analysis of how Mannheim's argument reproduces Western ideologies of youth.

13. "Synoptic illusion" is a term Pierre Bourdieu coined to characterize the failure of charts and diagrams to capture complex, temporally located social relationships. Bourdieu (1977, 1992) points out several problems associated with synoptic illusions. For example, the relations between things represented in the diagram may be artifacts of the diagram's production that do not exist in practice. More important, such diagrams obscure the work of time by making the part stand for the whole. As a result, synoptic illusions hide the underlying heterogeneity that is an important part of change.

14. See also Jean Comaroff's (1985, 8) observation that we need to attend more to "relations of synchrony and diachrony" in transformative bodily processes like alimentation, gestation, birth, and death.

15. For classic accounts of moral panics, see Young 1971 and Cohen 1972.

16. Kenda Mutongi (2007, 139ff.), for example, has described how in the early 1940s, fear of "wayward women" who worked as prostitutes in the cities circulated widely among Kenyan men and was quickly picked up by colonial officials. The panic over women's "shameless" behavior led to the further control of women. This was so not only for colonial officials, who worried about venereal disease. It was also true for the women's husbands, stationed in places like Burma for the colonial war effort, who then sought to control their women—sometimes by beating them—when they returned home. In this patrilineal group, where men are supposed to pay bridewealth for women and see their wives as an investment, the importance of controlling women as part of controlling social reproduction is placed front and center (Thomas 2003).

17. See Farquhar and Lock's (2007, 5) felicitous characterization of Marcel Mauss's 1973 [1935] argument.

1. The Betsimisaraka comprise two groups. The southern Betsimisaraka inhabit the area stretching from just below Tamatave around Andevoranto to just above Manan-jary. The northern Betsimisaraka occupy the area from Tamatave in the south to Maroansetra in the north. During the colonial period, more schools were in the northern part of the region. Consequently, northern Betsimisaraka tend to be better educated and hold more positions of power in Tamatave than do southern Betsi-misaraka. In addition, more lucrative crops—like cloves and vanilla—grow in the northern part of the province, further contributing to the economic imbalance be-tween the two regions.

2. When Radama's troops arrived in Tamatave about 1820, two métis brothers, Jean René and Fiche—and their nephew Corroller—controlled the town through a com-bination of trade and force. Jean René was the most powerful of the three. He had served as an interpreter to the French colonel-agent Sylvain Roux, who had come to the east coast earlier to investigate the investment opportunities for French interests. In a desperate effort to retain his political independence from the Merina, Jean René sought help first from the French and then from British colonial agents. His efforts failed. In 1822 he submitted to Radama and agreed to become his administrator in Tamatave. Despite recognizing Radama's sovereignty, Jean René was able to retain considerable regional autonomy (Esoavelomandroso 1980).

3. From 1823 until the French colonized Madagascar in 1895, the Merina oligarchy controlled the port, and Merina officers constituted an important segment of the local elite (Bois 1996; Esoavelomandroso 1979, 326; also see Rantoandro 1980). Al-liances between those merchants and middlemen who were involved in commerce and the Merina government agents who regulated that commerce channeled the power and resources that emanated from the port. Officers engaged in economic ac-tivities, while merchants used their connections with officers to benefit their business (Esoavelomandroso 1979). At that time, the Merina head of the province, Rainan-driamampandry, was one of the richest men in the area. His wealth came from land, rice fields, plantations, and money made in the fabric trade.

4. Although Ledoux wrote in the mid-twentieth century, schools date back to the ar-rival of the missions in the mid-nineteenth century. Although missionaries from the London Missionary Society (LMS) first debarked in Tamatave, they quickly focused their efforts on the city of Antananarivo in the high plateau, the center of the Merina kingdom. Creating schools was central to proselytizing. By 1824 missionaries from various Protestant denominations had created twenty-two new schools in the vicin-ity of Antananarivo, with 2,000 students (Raison-Jourde 1991). The Merina state used schools to forcibly pry children away from their parents—who resisted because they were needed on farms—and teach them the literacy required to work in the state bureaucracy. By the 1870s a system of compulsory primary education had been established.

5. By 1931, 32 percent of the school-age population actually attended school in Mad-agascar—considerably greater than for any other French territory (Kent 1962). By about 1934, almost 48 percent of Malagasy children went to school in 2,132 estab-lishments. Of these, 1,009 were state schools, and 538 were along the coasts (Ran-drianja 2001, 62).

6. Cultural conceptions of schooling and literacy partially illuminate why east coasters embrace schooling. During the precolonial period, political leaders of communities frequently collaborated with diviners or ritual specialists (Raison-Jourde 1983). Among the most powerful ritual specialists were those who controlled the *sora be*, a form of Arabic writing in the Malagasy language (Bloch 1968). The collaboration between political and ritual power in the making of polities continued when the Merina kingdom collaborated with the LMS missionaries during the nineteenth century and used the literacy skills they had gained to promote their political expansion (Raison-Jourde 1977, 1991; Larson 2009). Many peasants feared schooling, since the state used it to take children from their families. Such fear was mitigated, however, by a cultural appreciation of the powers of literacy and a respect for books. Many Malagasy see schooling and literacy (*mahay taratasy*) as a way to access the transformative potential of knowledge (Keller 2005).

7. Many families believed they could ensure their future success by having one child in the colonial administration while others continued to earn their living by farming. Rural families generally chose sons for further schooling, although some young women trained as midwives and teachers. However, families also recognized the transformative potential of schooling. During my first fieldwork, elder men who had grown up during the colonial period recounted how their families had longed to send at least one son to school. The desire to school children notwithstanding, they generally did not want that child to become a *tangalamena*, the person in charge of ritually mediating between the living and the dead, since they believed schooling changed personality, making a person less able to control anger, sine qua non for mediating between the living and the ancestors.

8. In Malagasy, the concept is fashioned by combining the word for person, *olo*, and the word for success or flourishing—*vanona* (Esoavelomandroso 1992, 406).

9. See, for example, the article "Comment Ikala a manqué son mariage" under the rubric of "La vie indigène," in *La Femme Coloniale*, December 1935.

10. These marriages are locally called by the Malagasy version of the French term—*mariazy*.

11. See, for example, a series of articles that appeared in *Isika Vehivavy* (We Women) in March 1960, all urging women to use their money for their children's well-being and education before spending it on themselves. These articles suggested that the honorable woman (*vehivavy mihaja*) was someone who behaved well and thought about her actions, rather than someone who simply dressed well.

12. See Cole 2006 for an analysis of how memories of this event affected subsequent political struggles.

13. At first glance, the principles that guided the socialist period appear to contradict the basic narrative I have sketched so far, in which Malagasy draw on outside power and foreign practices to create local social hierarchies (see also Rutherford 2002 for a comparable example in the Indonesian context). Nationalist rhetoric notwithstanding, the socialist ideology the government used was itself foreign. Moreover, the echoes of the 1968 student movement in France also influenced Madagascar during this period. As part of their national service, radicalized French students often came to teach and work in Madagascar, bringing with them their ideas about equality and self-determination (Raison-Jourde, personal communication, 2008).

14. In Malagasy the expression is "Basy ariary fito. Tsy ho any mahantra sady tsy ho any ny manakarena," literally, "Seven-guinea gun. Not for the rich man and not for the poor."

15. Malagasy refer to this policy either as *liberalisme* from the French or, in Malagasy, *fanalalahana*.

16. By the mid-1990s, the currency had been devalued twice. Throughout the first half of 1987, there were 750 Malagasy francs (fmg) to the U.S. dollar. By July 1987 the Malagasy franc had decreased in value by half and was worth only 1,300 fmg to the dollar. By 1994 it had been devalued again and was worth only 3,530. In 2000 and 2001, when some of this fieldwork was carried out, the exchange rate was 6,300 fmg to the dollar. It has remained fairly stable over the past several years.

17. New, officially registered businesses include transportation, telecommunications, and tourism; various industries devoted to producing food, leather, and metal; and construction and commerce. It is notable that of those establishments that occupy the tertiary sector, many were created only after 1995.

18. More clearly than many other contexts, the workers in the Champion store reflect a hierarchy of access to global business opportunities that the inhabitants of Tamatave feel keenly. The owners were South African. Although the general manager looked ethnically Merina, her employees referred to her to as *vazaha* (European). The floor managers were all Merina, while those washing the floors were southern Betsimisaraka. For a discussion of the meanings associated with the word vazaha, usually translated as European, see Cole and Middleton 2001.

19. Ever since the civil strike that ended the state-socialist Second Republic and ousted him from power in 1992, Ratsiraka had cast political struggles for national power in terms of an ethnic struggle pitting the Merina of the high plateau against the coastal populations (see Cole 2001, 2003). During his political struggle against Zafy Albert during the early 1990s, Ratsiraka consistently spread propaganda throughout the east coast. He claimed that if Zafy Albert won, the Merina ethnic group would once again enslave the coastal peoples as they had during the nineteenth century. Faced by competition from Ravalomanana, Ratsiraka revived these ethnic tactics, once again portraying himself as a savior of coastal peoples in the face of Merina hegemony.

20. When the results from the 2001 presidential elections were announced in January 2002, Ratsiraka at first appeared to be the winner. Marc Ravalomanana, however, accused him of massive vote theft. When the supreme court refused to order a recount, Ravalomanana pronounced himself the legitimate president on February 22, 2002. Although many people supported Ravalomanana, Ratsiraka responded with a physical blockade of the capital intended to force Ravalomanana to recognize his power. From February through June 2002, the blockade deprived Antananarivo of gasoline and other goods that debark at the port of Tamatave. Reciprocally, people in Tamatave were deprived of the meat, rice, and fresh vegetables produced on the high plateau. During the five months of the roadblocks, some people managed to earn significant amounts by illegally transporting gasoline and other products across the roadblocks. Tamatavians claimed that Pascale Lahady, then governor of Tamatave, was paid large sums to permit illegal trade. The vast majority of the population, however, found themselves unable to purchase the most basic foods.

　　At the same time, Ratsiraka's supporters mobilized youth into militias referred to as ZaToVo (Zanaka Toamasina Vonina, or Children of Toamasina Ready to Protect!), which were used to man the blockade at Brickaville and to terrify the local population, often by deliberately evoking memories of the anti-Merina riots of 1972. On March 12, 2002, what began as a peaceful march demanding the dismantling of the barricades ended with several deaths when the ZaToVo attacked the crowd and then looted local shops. By the end of June 2002, the conflict was resolved when Ravalomanana used military force to reconquer the provinces. Tamatave was the last to fall. When I visited Tamatave in December 2002, people still spoke animatedly about how terrified they had been when the Merina army first arrived. For over a year afterward, arrests continued of people suspected of supporting Ratsiraka. Many young men who had been recruited to work in Ratsiraka's militia, mainly for tiny sums, complained that the Merina who control many of the stores did not want to employ them. Through any sense of ethnic animosity was virtually irrelevant to the fieldwork I carried out in 1999 and 2000–2001, when I returned immediately after the political standoff in 2003, comments about Merina racism were increasingly frequent.

21. Not only are there inequalities within the city of Tamatave, but there are sharp socio-economic disparities between the city and the surrounding countryside. According to one report, between 1997 and 1999 urban consumer spending power rose by 18 percent, while rural power fell by 5 percent, leaving urban Malagasy with 56 percent more spending power than their rural counterparts. It is in the province of Tamatave that the greatest number of youth have abandoned the agricultural livelihood of their parents (INSTAT 2000).

22. When we consider that the majority of the population is young—the median age in Tamatave is twenty-one, and the average age is twenty-three—it becomes clear that a few middle-aged and late-middle-aged men control many of the stable, salaried jobs. While the overall official rate of unemployment is only 8.4 percent, the rate for people just entering the labor market is 62 percent. Among the most educated group, people who have college degrees, where one would expect to find the least unemployment, the rate was 11 percent, twice that of the other large urban centers in Madagascar (INSTAT 2000). Moreover, because the statistics are derived by calculating the demand for jobs against the number of new jobs offered, and because much of Tamatave's economy is in the informal sector, these statistics underestimate the rates of unemployment and underemployment. For every person who earns a stable salary, there are numerous dependents. One employed man, earning on average 523,000 fmg a month in a salaried job (less than $100), supports an average of 4.2 dependents.

23. A study by the National Bureau of Statistics reports that whereas in the past one could easily classify people as either government worker, manager, or employee, this is no longer true because today more than half of the population works in the informal sector. More young people are likely to end up in the unpredictable informal sector than will be able to replicate the status of their fathers (INSTAT 2000, 59). This trend is paired with a movement away from farming and commerce and toward industry and service.

CHAPTER THREE

1. In Malagasy, *Aomby mahia tsy lafina namana.*

2. Although the social dynamics and implications of these practices in Tamatave differ from what takes place in rural areas, this difference is not because of a rural/urban dichotomy or because of a teleological movement of history. For two hundred years Tamatave and the rural areas surrounding it have been part of a shared regional dynamic in which rural and urban experiences exist in relation to one another. Tamatave pulls from the surrounding rural areas and feeds people back to them, so that there is constant exchange between the two.

3. See, for example, Williams 1975 for an analysis of European discourse, and Ferguson 1997 for a discussion of this discourse in an African context.

4. Taylor's use of the term is similar to what Robin Horton (1967) identified as the lack of awareness that characterizes traditional African thought, making it "closed."

5. As this example implies, ancestral power works by binding people in place rather than letting them scatter over the land, a mechanism for controlling people and constituting them as subjects that has corollaries in many other parts of Madagascar (Cole 2001; Feeley-Harnik 1991; Graeber 1995; Lambek 2002; Lambek and Walsh 1999).

6. In Malagasy, *Vehivavy tsy mañaña tandindrazana. Nefa mañaña my.*

7. The tangalamena, who mediate between the living and the dead and preside over rituals, are the political players in this world. To be a tangalamena means one has control over the three sites that together constitute an autonomous political unit: the great house, a place for invoking the ancestors, and a tomb. Only men can become tangalamena. Given that those who mediate between the living and the dead have the potential to curse their descendants and that emotions can cause involuntary speech, a hot temper is a liability. Since men are said to control their emotions better than women, east coasters argue that men mediate ancestral power more successfully. Women can find other ways of accruing social resources, but they can never become the key political players who dominate many aspects of rural life.

8. A wide range of writing suggests that Malagasy tend to imagine personhood according to an Austronesian model in which only death and burial in a tomb finalize identity and personhood (Bloch 1971; Fox 1987; Middleton 1995). This general life course moves from the fluidity and potential associated with birth, childhood, and maturation toward the stillness and finality of death and ancestorhood. Both Rita Astuti (1995) and Maurice Bloch (1995) have described how the Vezo on the west coast, and the Zafimaniry of the eastern forest littoral, take great pleasure in the flexible, pliable nature of their children's bodies. By contrast, these groups symbolically associate their elders with hard, upright materials like the staffs old men use to invoke the ancestors. This symbolic movement from young to old and soft to hard maps onto the ideal trajectory in which a person progresses from a flexible, ephemeral, and vulnerable baby to a hard, enduring symbol of ancestral power. Intergenerational exchange is the medium through which this happens.

9. These progressive stages are relationally situated in daily life. For example, in any given interaction one person is likely to be dependent on another, becoming the junior party to that interaction, and by extension, a child. This set of associations helps explain why those who are chronologically old but socially dependent continue to be treated as children. At times they are even referred to by the word for children, *ankizy.* Not surprisingly, in the past ankizy also referred to slaves.

10. As inhabitants of the east coast say to express pride in their own caring capacities, "I can finish you" or "I can complete you" (*vitako anao*).

11. Yet local wisdom also has it that one should guard against the sense that one knows, based on present circumstances, what the outcome of any interaction will be. Generative potential (hasina) is often both unpredictable and hidden. Another proverb explicitly responds to the wisdom encapsulated in the "thin cow" proverb: "Do not push away [ignore] the runt, because you never know who will later bear twins." In other words, do not ignore the person who seems poor or weak now, because you never know who will generate wealth and prosperity in the future.

12. The government sponsors most sacrifices held in Tamatave, usually to commemorate important political events or to inaugurate new buildings. Though occasionally families hold sacrifices as well, these rituals are fairly truncated compared with what takes place in the countryside.

13. In Malagasy, *Irin'olona fa tsy haniry olona.*
14. In making this claim, I am not suggesting that the inhabitants of rural areas do not sometimes query the power of ancestors. To the contrary, it was a frequent topic of debate. Villagers I knew in the early 1990s loved to sit around and confer about their experiences, swapping stories about when the ancestors had helped them and describing ways they sought to test ancestral power. These stories were just as common when I returned to that area in 2007. But in rural villages the depth and density with which ideas about ancestors were woven into everyday practice through the taboos people had to honor and the places they had to live helped guard against individual doubts about ancestral power. This was not the case in the urban context.
15. According to one study carried out by the government's statistical bureau, 49 percent of Tamatavian adults claim they are Catholic, 28 percent say they are Protestant, and another 14 percent belong to one of the new evangelical churches (INSTAT 2001). Only 2 percent claim "traditional" religious affiliation or ancestral practice (INSTAT 2001).
16. As Eva Keller (2005, 177) remarks of Adventist practice in northeastern Madagascar, "I call the Adventist construction of *fombandrazana* a disembedded notion of 'religion,' because by treating 'supernatural entities,' in particular the ancestors, as separate from other spheres of life like kinship, this construction is clearly modeled on Christianity."
17. Some people have also converted to Adventism. See Keller 2005.
18. There have been several charismatic Christian revival movements in Madagascar since the arrival of Christianity in the nineteenth century.
19. It is likely that the new evangelical churches have had more success in Tamatave than in Antananarivo because in Antananarivo the Protestant church (AFJKM) in particular is so deeply rooted in the community that it has proved more difficult to entice people away. Nevertheless, Pentecostalism and the evangelical revivalist movement enjoy considerable success in Antananarivo and its surrounds as well (see Dubourdieu 2002).
20. The name literally means "many plates." It refers to the grave of a former prostitute where Tamatavians used to make vows until her family came and brought her bones back to Diego Suarez.
21. The meaning of *fivoarana* is similar to that of *fandrosoana* (verb form, *mandroso*, "to push forward"). Where *fandrosoana* means "progress" at the collective level and is used to refer to "developed" or "underdeveloped" nations, *mivoatra* refers to individual progress and evolution. In this respect the notion of *fivoarana* is closely tied to personal aspiration, a kind of reaching beyond the self, not for transcendence but for self-perfection. The two words—fandrosoana and fivoarana—have coexisted for a long time; one can find both in Richardson's Malagasy-English dictionary, first published in 1885. However, while *mandroso* has long meant "to increase in civilization," in the nineteenth century *mivoatra* meant "to arrange, to build, to make ready." The word first took on the meaning of inner spiritual work on the self in the context of Protestant teaching in the early twentieth century. Although I am not certain when it first moved from the spiritual to the secular realm, the switch may have begun around independence. Regardless of when the change in meaning took place, people's contemporary tendency to use fivoarana, which highlights individual progress, as opposed to the collectively oriented fandrosoana, fits well with the contemporary movement away from socialism, with its emphasis on collective, state-orchestrated programs as a route to success, and toward individual engagement with

the market. Many people claimed that the word, as it was applied to the idea of progress, became widespread after liberalization in 1991.

22. In no way am I seeking to analyze a scenario in which people living in a subsistence economy are suddenly introduced to money. Monetization is hardly new to Tamatave, as is evident from the history of the port in chapter 2. Nor is it new to Madagascar. In fact, several authors have used ethnography from various parts of Madagascar to argue against Western theories of money's allegedly universal and abstracting properties. As Michael Lambek (2001, 736) observes, "A study of the reception of money by people on the capitalist periphery requires a certain historical depth. Monetary practices and ideas about money are not necessarily only immediate responses—of acquiescence or resistance—to market relation or the policies of national or transnational financial institutions. They need to be understood as embedded within local systems of power, reproduction and meaning."

So too Maurice Bloch, whose theories emerged out of his Malagasy ethnography, has argued together with Jonathan Parry (Parry and Bloch 1989) that money has no intrinsic properties apart from the cultural world into which it is incorporated. While these arguments may hold true for the circumstances in which these authors conducted their fieldwork (among ritual specialists of the Sakalava monarchy and in rural Imerna respectively), in contemporary Tamatave money—how to get it and what it can do—has taken on an urgency and an intensity that are painfully palpable. Yet as both Bloch and Lambek suggest, the preexisting cultural ideas continue to matter.

CHAPTER FOUR

1. In Malagasy the speech might run something like this: *Jereo zanakay. Izy tsy poara maso, izy tsy fola-tagnana. Raha leo ianareo, dia miverina aty aminay.*

2. In Malagasy, *Vehivavy raha fanaka malemy.*

3. Villagers say that physical desire for a member of the opposite sex is natural and spontaneous, explaining that it comes from Zanahary, or God. For example, Ramarie's first marriage was to a man who had been married to his older brother's widow, a traditional levirate marriage. The wife bore no children, so the man decided to remarry to obtain an heir. But even Ramarie, who had grown up in a time when the demands of kinship had shaped one of her marriages, talked about how women choose partners in terms of personal preference and desire. As she explained, "Some girls choose lovers for looks, others seek their material comfort." She went on to tell me how an older man, comparatively wealthy by village standards, had come and greeted her, the traditional way a man seeks to establish sexual relations with a woman. The thought of sleeping with him made her cringe, so she refused the offer.

4. Although she was many years younger, Ramarie's daughter-in-law, Beberi, shared many of these assumptions about women's right to exchange their sexual and reproductive capacities for material support. Beberi was married to another young man who lived in the village at the time, but she spoke with admiration of Celine, who was the talk of the village because she had achieved a liaison with a relatively older wealthy man who came from upcountry. The man had bought a patent, the government permit required to sell rum legally. Celine became his local lover and then received money from him in exchange for selling the rum. Celine's ability to get things from the man sparked Beberi's admiration, and perhaps a bit of envy. Not long after I left the village Beberi had an affair with a government employee who came through

to work on the canal. She left her son, who was eight by then, with his father's family, took her daughter, and followed him.

5. For example, one woman who courted during the late 1950s described her experience thus when I asked if girls and boys were raised in the same way: "No. Girls were controlled more. They could not just go out strolling. Parents did not control boys because they never feared that boys would get pregnant. My father would warn my brothers not to make someone pregnant. But we girls, we were lectured about giving in to [the demands of] boys. Girls are very precious—you should wear the veil before you leave the house [have a church marriage]. If you don't get married, your family loses honor. My parents insisted we were virgins when we left the house. If we'd been with someone and got married then people would say we were not virgins and the marriage had no meaning. And you could not sneak off chatting in the shadows. Only when a boy came and introduced himself to your parents could you really start chatting with him. My husband and I met when he was a [Boy] Scout and I was a Theresette [the Catholic group for girls]; we went to pray in the morning, and we would meet. At that time we were just chatting—no sex. There was a time when we would go meet at the beach, or we would go to the cinema. But we had to go home at four o'clock because I had to be home by five o'clock. Eventually my husband sent me a letter [a declaration of intentions], and I answered him and said "I love you too." I asked him when he would contact my parents. At that time we were still checking out each other's characters, and he would come by all the time to see me.

6. In Malagasy, *Lehilahy manambola mampirafy.*

7. In some cases women who are angered by their husbands' infidelities may threaten to dissolve the marriage. They may return to their natal homes and wait for their husbands to come and coax them back in a scenario referred to as "to bring home" or "to coax" (*miampody, mitamby*). When her errant husband tried to win her back, Bernadette, a fifty-six-year-old woman who lived in Tamatave, demanded he buy her a house. She explained, "If there is a problem, and the man is caught cheating, you go home, and you don't go back until he comes to get you. . . . When that happened to me, I asked for a house! And he went home and wrote a letter testifying that he would build me a house. I tightened my belt at home to save money for that house, and that house, it isn't shared—it is written [legally] in my name."

Though the house (which we were sitting in at the time) was a traditional one made of thatch, and though she was in fact quite poor, owning her own house nevertheless gave her a permanent foothold in Tamatave, one considerably more secure than many other women could claim. Another woman, also in her fifties, told how her husband became increasingly violent after his military service in Algeria. They kept fighting, and she sometimes returned home to her mother's, where she would wait for him to lure her back with gifts. She explained, "He came to Tamatave three times to try and bring me home, but I wouldn't go. At first, I told him to buy me a sewing machine. And he said, "Where am I going to get the money to buy you a sewing machine?" That meant that he didn't really love me but was just teasing me. And I decided not to return to him." In all these examples, women take the amount and regularity of the gifts and support they receive as a direct measure of how much the man really cares for them. However, these women are comparatively old (late fifties), and the events they describe may have taken place in the late 1970s. It is not clear that a married woman today, whether she lived in the countryside or in Tamatave, could obtain the same treatment.

8. In Malagasy, *Tsy tia tamaigna mazava ila.*
9. To take just one example, Lalao, a young woman who worked for a brief time as my assistant, came from a middle-class family where her father worked at the local bank and her mother cared for the house. But her father took a lover and abandoned his first family, starting a new one. Lalao and her brother and mother were left to struggle. The father subsequently died. Having never really worked, the mother found it impossible to find a job. Eventually she was able to use his pension to buy a car, which they then used as a taxi to earn income. However, she remained constantly embroiled in fights with the taxi driver, who stole from them, so that they rarely received much of the money. Although Lalao was attending college when I knew her and was in fact a very strong and promising student, she lived in grinding poverty and was eventually forced to stop her studies. She eventually married a man from Réunion.
10. See Cole 2008a for a discussion of class in Tamatave.
11. In rural areas of Tamatave province it is customary to perform a funeral sacrifice, referred to in the southern part of the region as a *lofo*. For a more detailed discussion of cattle sacrifice among southern Betsimisaraka, see Cole 2001.
12. In Malagasy, *Mitovy amin'ny namana, mitovy amin'ny olona rehetra.*

CHAPTER FIVE
1. In French, and in the Malagasy use of the French word, *jeune* or *jeunes* can be used either as a noun or as an adjective (young or the young). I have followed the French convention of making jeune/jeunes singular or plural according to the context in which it was used.
2. In addition to *tanora*, which is also used on the high plateau, east coasters sometimes use the words *gona-lahy* and *gonavavy* to refer to this phase in the life course.
3. There is considerable evidence, at least for the high plateau, that this has been a problem for families of migrants to the city at least since the mid-1970s (Chandon-Möet 1976).
4. In Malagasy, *ny olona tia hanjary.*
5. The tension between the desire to retain an authentic cultural identity, marked as inferior in relation to the West, and the fear of loss that accompanies modernization has been noted by many postcolonial scholars (Fanon 1967 [1952]; Nandy 1983). So, too, the idea that the colonized try to achieve a modern identity but end up described by Homi Bhabha's famous aphorism "not quite/not white" (1994, 131) has been documented in many other postcolonial contexts. For many Tamatavians the experience of recent globalization clearly fuels a much older set of concerns at the same time that it enables partly new practices.
6. In Malagasy, *Tia ho vazaha nefa tsy maharaka ny fandrosoana vazaha.*
7. His evocation of "not on the bed, not on the floor" to express his predicament recalls the phrase from Karoland, Indonesia, "hanging without a rope" (Steedly 1993).
8. The slang word *ambassady* derives from the French *ambassadeur*, "ambassador," because these young women represent their families back in the countryside.

CHAPTER SIX
1. Anecdotal evidence suggests that the practice is most frequent in Diego Suarez, the large port town the northern tip of Madagascar. Though it was looked down on in Antananarivo in the past, it is becoming more widely accepted. See Cole 2008b and Pompey 2007.

2. It is possible that some of these "French" men are Malagasy or other Africans who have French nationality. Certainly some come from other parts of the French overseas empire, including Réunion and Martinique. However, my interviews at the French consulate suggest that the great majority were French men from metropolitan France and Réunion.

3. In a dictionary from the late eighteenth century, the scholar-traveler Barthelemy Huet de Froberville defined the vadimbazaha thus: "Literally the wife of the whites, the foreigners. It is not a question of referring to European women or foreign women . . . rather the natives use the term *vadimbazaha* to refer to the Malagasy women that the foreigners take on their arrival to care for their homes; [the vadimbazaha's] prerogatives go as far as to include all the traditional conjugal rights" (cited in Bois 1997, 64).

4. This was a common practice in many port towns of Africa. See Brooks 1976; Jean-Baptiste 2010.

5. For example, in an article titled "La femme aux colonies" the second governor-general, Victor Augagneur, lamented the effect of these unions. He argued that that the government needed to "facilitate the marriage of colonials with women of their own race. . . . Too many agents fall under the influence of indigenous women. . . . Cohabiting with the Ramatoa [local word for "miss"] whose education is nothing more than a small change in their personal habits, leads to intellectual and moral decline. . . . You need only to go into their houses in the bush to know to just what low levels some of our officers, functionaries or settlers descend" (cited in Bavoux 1997, 184).

6. What Simonin refers to as *simirires* is likely a misspelling of *tsimihoririna*, "those who do not sleep on their sides" (Grandidier 1942, cited in Bois 1997), which may be a reference to sexual position, since side-to-side is widely perceived to be the most discreet way to have sex in a crowded household (Kirsten Stoebenau, personal communication, 2007). Perhaps the "tsimirires" were so called because they did not see themselves as so constrained.

7. Like Luise White (1990), whose oral history work with prostitutes in Nairobi during the 1970s and 1980s showed that focusing on women's experience rather than men's switched the analytic language from disease, contagion, and control to labor, I focus on women's participation in the sexual economy as a particular kind of labor. Focusing on labor and exchange, as opposed to highlighting government and public health regulation, makes particular sense given that prostitution has *never* been an issue of state control in Madagascar.

8. For critiques of the category of prostitution in Africa, see Hunter 2002; Schoepf 1992; Standing 1992; Wojcicki 2002; and Zalduondo 1991. Some scholars have suggested "transactional sex" as a label that avoids much of the stigma associated with prostitution, and I used the term in my earlier writing on the topic (Cole 2004). However, the term poses its own problems, given that the idea of transacting individuals implies a kind of individual rational actor associated with economic theory.

9. The term *makorelina* likely comes from *maquereau*, the French word for pimp. It may have reached Madagascar during the colonial period when Réunionais women occasionally ran brothels. The term *mpivaro-tena* means literally "someone who sells herself." As mentioned above, the older term that one sometimes finds in travelers' accounts is tsimihoririna.

10. Of the major Internet sites Malagasy women use to seek vazaha online, Tamatavian women figure second after Diego Suarez in number of personal profiles, suggesting

that they are among the most active group pursuing this option in Madagascar. See Pompey 2007.

11. It is difficult to generalize about how much money these women receive from vazaha men. In some cases, when women marry vazaha the association is clearly life- and class-transforming, as in Mamitiana's story above. In other cases, however, women conducted liaisons with men who had gone home to France but promised to return (see Brennan 2004 for a comparable example from the Dominican Republic). Typically these men sent them money via the post or the bank. Although women in this position were more vulnerable than those who were legally married, the sums were vast compared with what most would earn in a regular job. In three cases I documented, young women who had worked as maids were in relationships with foreign men who sent over 1,000,000 fmg a month—about three hundred dollars at the time. Recall, also, Eudoxie's story above, where she dropped out of college as soon as she became involved with her French man because she assumed he would support her and that therefore she no longer needed to work. The amount women receive from Malagasy men also varies widely. In some cases women could be paid as little as 5,000 fmg (less than a dollar) for a *passe temps* (quick encounter), but one woman who worked as a maid for a European, earning 50,000 fmg a month, recounted how all the prostitutes in her neighborhood mocked her, claiming they earned in one night what she earned in a month. Several of the women I knew had worked as maids and argued that they fared better as prostitutes, even before they met the vazaha men they eventually stayed with.

12. Though no one I knew was able to identify the origins of the word, the root *jao* means an uncastrated, powerful bull and is also by extension frequently used as a name for men (Gillian Feeley-Harnik, personal communication, 2002). The word had a previous analogue in *jaoloka*, a term used in western Madagascar to refer to a man who had the misfortune to live uxorilocally, a situation associated with changing patterns of social reproduction that intensified after migrants came to the area following the introduction of wage labor (Waast 1980).

13. Though it might be tempting to compare the jaombilo who fulfills these duties to a pimp, this would be a mistake. Unlike the pimp/prostitute dyad in many other places, these women control the money they earn. They are on the whole in a more powerful position than the men who become their dependents, even if men occasionally try to turn the tables.

14. Although Dezy's remark about disease was uncommon in 2001–2003, it might be more common now, given the government's efforts to raise awareness about HIV/AIDS.

CHAPTER SEVEN

1. According to Richardson (1885, 298) *mijaly* implies not only physical suffering and pain but also punishment.

2. There is an enormous literature trying to explain why Pentecostalism has been taken up in so many parts of the world, and I can hardly do justice to it here (Robbins 2004b). Many scholars have drawn on deprivation and social disorganization arguments, pointing out that many of the people attracted to Pentecostalism are poor migrants to the cities, whose traditional lifeways have been disrupted by poverty and urbanization (Lalive d'Epinay 1969; Willems 1967). More recently, however, scholars have pointed out the positive features of Pentecostal spread, including a prominent focus on evangelization, an egalitarian ethos, a flexible social organiza-

tion, and an enjoyable, absorbing ritual life (see, for example, Brouwer, Gifford, and Rose 1996; Burdick 1998; Chestnut 1997; Stoll 1990).

3. Converts often used the Malagasy word *tahotra* to illuminate this idea of an internal transformation that transcends local contexts. As a concept tahotra combines fear and respect: a woman who has tahotra respects the rules intrinsic to social life, whereas a woman who lacks tahotra may "dare" (*sahy*) to commit evil deeds. A pervasive sense of tahotra indicates internal transformation.

4. From the perspective of those who believe in ancestral power, such a refusal is tantamount to insanity or witchcraft.

5. The reality of rural practice is far more complex and more imbued with the moral power of ancestors than this urban interpretation implies (see Cole 2001; Lambek 2002).

6. Other congregants criticized ancestors using a different but related logic. This logic holds that if one gains wealth either by stealing or through unexpected windfalls that do not rely on culturally valued forms of labor, the money will not produce a return or grow—it is a kind of *vola mafana* ("hot money") that must be quickly spent (see Cole 2005; Walsh 2003). One middle-aged woman recounted, "Before, I had lots of money, but I didn't get much from it. It was used up all the time on things without meaning." One could read her statement as implying that even when ancestors do bless their descendants and bestow material prosperity, that blessing is illegitimate because it comes from a false god. Like hot money, it is too easily squandered.

7. In Malagasy, *Jesosy ilay sakaiza indrindra, mamela heloka, manafaka, manasitrana, mahamaolona.*

8. Despite some shared general assumptions, each of the four churches I attended in rotation—the Assembly of God, the Power of Faith church, Pentekotista Afaka, and the Rhema—had slightly different emphases in doctrine and variations in styles of worship.

9. It is notable that Mamy, who had previously been possessed by *tromba* (spirits), explained speaking in tongues in terms quite similar to the way many people describe the experience of tromba, particularly speaking foreign languages. For an account of tromba in Tamatave, see Emoff 2002.

10. The religious practices of women in an Islamic revival movement in Cairo offer a useful foil for understanding Pentecostal practice with respect to clothing. Participants in this Islamic revival learn to acquire certain dispositions through self-conscious bodily training, seeking to achieve "rehearsed spontaneity" (Mahmood 2005). They believe that by adopting certain external behaviors one can model a more pious internal self. By contrast, Pentecostal doctrine holds that converts have had "their hearts touched" and they are already new people. Ideally, they should simply "express" the transformation God has already effected. Both traditions use clothing, but they do so in strikingly different ways.

11. As we've seen, Tamatavians use many different words to talk about life's difficulties. I've already mentioned *malahelo*—a word that combines the idea of sadness with bitterness, implying that people have not received the recognition they think they deserve from their social interlocutors (see chapter 3) and *mijaly*, which implies the endurance of physical pain or punishment. Women also use a colloquial expression, *raha mahazo ahy* (the thing that got me). Both malahelo and raha mahazo ahy connote the suffering that comes with disappointment and humiliation.

12. See Keller 2005 for a similar point regarding Adventist practice in northeastern Madagascar.

CHAPTER EIGHT

1. The mpiandry's search for medicines was in fact documented by a BBC reporter who was in Madagascar to cover political events. See http://news.bbc.co.uk/2/hi/africa/ 7948278.stm. In addition, news of the discovery also quickly traveled by word of mouth to Tamatave, where my former assistant reported that many people feared religious conflict, given that Andry Rajoelina is Catholic and Marc Ravalomanana belongs to the Malagasy Protestant Church.

2. Though the young women who seek vazaha were not visible in the political events, they have also become an accepted—if contested—part of national political culture. Only a few months before Rajoelina seized power, one of his supporters, a journalist, presented a summary of the Malagasy overseas diaspora in which he used photos of girls seeking vazaha husbands from Internet-based marriage agencies to illustrate the question of Malagasy acquisition of French citizenship today. These images had apparently become so familiar to urbanites that they did not even merit comment.

3. This is in some ways like what a text must go through to become extractable from the context in which it was born, what linguistic anthropologists call "entextualization" (Bauman and Briggs 1990). Webb Keane (2007, 14) notes that this entails the "elimination of features that anchor any stretch of discourse in some immediate context."

4. This feedback is loosely comparable to the looping effect described by Ian Hacking (1987).

5. For example, Sewell (2005, 248ff.) argues that heightened emotions always characterize major events like the French Revolution. What took place at the Bastille, including the killing of certain officials, cannot be understood without reference to the intense "collective effervescence" (Durkheim 1995 [1912]). For further discussion of the concept of affect from a very different perspective, see Hardt (1999, 2007).

WORKS CITED

Abbink, Jon. 2005. Being Young in Africa: The Politics of Despair and Renewal. In *Vanguard or Vandals: Youth, Politics and Conflict in Africa*, ed. Jon Abbink and Ineke van Kessel, 1–34. Leiden: Brill.

Abbink, Jon, and Ineke van Kessel, eds. 2005. *Vanguard or Vandals: Youth, Politics and Conflict in Africa*. Leiden: Brill.

Althabe, Gerard. 1969. *Oppression et libération dans l'imaginaire: Les communautés villageoises de la côte orientale de Madagascar*. Paris: Maspero.

Anderson, Benedict. 1972. *Java in a Time of Revolution: Occupation and Resistance*. Ithaca, NY: Cornell University Press.

Andrianjafy, Danielle N. 1990. Répresentations de la femme malgache dans la littérature française. *Dires* (Montreal) 8 (1): 131–151.

Antoine, Philippe, Mireille Razafindrakoto, and François Roubaud. 2001. Contraints de rester jeunes? Évolution de l'insertion dans trois capitals africaines: Dakar, Yaoundé et Antananarivo. *Autrepart* 18:17–36.

Archer, Robert. 1976. *Madagascar depuis 1972*. Paris: Éditions de l'Harmattan.

Asad, Talal. 1993. *Genealogies of Religion: Discipline and Reasons of Power in Christianity and Islam*. Baltimore, MD: Johns Hopkins University Press.

Astuti, Rita. 1995. *People of the Sea: Identity and Descent among the Vezo of Madagascar*. Cambridge: Cambridge University Press.

Austen, Ralph, ed. 1999. *In Search of Sunjata: The Mande Epic as History, Literature and Performance*. Bloomington: Indiana University Press.

Austin-Broos, Diane J. 1997. *Jamaica Genesis: Religion and the Politics of Moral Orders*. Chicago: University of Chicago Press.

Baker, Keith Michael. 1990. *Inventing the French Revolution*. Cambridge: Cambridge University Press.

Bauman, Richard, and Charles L. Briggs. 1990. Poetics and Performance as Critical Perspectives on Language and Social Life. *Annual Review of Anthropology* 19:59–88.

Bavoux, Claude. 1997. Les Réunionnais de Madagascar de 1889 à 1925. PhD diss., University of Paris 7.

Berger, Laurent. 2006. Les raisons de la colère des ancêtres Zafinifotsy (Ankarana, Madagascar): L'anthropologie au défi de la mondialisation. PhD diss., École des Hautes Études en Sciences Sociales.

Bhabha, Homi. 1994. *The Location of Culture*. London: Routledge.

Bloch, Maurice. 1968. Astrology and Writing in Madagascar. In *Literacy in Traditional Societies*, ed. Jack Goody, 277–297. Cambridge: Cambridge University Press.

———. 1971. *Placing the Dead: Tombs, Ancestral Villages and Kinship in Madagascar*. New York: Seminar Press.

———. 1989. *Ritual, History and Power: Selected Papers in Anthropology*. London: Athlone Press.

———. 1995. People into Places: Zafimaniry Concepts of Clarity. In *The Anthropology of Landscape*, ed. Eric Hirsch and Michael O'Hanlon, 63–77. Oxford: Oxford University Press.

———. 1998a. *How We Think They Think: Anthropological Approaches to Cognition, Memory and Literacy*. Boulder, CO: Westview Press.

———. 1998b. What Goes without Saying: The Conceptualization of Zafimaniry Society. In *How We Think They Think: Anthropological Approaches to Cognition, Memory and Literacy*, 23–38. Boulder, CO: Westview Press.

———. 1999. "Eating" Young Men among the Zafimaniry. In *Ancestors, Power and History in Madagascar*, ed. Karen Middleton, 175–190. Leiden: Brill.

Bois, Dominique. 1996. Vazaha et autochtones sur la côte est de Madagascar: Médiation et métissage entre 1854 et 1885. PhD diss., University of Paris 7.

———. 1997. Tamatave, la cité des femmes. *CLIO* 6:61–86.

———. 2001. Les métis à Tamatave dans la seconde moitié du xixème siècle. *Annuaire des Pays de l'Océan Indien* 17:123–142.

Bornstein, Erica. 2003. *The Spirit of Development: Protestant NGO's, Morality and Economics in Zimbabwe*. New York: Routledge.

Bourdieu, Pierre. 1977. *Outline of a Theory of Practice*. Cambridge: Cambridge University Press.

———. 1992. *The Logic of Practice*. Trans. Richard Nice. Stanford, CA: Stanford University Press.

Brennan, Denise. 2004. *What's Love Got to Do with It? Transnational Desires and Sex Tourism in the Dominican Republic*. Durham, NC: Duke University Press.

Brodwin, Paul. 2003. Pentecostalism in Translation: Religion and the Production of Community in the Haitian Diaspora. *American Ethnologist* 30 (1): 85–101.

Brooks, George. 1976. The Signares of Saint Louis and Gorée: Women Entrepreneurs in Eighteenth Century Senegal. In *Women in Africa: Studies in Social and Economic Change*, ed. Nancy Hafkin, 19–44. Stanford, CA: Stanford University Press.

Brouwer, Steve, Paul Gifford, and Susan D. Rose. 1996. *Exporting the American Gospel: Global Christian Fundamentalism*. New York: Routledge.

Brusco, Elizabeth. 1995. *The Reformation of Machismo: Evangelical Conversion and Gender in Colombia*. Austin: University of Texas Press.

Burdick, John. 1998. *Blessed Anastácia: Women, Race and Popular Christianity in Brazil*. New York: Routledge.

Burke, Timothy. 1996. *Lifebuoy Men, Lux Women: Commodification, Consumption, and Cleanliness in Modern Zimbabwe*. Durham, NC: Duke University Press.

Burley, Natasha C. 2004. Rebirth of a French Farm Village, via Madagascar. *Herald Tribune*, September 8.

Cannell, Fenella. 2006. Introduction. In *The Anthropology of Christianity*, ed. Fenella Cannell, 1–50. Durham, NC: Duke University Press.

Castañeda, Claudia. 2002. *Figurations: Child, Bodies, Worlds*. Durham, NC: Duke University Press.

Centre d'Archives d'Outre Mer, Aix en Provence. 1938. *Prostitution.* MAD/PT 194.

Chandon-Möet, Bernard. 1976. Les catholiques de la région d'Ambositra-Fandriana-Ambatofinandrahana: Esquisse de situation. Étude Réalisée pour le diocèse de Fianarantsoa (Madagascar) à l'occasion du centenaire de l'église catholique à Ambositra (1876–1976).

Chestnut, R. Andrew. 1997. *Born Again in Brazil: The Pentecostal Boom and the Pathogens of Poverty.* New Brunswick, NJ: Rutgers University Press.

Chow, Tse-tsung. 1967. *The May Fourth Movement: Intellectual Revolution in Modern China.* Cambridge, MA: Harvard University Press.

Christiansen, Catrine, Mats Utas, and Henrik E. Vigh, eds. 2006. *Navigating Youth, Generating Adulthood: Social Becoming in an African Context.* Uppsala: Nordsika Afrikainstitutet.

Cohen, Stanley. 1972. *Folk Devils and Moral Panics: The Creation of the Mods and Rockers.* London: MacGibbon and Kee.

Cole, Jennifer. 1998. The Work of Memory in Madagascar. *American Ethnologist* 25 (4): 610–633.

———. 2001. *Forget Colonialism? Sacrifice and the Art of Memory.* Berkeley: University of California Press.

———. 2003. Narratives and Moral Projects: Generational Memories of the Malagasy 1947 Rebellion. *Ethos* 31 (1): 95–126.

———. 2005. The Jaombilo of Tamatave (Madagascar), 1992–2004: Reflections on Youth and Globalization. *Journal of Social History,* Summer, 891–914.

———. 2006. Malagasy and Western Conceptions of Memory: Implications for Post-colonial Politics and the Study of Memory. *Ethos* 34 (2): 211–243.

———. 2008a. Fashioning Distinction: Youth and Consumerism in Urban Madagascar. In *Figuring the Future: Youth and Temporality in a Global Era,* ed. Jennifer Cole and Deborah Durham, 99–124. Santa Fe, NM: School of American Research Press.

———. 2008b. "Et Plus Si Affinités": Malagasy Internet Marriage, Shifting Post-colonial Hierarchies, and National Honor. In *Emotional Latitudes: The Ambiguities of Colonial and Post-colonial Sentiment.* Special Issue of *Historical Reflections/Réflexions Historiques,* ed. Matt Matsuda and Alice Bullard 34 (1): 26–49.

———. 2009. Love, Money, and Economies of Intimacy in Tamatave, Madagascar. In *Love in Africa,* ed. Jennifer Cole and Lynn Thomas, 109–134. Chicago: University of Chicago Press.

Cole, Jennifer, and Deborah Durham, eds. 2007. *Generations and Globalization: Youth, Age, and Family in the New World Economy.* Bloomington: Indiana University Press.

———, eds. 2008a. *Figuring the Future: Globalization and the Temporalities of Children and Youth.* Santa Fe, NM: School of American Research Press.

———. 2008b. Globalization and the Temporality of Children and Youth. In *Figuring the Future: Globalization and the Temporalities of Children and Youth,* ed. Jennifer Cole and Deborah Durham, 3–23. Santa Fe, NM: School of American Research Press.

Cole, Jennifer, and Karen Middleton. 2001. Rethinking Ancestors and Colonial Power in Madagascar. *Africa* 71 (1): 1–37.

Cole, Jennifer, and Lynn Thomas, eds. 2009. *Love in Africa.* Chicago: University of Chicago Press.

Cole, Michael, and Sheila Cole. 1989. *The Development of Children.* New York: Scientific American Books.

Cole, Michael, Sheila Cole, and C. Lightfoot. 2005. *The Development of Children.* 5th ed. New York: Worth Publishing.

Comaroff, Jean. 1985. *Body of Power, Spirit of Resistance: The Culture and History of a South African People*. Chicago: University of Chicago Press.

Comaroff, Jean, and John Comaroff. 1999. Occult Economies and the Violence of Abstraction: Notes from the South African Postcolony. *American Ethnologist* 26 (2): 279–303.

———. 2000. Millennial Capitalism: First Thoughts on a Second Coming. *Public Culture* 12 (2): 291–343.

———. 2003. Second Comings: Neo-Protestant Ethics and Millennial Capitalism in Africa, and Elsewhere. In *2000 Years and Beyond: Faith, Identity and the Common Era*, ed. Paul Gifford with David Archard, Trevor A. Hart, and Nigel Rapport, 106–126. London: Routledge.

———. 2004. Notes on Afromodernity and the Neo World Order: An Afterword. In *Producing African Futures: Ritual and Reproduction in a Neoliberal Age*, 529–48. Leiden: Brill.

———. 2005. Reflections on Youth. In *Makers and Breakers: Children and Youth in Postcolonial Africa*, ed. Alcinda Honwana and Filip de Boeck, 19–30. Oxford: James Curry.

Condominas, George. 1960. *Fokonolona et collectivités rurales en Imerina*. Paris: Berger-Levrault.

Connerton, Paul. 1989. *How Societies Remember*. Cambridge: Cambridge University Press.

Constable, Nicole. 2003. *Romance on a Global Stage: Pen Pals, Virtual Ethnography and "Mail Order" Brides*. Berkeley: University of California Press.

———, ed. 2005. *Cross-Border Marriages: Gender and Mobility in Transnational Asia*. Philadelphia: University of Pennsylvania Press.

Cooper, Frederick. 2001. What Is the Concept of Globalization Good For? An African Historian's Perspective. *African Affairs* 100:189–213.

———. 2005. *Colonialism in Question: Theory, Knowledge and History*. Berkeley: University of California Press.

Cooper, Frederick, and Ann Stoler, eds. 1997. *Tensions of Empire: Colonial Cultures in a Bourgeois World*. Berkeley: University of California Press.

Covell, Maureen. 1987. *Madagascar: Politics, Economics, and Society*. New York: Frances Pinter.

Crise. 1991. *Tribune de Madagascar*, January 7.

Cruise-O'Brien, Donal B. 1996. A Lost Generation? Youth Identity and State Decay in West Africa. In *Postcolonial Identities in Africa*, ed. Richard Werbner and Terence Ranger, 55–74. London: Zed Books.

Csordas, Thomas. 1992. Religion and the World System: The Pentecostal Ethic and the Spirit of Monopoly Capital. *Dialectical Anthropology* 17:3–24.

Decary, R. 1938. Enquête no. 4 sur le problème des métis. Papiers Raymond Decary, 2984. Bibliothèque Centrale, Muséum National d'Histoire Naturelle.

Delval, Raymond. 1972. *Radama II: Prince de la Renaissance Malgache, 1861–1863*. Paris: Éditions de l'École.

———. 1992. Les débuts du mouvement scout et notamment du guidisme à Madagascar. In *Les jeunes en Afrique*, vol. 1, *Évolution et rôle (xix–xx siècle)*, ed. Hélène Almeida-Topor, Catherine Coquery-Vidrovitch, and Odile Goerg, 286–306. Paris: Éditions de l'Harmattan.

Deschamps, Hubert Julius. 1949. *Les pirates à Madagascar aux xviie et xviiie siècles*. Paris: Éditions Berger-Levrault.

Donham, Donald L. 1999. *Marxist Modern: An Ethnographic History of the Ethiopian Revolution*. Berkeley: University of California Press.

Dubourdieu, Lucile Jacquier. 2002. De la guérison des corps à la guérison de la nation:

Réveil et mouvements évangeliques à l'assaut de l'espace publique. In *Madagascar, les urnes et la rue. Politique Africaine* 86: 70–85.

Durham, Deborah. 2004. Disappearing Youth: Youth as Social Shifter in Botswana. *American Ethnologist* 31 (4): 589–605.

———. 2008. Apathy and Agency: The Romance of Youth in Botsawana. In *Figuring the Future: Globalization and the Temporalities of Children and Youth*, ed. Jennifer Cole and Deborah Durham, 151–179. Santa Fe, NM: School of American Research Press.

Durkheim, Émile. 1995 [1912]. *Elementary Forms of Religious Life*. Trans. Karen E. Fields. London: Free Press.

Elder, Glen H. 1999. *Children of the Great Depression: Social Change in Life Experience*. Twenty-fifth anniversary edition. Boulder, CO: Westview Press.

Ellis, William. 1838. *History of Madagascar*. London: Fisher.

———. 1858. *Visits to Madagascar*. London: John Murray.

———. 1862. *Madagascar Revisited*. London: John Murray.

Emoff, Ron. 2002. *Recollecting from the Past: Musical Practice and Spirit Possession on the East Coast of Madagascar*. Middletown: CT: Wesleyan University Press.

Erikson, Erik H. 1968. *Identity, Youth, and Crisis*. New York: W. W. Norton.

Esoavelomandroso, Faranirina. 1981. Différentes lectures de l'histoire: Quelques réflexions sur le V.V.S. *Recherche, Paedagogie et Culture* 50:101–111.

———. 1992. Ainés et cadets: Le foyer chrétien des jeunes gens d'Antananarivo (1924–1960). In *Les jeunes en Afrique*, vol. 1, *Évolution et rôle (xix–xx siècle)*, ed. Hélène Almeida-Topor, Catherine Coquery-Vidrovitch, and Odile Goerg, 400–415. Paris: Éditions de l'Harmattan.

Esoavelomandroso, Manassé. 1978. Religion et politique: L'évangélisation du pays Betsimisaraka à la fin du xixième siècle. *Omaly Sy Anio: Revue d'Études Historiques* 7–8: 7–40.

———. 1979. *La province maritime orientale du royaume de Madagascar à la fin du xixe siècle (1882–1895)*. Antananarivo: FTM Antananarivo, Madagascar.

———. 1980. The "Malagasy Creoles" of Tamatave in the 19th Century. *Diogenes* 28: 50–63.

Evers, Sandra. 2002. *Constructing History, Culture and Inequality: The Betsileo in the Extreme Southern Highlands of Madagascar*. Leiden: Brill.

Fanon, Franz. 1967 [1952]. *Black Skins, White Masks*. New York: Grove Press.

Farquhar, Judith, and Margaret Lock. 2007. Introduction. In *Beyond the Body Proper*, ed. Margaret Lock and Judith Farquhar, 1–16. Durham, NC: Duke University Press.

Farrer, James. 2002. *Opening Up: Youth Sex Culture and Market Reform in Shanghai*. Chicago: University of Chicago Press.

Fass, Paula S. 2007. *Children of a New World: Society, Culture, and Globalization*. New York: New York University Press.

Feeley-Harnik, Gillian. 1984. The Political Economy of Death: Communication and Change in Malagasy Colonial History. *American Ethnologist* 8:231–254.

———. 1991. *A Green Estate: Restoring Independence in Madagascar*. Washington, DC: Smithsonian Institution Press.

Ferguson, James. 1997. The Country and the City on the Copperbelt. In *Culture, Power, Place: Explorations in Critical Anthropology*, ed. Akhil Gupta and James Ferguson, 137–154. Durham, NC: Duke University Press.

———. 1999. *Expectations of Modernity: Myths and Meanings of Urban Life on the Zambian Copperbelt*. Berkeley: University of California Press.

————. 2006. *Global Shadows: Africa in the Neoliberal World Order*. Durham, NC: Duke University Press.

Flavell, J. H. 1971. Stage-Related Properties of Cognitive Development. *Cognitive Psychology* 2:421–453.

Fortes, Meyer. 1984. Age, Generation and Social Structure. In *Age and Anthropological Theory*, ed. David I. Kertzer and Jennie Keith, 99–122. Ithaca, NY: Cornell University Press.

Foucault, Michel. 1978. *The History of Sexuality*, vol. 1. New York: Pantheon.

————. 1994. The Subject and Power. In *The Essential Foucault*, ed. Paul Rabinow and Nikolas Rose, 126–144. New York: New Press.

Fox, James. 1987. The House as a Type of Social Organization on the Island of Roti. In *De la hutte au palais*, ed. Charles Macdonald, 171–178. Paris: Éditions du CNRS.

Fremigacci, Jean. 1999. Bilan provisoire de l'insurrection de 1947: Nécessité de nouvelles recherches. In *Madagascar 1947: La tragédie oubliée*, ed. Francis Arzalier and Jean Suret-Canale, 177–189. Pantin, France: Temps des Cerises.

Frenée, M. 1931. *Madagascar: Guide des colonies françaises*. Paris: Société d'Éditions Géographiques, Maritimes et Coloniales.

Fussell, Paul. 2000 [1975]. *The Great War and Modern Memory*. New York: Oxford University Press.

Gal, Susan, and Gail Kligman. 2000. *The Politics of Gender after Socialism: A Comparative-Historical Essay*. Princeton, NJ: Princeton University Press.

Galibert, Didier. 2009. Mobilisation populaire et répression à Madagascar: La cité culturelle dans l'impasse? In *Afrique, la globalisation par les Suds. Politique Africaine* 113: 139–151.

Geertz, Clifford. 1983. "From the Native's Point of View": On the Nature of Anthropological Understanding. In *Local Knowledge: Further Essays in Interpretive Anthropology*, 55–71. New York: Basic Books.

Gifford, Paul. 2004. *Ghana's New Christianity: Pentecostalism in a Globalizing African Economy*. Bloomington: Indiana University Press.

Gill, Lesley. 1990. "Like a Veil to Cover Them": Women and the Pentecostal Movement in La Paz. *American Ethnologist* 17 (4): 708–721.

Goffman, Erving. 1963. *Stigma: Notes on the Management of Spoiled Identity*. Englewood Cliffs, NJ: Prentice-Hall.

Gogul, Anne-Marie. 2006. *Aux origines du mai malgache: Désir d'école et compétition sociale, 1951–1972*. Paris: Karthala.

Gondola, Didier. 1999. Dream and Drama: The Search for Elegance among Congolese Youth. *African Studies Review* 42 (1): 23–48.

Goody, Esther. 1982. *Parenthood and Social Reproduction: Fostering and Occupational Roles in West Africa*. Cambridge: Cambridge University Press.

Gould, Stephen Jay. 1996. *The Mismeasure of Man*. 2nd ed. London: W. W. Norton.

Graeber, David. 1995. Dancing with Corpses Reconsidered: An Interpretation of *Famadihana* (in Arivonimamo, Madagascar). *American Ethnologist* 22:258–278.

————. 2001. *Toward an Anthropological Theory of Value: The False Coin of Our Own Dreams*. New York: Palgrave.

————. 2007. *Lost People: Magic and the Legacy of Slavery in Madagascar*. Bloomington: Indiana University Press.

Grandidier, Guillaume. 1913. *Le mariage à Madagascar*. Bulletins et mémoires de la Société d'Anthropologie de Paris, vol. 4, ser. 6. Paris: Société d'Anthropologie de Paris.

————. 1942. *Histoire politique et colonial*, t. 1, vol. 5, p. 320, n. 4, notule B. Éditions Imprimerie Officielle de Tananarive.

Gregg, Jessica. 2006. He Can Be Sad Like That: Liberdade and the Absence of Romantic Love in a Brazilian Shantytown. In *Modern Loves: The Anthropology of Romantic Courtship and Companionate Marriage,* ed. Jennifer S. Hirsch and Holly Wardlow, 157–173. Ann Arbor: University of Michigan Press.

Grimes, Ronald. 2000. *Deeply into the Bone: Reinventing Rites of Passage.* Berkeley: University of California Press.

Gupta, Akhil. 1998. *Postcolonial Developments.* Durham, NC: Duke University Press.

Hackett, Rosalind. 1995. The Gospel of Prosperity in West Africa. In *Religion and the Transformation of Capitalism,* ed. Richard H. Roberts, 199–214. London: Routledge.

Hacking, Ian. 1987. Making Up People. In *Reconstructing Individualism: Autonomy, Individuality, and the Self in Western Thought,* ed. Thomas C. Heller, Morton Sosna, and David E. Welberry, with Arnold I. Davidson and Ann Swidler, 222–236. Stanford, CA: Stanford University Press.

Hall, Stuart, and Tony Jefferson. 2000 [1975]. *Resistance through Rituals: Youth Subcultures in Post-war Britain.* London: Routledge.

Hansen, Karen T. 2005. Getting Stuck in the Compound: Some Odds against Social Adulthood in Lusaka, Zambia. *Africa Today* 51 (4): 3–16.

Harding, Susan Friend. 1987. Convicted by the Holy Spirit: The Rhetoric of Fundamental Baptist Conversion. *American Ethnologist* 14 (1): 167–181.

———. 2000. *The Book of Jerry Falwell: Fundamentalist Language and Politics.* Princeton, NJ: Princeton University Press.

Hardt, Michael. 1999. Affective Labor. *Boundary 2* 26 (2): 89–100.

———. 2007. Foreword: What Affects Are Good For. In *The Affective Turn: Theorizing the Social,* ed. Patricia Ticeneto Clough with Jean Halley, ix–xiii. Durham, NC: Duke University Press.

Harvey, David. 2005. *A Brief History of Neoliberalism.* Oxford: Oxford University Press.

Hatzfeld, O. 1953. Évolution actuelle de la société malgache. *Le Monde Non Chrétien* 27: 294–304.

Hebdige, Dick. 1979. *Subculture: The Meaning of Style.* New York: Routledge.

———. 2000 [1975]. The Meaning of Mod. In *Resistance through Rituals: Youth Subcultures in Post-war Britain,* ed. Stuart Hall and Tony Jefferson, 87–98. New York: Routledge.

Herdt, Gilbert, ed. 2009. *Moral Panics, Sex Panics: Fear and the Fight over Sexual Rights.* New York: New York University Press.

Ho, Engseng. 2004. *The Graves of Tarim: Genealogy and Mobility across the Indian Ocean.* Berkeley: University of California Press.

Hodgson, Dorothy, and Sheryl McCurdy. 2001. *"Wicked" Women and the Reconfiguration of Gender in Africa.* Portsmouth, NH: Heinemann.

Honwana, Alcinda, and Filip de Boeck. 2005a. Introduction. In *Makers and Breakers: Children and Youth in Postcolonial Africa,* ed. Filip de Boeck and Alcinda Honwana. Oxford: James Curry.

———, eds. 2005b. *Makers and Breakers: Children and Youth in Postcolonial Africa.* Oxford: James Curry.

Horton, Robin. 1967. African Traditional Thought and Western Science. *Africa* 37 (2): 155–187.

Hunt, Nancy Rose. 1999. *A Colonial Lexicon of Birth Ritual, Medicalization, and Mobility in the Congo.* Durham, NC: Duke University Press.

Hunter, Mark. 2002. The Materiality of Everyday Sex: Thinking beyond "Prostitution." *African Studies* 61 (1): 99–120.

Hurbon, Laënnec. 2001. Pentecostalism and Transnationalism in the Caribbean. In

Between Babel and Pentecost: Transnationalism in Africa and Latin America, ed. André Coron and Ruth Marshall-Fratani, 124–141. Bloomington: Indiana University Press.

INSTAT. 1975. Recensement 1975: Série études et analyse. Analyse des données démographiques. Antananarivo, Madagascar: Ministre des Finances et de l'Économie, Institut National de la Statistique.

——. 2000. Tableau de bord social: Appui à la mise en place d'un système national intégré de suivi de la pauvreté. Antananarivo, Madagascar: Ministre des Finances et de l'Économie, Institut National de la Statistique.

——. 2001. L'emploi, le chomage et les conditions d'activité des ménages dans les sept grandes villes de Madagascar. Antananarivo, Madagascar: Ministre des Finances et de l'Économie, Institut National de la Statistique.

——. 2003. Tableau de bord social: Toamasina. Antananarivo, Madagascar: Ministre des Finances et de l'Économie, Institut National de la Statistique.

Jameson, Frederic. 1991. *Postmodernism, or The Cultural Logic of Late Capitalism*. Durham, NC: Duke University Press.

Jaofeno, Sonny. 2006. Les jeunes bachelières malgaches: Hérauts de la révolution (1975–1991). Master's thesis, University of Paris 7.

Jean-Baptiste, Rachel. 2010. "A Black Girl Should Not Be with a White Man": Sex, Race and African Women's Social and Legal Status in Colonial Gabon, c. 1900–1946. *Journal of Women's History* 2 (3): 56–82.

Jeffrey, Craig, Patricia Jeffrey, and Roger Jeffrey. 2008. *Degrees without Freedom? Education, Masculinities, and Unemployment in North India*. Stanford, CA: Stanford University Press.

Johnson-Hanks, Jennifer. 2002. On the Limits of Life Stages in Ethnography: Toward a Theory of Vital Conjunctures. *American Anthropologist* 104 (3): 865–880.

——. 2006. *Uncertain Honor: Modern Motherhood in an African Crisis*. Chicago: University of Chicago Press.

——. 2007. Women on the Market: Marriage, Consumption and the Internet in Urban Cameroon. *American Ethnologist* 34 (4): 642–658.

Keane, Webb. 2007. *Christian Moderns: Freedom and Fetish in the Mission Encounter*. Berkeley: University of California Press.

Keenan, Elinor Ochs. 1974. Norm-Makers, Norm-Breakers: Uses of Speech by Men and Women in a Malagasy Community. In *Explorations in the Ethnography of Speaking*, ed. Richard Bauman and Joel Sherzer, 125–143. Cambridge: Cambridge University Press.

Keller, Eva. 2005. *The Road to Clarity: Seventh-Day Adventism in Madagascar*. New York: Palgrave Macmillan.

Kelsky, Karen. 2001. *Women on the Verge: Japanese Women, Western Dreams*. Durham, NC: Duke University Press.

Kent, Raymond. 1962. Malagasy Republic. In *The Educated African: A Country-by-Country Survey of Educational Development in Africa*, ed. Helen Kitchen, 249–266. New York: Praeger.

Koselleck, Reinhart. 1985. *Figures Past: On the Semantics of Historical Time*. Trans. Keith Tribe. Cambridge, MA: MIT Press.

Lacan, Jacques. 1968 [1949]. The Mirror-Phase as Formative of the Function of the I. *New Left Review* 1 (51): 71–77, September–October.

Lacaze, Honoré. 1881. *Souvenirs de Madagascar: Voyage à Madagascar, histoire, population, moeurs, institutions*. Paris: Berger-Levrault.

Lacombe, Legueval de. 1840. *Voyage à Madagascar et aux îles Comores*. Paris.

Lalive d'Epinay, Christian. 1969. *Haven of the Masses: A Study of the Pentecostal Movement in Chile*. London: Lutterworth.

Lambek, Michael. 2001. The Value of Coins in a Sakalava Polity: Money, Death and Historicity in Mahajanga, Madagascar. *Comparative Studies in Society and History* 43: 735–762.

———. 2002. *The Weight of the Past: Living with History in Mahajanga, Madagascar*. New York: Palgrave Macmillan.

Lambek, Michael, and Andrew Walsh. 1999. The Imagined Community of the Antankaraña: Identity, History, and Ritual in Northern Madagascar. In *Ancestors, Power and History in Madagascar*, ed. Karen Middleton, 145–174. Leiden: Brill.

Larson, Pier. 2009. *Ocean of Letters: Language and Identity in an Indian Ocean Diaspora*. Cambridge: Cambridge University Press.

LCHC (Laboratory of Comparative Human Cognition). 1983. Culture and Cognition. In *Handbook of Child Psychology*, ed. P. Mussen, vol. 1, *History, Theory and Methods*, ed. W. Kessen, 295–356. New York: Wiley.

Ledoux, Marc André. 1951. La jeunesse malgache. *Cahiers Charles de Foucauld*. Numero spécial sur Madagascar, 1 trimestre.

Lepovetsky, Gilles. 1994. *The Empire of Fashion: Dressing Modern Democracy*. Trans. Catherine Porter. Princeton, NJ: Princeton University Press.

LeVine Robert, and Barbara LeVine, 1966. *Nyansongo: A Gusi Community in Kenya*. New York: Wiley.

Liechty, Mark. 2003. *Suitably Modern: Making Middle-Class Culture in a New Consumer Society*. Princeton, NJ: Princeton University Press.

Lindsay, Lisa, and Stephen Meischer, eds. 2003. *Men and Masculinities in Modern Africa*. Portsmouth, NH: Heinemann.

Livingston, Julie. 2009. Suicide, Risk, and Investment in the Heart of the African Miracle. *Cultural Anthropology* 23 (4): 652–680.

Luhermann, Sonja. 2004. Mediated Marriage: Matchmaking in Provincial Russia. *Europe Asia Studies* 56 (6): 857–875.

Luhrmann, Tanya M. 2004. Metakinesis: How God Becomes Intimate in Contemporary US Christianity. *American Anthropologist* 106 (3): 518–528.

Lukose, Ritty. 2005. Consuming Globalization: Youth and Gender in Kerala, India. *Journal of Social History* 38 (4): 915–936.

———. 2009. *Liberalization's Children: Gender, Youth and Consumer Citizenship in South India*. Durham, NC: Duke University Press.

Mahmood, Saba. 2005. *The Politics of Piety*. Princeton, NJ: Princeton University Press.

Mains, Daniel. 2007. Neoliberal Times: Progress, Boredom and Shame among Young Men in Urban Ethiopia. *American Ethnologist* 34 (4): 659–667.

Maira, Sunaina, and Elizabeth Soep. 2005. *Youthscapes: The Popular, the National, the Global*. Philadelphia: University of Pennsylvania Press.

Mallet, Robert. 1964. *Région inhabitée*. Paris. Éditions Gallimard.

Mannheim, Karl. 1993 [1927]. The Problem of Generations. In *From Karl Mannheim*, ed. Kurt H. Wolff, 351–398. New Brunswick, NJ: Transaction.

Marguerat, Yves. 2005. From Generational Conflict to Renewed Dialogue: Winning the Trust of Street Children in Lomé, Togo. In *Vanguard or Vandals: Youth, Politics and Conflict in Africa*, ed. Jon Abbink and Ineke van Kessel, 207–227. Leiden: Brill.

Marshall, Ruth. 2009. *Political Spiritualities: The Pentecostal Revolution in Nigeria*. Chicago: University of Chicago Press.

Marx, Karl. 1978 [1972]. Economic and Philosophic Manuscripts of 1844. In *The Marx-Engels Reader*, 2nd ed., ed. Robert C. Tucker, 66–125. New York: W. W. Norton.

Masquelier, Adeline. 2005. The Scorpion's Sting: Youth, Marriage and the Struggle for Social Maturity in Niger. *Journal of the Royal Anthropological Institute* 3:59–83.

Mathiau, Alexandre. 1930. Préface de Delélée Desloges. In *Soliloques de brousse*. Paris: Pyronnet.

Mauss, Marcel. 1973 [1935]. Techniques of the Body. *Economy and Society* 2:70–88.

———. 1990 [1950]. *The Gift: The Form and Reason for Exchange in Archaic Societies*. New York: W. W. Norton.

Mead, Margaret. 1970. *Culture and Commitment: A Study of the Generation Gap*. Garden City, NY: Natural History Press.

Memmi, Albert. 1966. *The Colonizer and the Colonized*. Boston: Beacon Press.

Meyer, Birgit. 1999. *Translating the Devil: Religion and Modernity among the Ewe in Ghana*. Edinburgh: Edinburgh University Press.

Middleton, Karen. 1995. Tombs, Umbilical Cords and the Syllable "Fo." In *Cultures of Madagascar*, ed. S. E. Versa and M. Spindler, 223–235. Working Papers, ser. 2. Leiden: International Institute for Asian Studies.

———, ed. 1999. *Ancestors, Power and History in Madagascar*. Leiden: Brill.

Mills, Mary-Beth. 1997. Contesting the Margins of Modernity: Women, Migration, and Consumption in Thailand. *American Ethnologist* 24 (1): 37–61.

Mitchell, Timothy. 1998. Fixing the Economy. *Cultural Studies* 12:82–101.

———. 2002. *Rule of Experts: Egypt, Techno-politics, Modernity*. Berkeley: University of California Press.

Munn, Nancy. 1992. The Cultural Anthropology of Time: A Critical Essay. *Annual Review of Anthropology* 21:93–123.

Mutongi, Kenda. 2007. *Worries of the Heart: Widows, Family and Community in Kenya*. Chicago: University of Chicago Press.

Nandy, Ashis. 1983. *The Intimate Enemy: Loss and Recovery of Self under Colonialism*. Delhi: Oxford University Press.

Natokana ho fanolokolana ny tena, saina amam-panahin'ny vehivavy. 1960. *Isika Vehivavy* [We Women] (Tananarive), March.

Newman, Katherine. 1996. Ethnography, Biography and Cultural History: Generational Paradigms in Human Development. In *Ethnography and Human Development: Context and Meaning in Social Inquiry*, ed. Richard Jessor, Anne Colby, and Richard Shweder, 371–393. Chicago: University of Chicago Press.

Nyamnjoh, Francis. 2005. Fishing in Troubled Waters: Disquettes and Thiofs in Dakar. *Africa* 27 (3): 295–324.

Parny, Évariste de. 1787. *Chansons madécasses*. Paris: Arrière-Boutique.

Parry, Jonathan, and Bloch, Maurice, eds. 1989. *Money and the Morality of Exchange*. Cambridge: Cambridge University Press.

Parsons, Talcott. 1961. Youth in the Context of American Society. In *Youth: Change and Challenge*, ed. Erik Erikson, 93–119. New York: Basic Books.

Perry, Donna. 2009. Fathers, Sons, and the State: Discipline and Punishment in a Wolof Hinterland. *Cultural Anthropology* 24 (1): 33–67.

Piaget, Jean. 1977. *The Development of Thought: Equilibration of Cognitive Structures*. New York: Viking Press.

Pigg, Stacy Leigh. 1996. The Credible and the Credulous: The Question of "Villagers' Beliefs" in Nepal. *Cultural Anthropology* 11 (2): 160–201.

Pompey, Fabienne. 2007. Les petites fiancées de l'Internet. *Le Monde*, October 11.

Prestholdt, Jeremy. 2004. On the Global Repercussions of East African Consumerism. *American Historical Review* 109 (3): 1–38.

———. 2008. *Domesticating the World: African Consumerism and the Genealogies of Globalization.* Berkeley: University of California Press.

Raintsoa, Andy. 1995. Ny vola sy ny aina. *Tribune de Madagascar,* July 19.

Raison-Jourde, Françoise. 1977. L'échange inégal de la langue: La pénétration des techniques linguistiques dans une civilisation de l'oral (Imerinia, début du xix siècle). *Annales ESC* 32–34:639–669.

———. 1983. *Les souverains de Madagascar: L'histoire royale et ses résurgences contemporaines.* Paris: Karthala.

———. 1991. *Bible et pouvoir à Madagascar au xix siècle: Invention d'une identité chrétienne et construction de l'état.* Paris: Karthala.

———. 1997. Les prolongements du soulèvement dans la mémoire et dans le contact avec des administrés. Paper presented at Colloque Internationale sur le Cinquantenaire de l'Insurrection de 1947. Département de l'Histoire, Université d'Antananarivo, Madagascar.

Raison-Jourde, Françoise, and Pierre Raison. 2002. Ravalomanana et la Troisième Indépendence? *Politique Africaine* 86:5–17.

Rajaonah, Faranirina. 2001. Enquêtes sur les métis à Antananarivo pendant la période coloniale. *Annuaire des Pays de l'Océan Indien* 17:73–86.

Rakotonirina, Michel-Guste. 1960. *Lalan Fiton'ny Tokantrano.* Antananarivo: Imprimerie Volamahitsy.

Randriamaro, Jean-Roland. 2008. Identité culturelle et métissage chez les descendents d'esclaves de Tananarive. Paper presented at the conference Multiculturalisme, échanges et métissages culturels dans les villes de l'océan Indien Occidental, xvii-xxi. University of Paris 7, November 13–15.

Randrianja, Solofo. 2001. *Société et luttes anticoloniales à Madagascar, 1896–1946.* Paris: Karthala.

Rantoandro, Gabriel Andriamiarintsoa. 1980. Le gouvernement de Tamatave, de 1845 à 1865: Développement économique. PhD diss., University of Madagascar.

———. 2001. Hommes et réseaux malata de la côte orientale de Madagascar. *Annuaire des Pays de l'Océan Indien* 17:103–121.

Ratsiraka, Didier. 1975. *Charte de la révolution socialiste malgache tous azimuts.* Antananarivo: Imprimerie d'Ouvrages Éducatifs.

Rémy, Jean-Philippe, with Sébastien Hervieu. 2009. Madagascar: Qui est l'étrange Andry Rajoelina? À Madagascar, l'ascension fulgurante d'un jeune homme happé par la politique. *Le Monde,* March 27.

Renel, Charles. 1998 [1923]. *Le décivilisé.* Isle de la Réunion: Grand Océan.

Richards, Paul. 1996. *Fighting for the Rainforest: War, Youth, and Resources in Sierra Leone.* Oxford: James Curry.

Richardson, J. 1885. *A New Malagasy-English Dictionary.* Antananarivo: London Missionary Society.

Robbins, Joel. 2004a. *Becoming Sinners: Christianity and Moral Torment in a Papua New Guinea Society.* Berkeley: University of California Press.

———. 2004b. The Globalization of Pentecostal and Charismatic Christianity. *Annual Reviews in Anthropology* 33:117–143.

Rofel, Lisa. 2007. *Desiring China: Experiments in Neoliberalism, Sexuality, and Public Culture.* Durham, NC: Duke University Press.

Rose, Sonya O. 1999. Cultural Analysis and Moral Discourses: Episodes, Continuities and

Transformations. In *Beyond the Cultural Turn: New Directions in the Study of Society and Culture,* ed. Victoria E. Bonnell and Lynn Hunt, 217–240. Berkeley: University of California Press.

Rosenwein, Barbara. 2006. *Emotional Communities in the Early Middle Ages.* Ithaca, NY: Cornell University Press.

Rubin, Gayle. 1984. Thinking Sex: Notes for a Radical Theory of the Politics of Sexuality. In *Pleasure and Danger: Exploring Female Sexuality,* ed. Carole S. Vance, 267–317. Boston: Routledge and Kegan Paul.

Rushdie, Salman. 1992 [1988]. *The Satanic Verses.* Delaware: Consortium.

Rutherford, Danilyn. 2002. *Raiding the Land of the Foreigners: The Limits of the Nation on an Indonesian Frontier.* Princeton, NJ: Princeton University Press.

———. 2008. *Enchantments of Secular Belief.* http://divinity.uchicago.edu/martycenter/publications/webforum/archive.shtml.

Ryder, Norman B. 1965. The Cohort as a Concept in the Study of Social Change. *American Sociological Review* 30:843–861.

Saada, Emmanuelle. 2007. *Les enfants de la colonie: Les métis de l'empire français entre sujétion et citoyenneté.* Paris: Découverte.

Sahlins, Marshall. 1985. *Islands of History.* Chicago: University of Chicago Press.

Schaeffer-Grabiel, Felicity. 2004. Cyberbrides and Global Imaginaries: Mexican Women's Turn from the National to the Foreign. *Space and Culture* 7 (1): 33–48.

———. 2005. Planet-Love.com: Cyberbrides in the Americas and the Transnational Routes of US Masculinity. *Signs: Journal of Women in Culture and Society* 31 (2): 331–356.

Schlegel, Alice. 2000. The Global Spread of Adolescent Culture. In *Negotiating Adolescence in Times of Change,* ed. Lisa J. Crockett and Rainer K. Silbereisen, 71–88. Cambridge: Cambridge University Press.

Schoepf, Brooke Grundfest. 1992. Women at Risk: Case Studies from Zaire. In *The Time of AIDS: Social Analysis, Theory, and Method,* ed. Gilbert Herdt and Shirley Lindenbaum, 259–286. London: Sage.

Sewell, William H., Jr. 2005. *Logics of History: Social Theory and Social Transformation.* Chicago: University of Chicago Press.

Shanahan, M. J. 2000. Pathways to Adulthood in Changing Societies: Variability and Mechanisms in Life Course Perspective. *Annual Review of Sociology* 26:667–692.

Sharp, Lesley A. 1993. *The Possessed and the Dispossessed: Spirits, Identity, and Power in a Madagascar Migrant Town.* Berkeley: University of California Press.

———. 2002. *The Sacrificed Generation: Youth, History, and the Colonized Mind in Madagascar.* Berkeley: University of California Press.

Sibree, J. 1870. *Madagascar, the Great African Island.* London: Trübner.

Simmel, Georg. 1971 [1904]. Fashion. In *Georg Simmel on Individuality and Social Forms,* ed. Donald N. Levine, 294–323. Chicago: University of Chicago Press.

Simonin, L[ouis]. 1867. Notes de voyage (La Californie, Maurice, Aden, Madagascar). Paris: Challamel Ainé.

Smith-Rosenberg, Carroll. 1990. Sex as Symbol in Victorian Purity. In *Culture and Society: Contemporary Debates,* ed. Jeffrey C. Alexander and Steven Seidman, 160–170. Cambridge, MA: Harvard University Press.

Somda, Dominique. 2009. Et le réel serait passé: Le secret de l'esclavage et l'imagination de la société (Anôsy, sud de Madagascar). PhD diss., Université de Paris, Laboratoire d'Ethnologie et Sociologie Comparative.

Standing, Hilary. 1992. AIDS: Conceptual and Methodological Issues in Researching Sexual Behaviour in Sub-Saharan Africa. *Social Science and Medicine* 34 (5): 475–483.

Steedly, Mary Margaret. 1993. *Hanging without a Rope: Narrative Experience in Colonial and Postcolonial Karoland.* Princeton, NJ: Princeton University Press.

Stoebenau, Kirsten. 2006. From Those Who "Have to Carry Men" to Those Who "Look to Marry Men": The Social Organization of Women's Sex Work in Antananarivo, Madagascar. PhD diss., Johns Hopkins University.

Stoler, Ann. 2002. *Carnal Knowledge and Imperial Power: Race and the Intimate in Colonial Rule.* Berkeley: University of California Press.

Stoll, David. 1990. *Is Latin America Turning Protestant? The Politics of Evangelical Growth.* Berkeley: University of California Press.

Straker, Jay. 2007. Youth, Globalisation, and Millennial Reflection in a Guinean Forest Town. *Journal of Modern African Studies* 45 (2): 299–319.

Sundkler, Bengt. 1961 [1948]. *Bantu Prophets in South Africa.* London: Lutterworth.

Sylla, Yvette. 1985. Les Malata: Cohésion et disparité d'un "groupe." *Omaly Sy Anio* 21:-19–32.

Tanora Malagasy: Aza ariana ny kolontsainao. 1995. *Tribune de Madagascar,* March 15, 9.

Taylor, Charles. 2007. *A Secular Age.* Cambridge, MA: Belknap Press of Harvard University Press.

Thomas, Lynn M. 2003. *The Politics of the Womb: Women, Reproduction and the State in Kenya.* Berkeley: University of California Press.

Thomas, Lynn M., and Jennifer Cole. 2009. Thinking through Love in Africa. In *Love in Africa,* ed. Jennifer Cole and Lynn Thomas, 1–30. Chicago: University of Chicago Press.

Thomas, Phillip. 1996. Place, Person and Ancestry among the Temanambondro of Southeast Madagascar. PhD diss., London School of Economics.

Thompson, Virginia, and Richard Adloff. 1965. *The Malagasy Republic: Madagascar Today.* Stanford, CA: Stanford University Press.

Thorne, Barrie. 1993. *Gender Play: Boys and Girls in School.* New Brunswick, NJ: Rutgers University Press.

Tisseau, Violaine. 2007. Les femmes métisses dans les hautes terres centrales de Madagascar pendant la période coloniale. In *Perspectives historiques sur le genre en Afrique,* ed. Odile Goerg, 97–117. Cahiers du Groupe Afrique 23. Paris: Éditions de l'Harmattan.

Tronchon, Jacques. 1986. *L'insurrection malgache de 1947.* Paris: Karthala.

Tsing, Anna Lowenhaupt. 2005. *Friction: An Ethnography of Global Connection.* Princeton, NJ: Princeton University Press.

Valette, Jean. 1967. Note sur une coutume betsimisaraka du xviii siècle, les vadimbazaha. *Cahiers du Centre d'Étude des Coutumes,* vol. 3.

Vaovaon'I Toamasina, Trano Fandizana. 1995. *Tribune de Madagascar,* March 22, 6.

Veblen, Thorstein. 1992 [1899]. *The Theory of the Leisure Class.* London: Transaction.

Waast, Roland. 1980. Les concubins de Soalala. In *Changements sociaux dans l'ouest Malagache,* ed. R. Waast, E. Faroux, B. Schlemmer, F. Le Bourdic, J. P. Raison, and G. Dandoy, 153–188. Paris: Orstom.

Walkowitz, Judith. 1992. *City of Dreadful Delight: Narratives of Sexual Danger in Late-Victorian London.* Chicago: University of Chicago Press.

Walley, Christine J. 2004. *Rough Waters: Nature and Development in an East African Marine Park.* Princeton, NJ: Princeton University Press.

Walsh, Andrew. 2003. Hot Money and Daring Consumption in a Northern Malagasy Sapphire-Mining Town. *American Ethnologist* 30 (2): 290–305.

Wardlow, Holly. 2002. "Hands-Up"-ing Buses and Harvesting Cheese Pops: Gendered Mediation of Modern Disjuncture in Melanesia. In *Critically Modern: Alternatives, Alteri-*

ties, Anthropologies, ed. Bruce M. Knauft, 144–172. Bloomington: Indiana University Press.

———. 2004. Anger, Economy and Female Agency: Problematizing "Prostitution" and "Sex Work" among the Huli of Papua New Guinea. *Signs: Journal of Women in Culture and Society* 29 (4): 1017–1040.

Weber, Max. 1958 [1904–1905]. *The Protestant Ethic and the Spirit of Capitalism.* New York: Charles Scribner's Sons.

Weiss, Brad. 2002. Thug Realism: Inhabiting Fantasy in Urban Tanzania. *Cultural Anthropology* 17 (1): 93–128.

———, ed. 2004. *Producing African Futures: Ritual and Reproduction in a Neoliberal Age.* Leiden: Brill.

———. 2009. *Street Dreams and Hip Hop Barbershops: Global Fantasy in Urban Tanzania.* Bloomington: Indiana University Press.

White, Luise. 1990. *The Comforts of Home: Prostitution in Colonial Nairobi.* Chicago: University of Chicago Press.

White, Owen. 2000. *Children of the French Empire: Miscegenation and Colonial Society in French West Africa, 1895–1960.* Oxford: Oxford University Press.

Willems, Emilio. 1967. *Followers of the New Faith: Culture Change and the Rise of Protestantism in Brazil and Chile.* Nashville, TN: Vanderbilt University Press.

Williams, Raymond. 1975. *The Country and the City.* New York: Oxford University Press.

Wohl, Robert. 1979. *The Generation of 1914.* Cambridge: Cambridge University Press.

Wojcicki, Janet Maia. 2002. Commercial Sex Work or Ukuphanda? Sex-for-Money Exchange in Soweto and Hammanskraal Area, South Africa. *Culture, Medicine, and Psychiatry* 26 (3): 339–370.

Young, Jock. 1971. *The Drugtakers: The Social Meanings of Drug Use.* London: Paladin.

Zalduondo, Barbara. 1991. Prostitution Viewed Cross-Culturally: Toward Recontextualizing Sex Work in AIDS Intervention Research. *Journal of Sex Research* 28 (2): 223–248.

Zemon-Davis, Nathalie. 1983. *The Return of Martin Guerre.* Cambridge, MA: Harvard University Press.

Zhen, Zhang. 2000. Mediating Time: The "Rice Bowl of Youth" in Fin de Siècle Urban China. *Public Culture* 12 (1): 93–113.

INDEX

Italicized page numbers refer to figures.

abortions, 87, 93
administrative posts. *See* bureaucracy, government
adriambaventy, 26
adulthood, 5–8, 10–11, 14, 19, 28–29, 32, 42, 154, 181, 183–84; and ancestors, 52, 57, 198n10; and jeunes, 93–97, 104–5, 110, 181; and social economy, 70–71, 82, 86, 91; and vazaha, 118, 125, 142, 148–49
Adventists, 1–4, 11, 199nn16–17, 205n12
affective dimension, 52, 90, 143–45, 188–90
agriculture, 39, 42, 197n21, 197n23; and ancestors, 51, 54, 56–57, 62; in colonial period, 29, 194n4, 195n7; and humiliation of poverty, 58–59; in precolonial era, 25–26, 28, 194n1; and social economy, 71, 74, 83. *See also* rural culture
AIDS, 1–2, 4, 204n14
Albert, Zafy, 42, 180, 196n19
ambassady, 105–6, 202n8
ancestors, 10, 18–19, 25, 50, 51–59, *53*, 152, 184, 198n5, 198nn7–8; ancestor-descendant relationships, 51–56, *53*, 60–62, 69, 161; blessings of, 51, *53*, 54, 56–58, 64, 161, 184, 205n6; and bone turnings, 61, 158, 161, 184; and Christianity, 62–64, 199nn15–19; and jeunes, 97–99, 102, 105, 112, 135; and Pentecostalism, 63, 155, 157–61, 172,

174–75, 199n19, 205nn4–6; power of, 51–52, 56–57, 59–60, 63, 198n5, 199n14; and rural culture, 10, 18–19, 25, 50, 51–59, *53*, 60–62, 67–69, 198n5, 198nn7–8, 199n14; as saints, 62–63; second burial of, *53*, 54, 60, 85; taboos of, 51, 56–58, 93, 170–71, 199n14; tombs of, 51, 54, 56–57, 59–64, 85, 135, 161, 198n7; and urban culture, 59–65, 67–69, 199n14
anjara, 56
Antananarivo, 1, 21, 42–44, 85, 185, 196–97n20, 199n19; in colonial/neo-colonial periods, 31–33, 38, 194n4; and Rajoelina, 179–80; in socialist period, 40–41; and vazaha, 131, 202n1
Arapilazantsara (the Good Word), 63
Assembly of God church, 63, 89, 161, 165, 170, 205n8
Astuti, Rita, 198n8
Augagneur, Victor, 31, 124, 203n5

Be L'assietty, 63, 199n20
Berger, John, 108
Berger, Laurent, 10
Betsimisaraka, 18, 25, 37, 39, *53*, 56, 83, 194n1, 196n18
Betsimisaraka Federation, 25–26
Bezaka, Alexis, 102
Bhabha, Homi, 202n5

bilateral inheritance patterns, 26, 51–52, 78
birth control, 1–2, 93
biznesy, 111–12, 114, 121
Bloch, Maurice, 198n8, 200n22
Bourdieu, Pierre, 193n13
Boy Scouts movement, 31, 33, 201n5
bridewealth, 34, 72, 113, 137
bureaucracy, government, 24, 45, 60, 132;
    in colonial period, 29–34, 75, 194n4,
    195n7; in precolonial era, 26–28, 98;
    and social economy, 75–76, 83–84; in
    socialist period, 39, 41

Cannell, Fenella, 176
capitalism, 3–4, 6, 10–12, 17, 44, 49, 191–
    92n3, 200n22. See also globalization
caring, 54, 68, 72–74, 76, 78, 81–82, 90,
    141, 173
cash crops, 29, 44, 59
Catholicism, 2, 123, 131, 152; and ances-
    tors, 62–64, 199n15; in colonial period,
    26, 31, 33, 99–100, 201n5; and Pente-
    costalism, 158–61, 165, 172–74, 177;
    and Rajoelina, 206n1
cattle, 17, 25–26, 37; and masculinity,
    3–4, 95, 98–99; sacrifice of, 53, 57–60,
    62–64, 68, 88, 135, 158, 161, 198n12,
    202n11
cell phones, 43, 66, 96, 108, 188–89
Charter for the Malagasy Revolution (Red
    Book), 39
cheating, 77, 80, 83, 85, 88, 122, 131, 134,
    144, 201n7
childbearing, 8, 11, 56, 73, 80–83, 85, 87,
    152
children, 52–56, 55, 58, 69–70, 198nn8–9;
    and jeunes, 93–94, 96, 100–101, 104,
    133; and Pentecostalism, 152–53, 167,
    168, 173; and social economy, 71–72,
    76, 80–91, 84; and vazaha, 123–24,
    133, 146–47
Chinese, 23, 28, 43, 104, 131
Christianity, 34, 50, 65, 125, 176; and
    ancestors, 62–64, 199nn15–19; in colo-
    nial period, 33, 37, 74, 99; and jeunes,
    99–100, 103, 109. See also Catholicism;
    Pentecostalism; Protestants
Church of Jesus Christ in Madagascar. See
    FJKM (Fiangonan'i Jesoa Kristy eto
    Madagasikara)

class distinctions, 26; and jeunes, 106,
    109–10
colonial period (1895–1960), 18, 21,
    23–25, 27, 29–37, 30, 41–42, 45, 65–
    66, 187, 192n4, 193n16, 194nn1–5,
    195nn6–7; education in, 24, 29–33,
    194nn4–5, 195n6; jeunes compared
    to, 98–102, 105; marriage in, 33–37,
    74, 201n5, 201n7; and vazaha, 120–21,
    123–25, 203nn5–7, 203n9
Comaroff, Jean, 193n14
competition, social, 50, 59, 66–69; and
    jeunes, 96, 108; and Pentecostalism,
    153–54, 162–63, 174–77; and vazaha,
    146
computers, 66, 95, 107–8, 180
concubines, 73, 121–23
Connerton, Paul, 9
constitution, Malagasy, 180
consumerism, 2–6, 11, 43, 50, 64, 191–
    92n3, 197n21; in colonial/neocolonial
    periods, 32, 35–37, 36, 195n11; east
    African, 10; and jeunes, 93–94, 96–97,
    100, 104, 108–10, 114; and marriage,
    35–37, 36; and Pentecostalism, 157;
    and progress, 66–68; in socialist period,
    40–41, 195n14
continuity, cultural/historical, 5–9, 11,
    18–19, 176, 182–83, 191–92n3, 192n5;
    and ancestors, 48, 55, 56, 67; and
    jeunes, 98–99, 104; and Pentecostalism,
    160–64
Corroller, 28, 194n2
courtships, 72–75, 85, 185, 200n3, 201n5
Creoles, 24, 123–24
créoles malgaches, 26–28
crisis, language of, 6–9, 95, 182, 192nn4–5
cultural identity, 3–5, 186; and jeunes, 98–
    99, 102–4, 114, 119; and vazaha, 119

devil, 63–64, 100, 159, 166–70, 173, 175,
    181
Diego Suarez, 117, 129–30, 147, 199n20,
    202n1, 203–4n10
disembedding, 50, 59–69, 183–90, 198n4;
    and Pentecostalism, 152, 154–60, 175,
    177
diviners, 51, 63, 195n6; and jeunes, 105,
    128
divorce, 34, 73, 80, 83, 88, 131, 134, 146

domestic violence, 72, 142, 144–45, 153, 168, 173
Durham, Deborah, 192n8

economic factors, 21, 23–24, 44–45, 182–83, 187, 196nn16–17, 197nn21–22; in colonial/neocolonial periods, 29, 34–37, 36, 38; and devaluation of currency, 41, 93, 196n16; free trade zones, 42; and humiliation of poverty, 47–50, 60, 68, 200n22; informal economy, 44, 68, 83–86, 88, 197nn22–23; and jeunes, 93–95, 100, 106–7, 109–10, 202n3; and Pentecostalism, 153, 174, 176; in precolonial era, 25–28, 194n3; and privatization, 42, 44; and progress, 65–66, 199–200n21; and social economy, 71, 75–76, 82–83; in socialist period, 39–42, 45, 179; and vazaha, 120–21, 126. See also economic liberalization; money; resources; wealth
economic liberalization, 1, 3–5, 11–12, 20, 24, 42, 44–45, 179, 196n15; and humiliation of poverty, 49, 68; and jeunes, 93, 95, 126; and Pentecostalism, 152; and progress, 65–66, 199–200n21; and vazaha, 126, 149, 152
education, 15, 48–49; in colonial/neocolonial periods, 24, 29–34, 37–38, 194nn4–5, 195n6, 195n11; housekeeping schools, 34; and jeunes, 93–94, 103–9, 111, 129–31, 133, 180, 188, 204n11; in precolonial era, 26, 28–29, 194n1, 195n6; and social economy, 70–71, 76, 78, 81, 83, 85–88, 202n9; in socialist period, 39–40, 42; and vazaha, 117–18, 124, 129–31, 133–34, 204n11
elections, 42, 44, 112, 179–81, 196–97n20
elites, 67, 98; in colonial/neocolonial periods, 29, 31–32, 38, 98; in precolonial era, 24, 28, 194n3; and Rajoelina, 181
Ellis, William, 28, 34, 44
Esoavelomandroso, Manasse, 25, 28
Europeans, 196n18; in colonial period, 29, 32–33, 100–104; European men as husbands, 2, 13, 15, 17–18, 87, 101, 104, 116–50, 185; and jeunes, 100–104, 108, 128–30, 133; in precolonial era, 23, 25, 28; and progress, 65–66, 99. See also France/French; vazaha

evangelical churches, 1–2, 63, 100, 152, 181–82, 199n15, 199n19, 206n1. See also Pentecostalism; names of churches
exchange, networks of, 52–54, 66, 68–69, 97, 149, 198nn8–10; and Pentecostalism, 153, 173; and social economy, 71–74, 80–81, 86, 90–91, 200–201n4
experience-near view, 6, 14, 19, 183, 191n1
extended families, 48, 139. See also kin relationships

fandrosoana, 64–65, 199–200n21
fashions, 35, 41, 195n11, 195n14; and jeunes, 93, 96, 100, 106, 108–12, 114, 119, 127–29; and Pentecostalism, 157–60, 172, 177, 205n10
Ferguson, James, 8, 65
Fiche, 194n2
fitiavana, 54, 58, 68–69, 143–45, 150, 153, 173
fivoarana, 64, 199–200n21; and jeunes, 92–93, 99–100. See also progress
FJKM (Fiangonan'i Jesoa Kristy eto Madagasikara), 62
foreign/foreigners, 11, 43, 45, 73, 188; in colonial period, 29, 33, 102; and jeunes, 94, 97–98, 102–3, 108, 126, 128, 130; in precolonial era, 25–26, 28, 44, 98; and progress, 65–66; in socialist period, 38–41, 195n13. See also Europeans; vazaha
France/French, 43, 66, 188; in colonial/neocolonial periods, 29–39, 74, 76, 98–103, 194n3, 195n10; and jeunes, 108–9, 111, 126, 130–31, 136; in precolonial era, 25–26, 28, 62; student movement (1968), 195n13; and vazaha, 120–26, 130–31, 135, 136, 147, 203n2, 204n11, 206n2
future. See imagined futures

Gallieni, Joseph, 31–32
Geertz, Clifford, 191n1
gender inversions, 140–43
generations, 5–7, 13–16, 19, 30, 58, 179, 182–83, 186–87, 190, 192n5, 198n8; and jeunes, 95–96, 98, 100, 114, 129, 181; and Pentecostalism, 154, 178; and Rajoelina, 181–82; and vazaha, 118–19, 129, 137–40, 149

mistresses, 41, 65, 73, 80, 132, 138, 200–201n4

Mitchell, Timothy, 16

mixing. *See* intermarriage

mobility, social, 26, 69, 152; in colonial/neocolonial periods, 29–31, 33–34, 37–38; and jeunes, 99, 113, 133; in socialist period, 42, 45; and vazaha, 123, 133

models. *See* lasa maodely

modernity, 31, 50, 62, 64–67, 69; and jeunes, 93–94, 96–99, 103–6, 114, 202n5

modernization, 7–10; and ancestors, 64–67; in colonial period, 31, 64; theories of, 7–8, 65

money, 5, 11, 24, *36*, 37, 41, 184; and ancestors, 54, 59–62, 64; and humiliation of poverty, 47–50, 68–69, 200n22; and jeunes, 96, 106–7, 109–12, 119, 128, 131, 133; and Pentecostalism, 153, 162–64, 167–68, 171, 177; and social economy, 73, 77–84, 88, 90–91, 201n7; and vazaha, 119, 125, 128, 131, 133–35, 137, 139–42, 144–47, 204nn11–12. *See also* resources; wealth

moral corruption, 32–33, 124–25, 137, 195n8

moral panics, 18, 193n16

mothers: and bilateral inheritance patterns, 26, 51–52, 55, 78; and childbearing, 8, 11, 56, 73, 80–83, 85, 87, 152; and jeunes, 92, 102–3; mother-daughter bonds, 54, 138–39, 150; and Pentecostalism, 152, 173; and social economy, 71, 73, 79–81, 83, 85–86, 88–89; and vazaha, 117, 123, 129–33, 138–39, 146–47, 150

mpiandry, 181, 206n1

mpivaro-tena, 203n9

multiple temporalities. *See* temporal complexity

music videos, 93–94, 108

Mutongi, Kenda, 193n16

Myres de Villiers school, Le, 32

National Bureau of Statistics (INSTAT), 42–43, 197n23

nationalism, 38–40, 98–100, 102–4, 195n13

neocolonial period (1960–72), 4, 24, 29, 32, 37–39

neoliberal economics, 42, 45, 149, 196n15. *See also* economic liberalization

newness, 95, 119

newspapers, 3–4, 35, 42, 49, 126

NGOs (nongovernmental organizations), 1, 10, 111

nightclubs, 3, 17, 21, 87, 152; and vazaha, 126–27, *127*, 129–32, 134–35, 137–38, 141

OK Podium, 108

olombanona, 33, 195n8

PADESM ("party of the disinherited of Madagascar"), 37–38

Parry, Jonathan, 200n22

patrilineal, 18, 193n16; patrilineal bias, 52, 56

patrons, political, 111–12

Pentecostalism, 3, 10–11, 13–15, 17, 20, 33, 91, 151–78, *156*, 183, 186–87, 189, 192–93n10, 204–5nn2–3; and ancestors, 63, 155, 157–61, 199n19, 205nn4–6; continuities of, 160–64; conversion to, 63, 153, 155, 157–61, 163–65, 172–78, 190, 205n3, 205n10; and disembedding, 152, 155–60; emotional practice in, 168–69, 177, 205nn8–9; and evangelizing, 165–66, 170, 173, 176, 186; and exorcisms, 169, 181; and fashions, 157–60, 172, 177, 205n10; and fitsapana, 170; in Ghana, 63; and jeunes, 100, 152, 154–55; and manao vavolombelona, 170–71; and performing new self, 171–77, 205n11; and Rajoelina, 181; and reforming men's behavior, 163–64; and salvation, 155, 160, 164, 178, 186–87; and sermons, 166–68, 170–78; and speaking in tongues, 168–69, 205n9; and tithing, 167; and wealth, 158, 160–63, 205n6

Pentekotista Afaka (Pentecostals Saved), 63, 169, 172, 205n8

Perry, Donna, 192n5

Piaget, Jean, 192n7

Picquié, Albert, 31

pimps, 203n9, 204n13

pirates, 25